REILLY – A LIFE IN RUGBY LEAGUE

REILLY

A Life in
Rugby League

Malcolm Reilly with Harry Edgar

MAINSTREAM
PUBLISHING
EDINBURGH AND LONDON

Acknowledgements

Grateful thanks are due to Ian Heads in Sydney for his considerable efforts in putting together the original version of this story, published in Australia, and for giving kind permission that his work be used as a basis for this book.

In addition there is grateful acknowledgement of the invaluable research and interview work carried out by Neil Hanson covering Malcolm Reilly's early years.

First published in Great Britain in 1999 by
MAINSTREAM PUBLISHING COMPANY (EDINBURGH) LTD
7 Albany Street
Edinburgh EH1 3UG

This editon 2002

ISBN 1 84018 274 1

A catalogue record for this book is available from the British Library

Typeset in 10 on 13.5pt Janson Text

The Random House Group Limited supports The Forest Stewardship Council (FSC®), the leading international forest certification organisation. Our books carrying the FSC label are printed on FSC® certified paper. FSC is the only forest certification scheme endorsed by the leading environmental organisations, including Greenpeace. Our paper procurement policy can be found at www.randomhouse.co.uk/environment

MIX
Paper from
responsible sources
FSC® C018072
www.fsc.org

Printed and bound in Great Britain by Clays Ltd, St Ives PLC

Contents

This book, telling my story, is for my mother Annie and my late father Robert, who with their love and support have been, and are, so much a part of everything I achieved.

Foreword

I remember a conversation I had with Malcolm Reilly in the early months after he had joined us at Manly in 1971. His form had been great, but for a time he had seemed a little bit 'down'. I pulled him aside after training one night. 'Mate, are you all right?' I asked.

'Yeah, Kenny,' he said. 'I'm just missing my mum.'

The exchange always stuck in my mind, such an unexpected answer from this hard, tough – sometimes ferocious – footballer who was making such a mark in Australia. But it was just Malcolm – a bloke for whom such things as family, love of home, loyalty to friends always meant the world. It was for those sort of reasons of course that Mal Reilly headed home to England for good, at the end of the 1998 season.

To the Manly club, Mal Reilly is many things: one of the best buys we ever made, one of the finest footballers we ever had in our ranks, a stranger from a strange land who became so much a part of the place in so many ways. Malcolm holds a special place in the hearts of all Manly people who watched him play and got to know him. I saw him first on the 1970 British tour out here, then again when I managed Australia's team in the World Cup in England later that same year. He was young, but already hard, confident and immensely talented. I remember talking to the legendary Derek 'Rocky' Turner about him in England in late 1970. Turner rated him enormously highly; I'm sure he saw a lot of his own tough, uncompromising style in Malcolm. At our training sessions on that World Cup campaign, which ended in some glory for us Aussies when we won the trophy against the odds, I noticed that Reilly's name was mentioned far more often by our blokes than that of any other British player. Even then it was obvious he was very special.

As secretary of the Manly club, I had been searching for the 'missing link' to make our team whole. For almost a quarter of a century we had been tilting at the premiership – getting close, but always falling at the last hurdle. By then we had the genius of Bob Fulton in our ranks, and as 1970 unfolded I became more and more certain that Reilly was the final 'X factor'. It was no easy operation to get him; obviously his club

Castleford didn't want to see him go, despite Malcolm's own ambitions to play in Australia. Finally I said to him, 'Look, just hop on a plane and come out . . . we'll battle through it when you get here.' And that's the way it worked, Malcolm arriving one night at Mascot, and me spiriting him across the Harbour Bridge to the Manly Pacific Hotel. Weeks later, after lots of phone calls back and forth to the straight-talking Phil Brunt in Castleford, and daily dealings with solicitor Jim Comans, Malcolm Reilly became a Manly player.

It was the beginning of a wonderful partnership. Malcolm, so devastating in so many ways on the football field, did indeed prove to be our missing link. And Manly – its beaches, its lifestyle, its people – permeated his own life to the extent that it will forever be a second home for him. On the field he was often magnificent, a mix of toughness and delicate skills. He added the hard edge we needed up front, and in many ways he turned the game on its head with his wonderful ball skills – the ability to get passes away under unbelievable pressure – and a kicking game that was a mixed bag of wonderful examples of the kicking art. Very often it seemed he had the ball on a string. All of it was made more remarkable by the fact that, as the seasons went by with Manly, he was increasingly hampered by the notoriously damaged Reilly knee, which became the most talked about piece of anatomy in the history of the game!

I rate him as one of the toughest players I have ever seen, a man who would never take a backward step. People have said to me, 'Jeez, he dealt it out!' Well, yes, he did. But the fact was that Malcolm was a target *every* time he went out on to a football field in Australia. He never asked for any quarter, and never got any. His attitude was that if he was going to hand it out, then he was going to cop it back. And that's the way he lived, and the way it worked. I remember in a match early in 1973, he caught Australia's World Cup hooker Ron Turner with a shot that cut Turner badly and put him into dreamland. In the grand final later that year, when Cronulla played Manly, Turner got square, nailing Reilly off the ball very early on. From Malcolm, there was no complaint. That was merely the reality of football . . . the way it was back then.

Malcolm came to us with a tough reputation. There had been an off-field incident or two, well documented in the pages of this book, on the Great Britain tour to Australia in 1970. But I can't speak highly enough about the way he was at Manly, and what he came to mean to the club. In every possible respect he was an ideal citizen, a considerate, modest and responsible bloke. A gentle man. And a gentleman, wonderfully loyal to family, friends and club. People who know me well will recognise that the quality of loyalty means the world to me. Its absence in some and its abundance in others will stay in my mind, never forgotten, from those long and ugly days of the Super League war when a corporate interloper tried to steal rugby league away – and went pretty close to wrecking the game in the process. Malcolm Reilly stuck solid with us (the ARL) then, as I knew he would.

I remember a night long ago at Brookvale: the aftermath of a game, with the players still in the rooms and the crowd drifting away. I was outside, chatting to several of the players' wives, in the lee of the grandstand. Up in the stand a bunch of young louts, well fuelled by booze, were making pests of themselves. On finishing their cans of beer, they were hurling them down the stand. Eventually, I went up and remonstrated with them, copping a torrent of abuse for my trouble. At just that point, Malcolm Reilly came out of the dressing-room, bag in hand. Malcolm glanced up at the commotion and summed up what was going on. In a flash he had dropped his bag and was sprinting up the steps. Well, you've never seen a bunch of blokes scatter so quickly. Loyal, tough and fearless, Malcolm would be just the bloke to have alongside in the trenches in any battle . . .

In late 1994 I had the great pleasure of strongly recommending Malcolm to the Newcastle club when they had him in their sights as coach. Malcolm was established as one of the finest coaches in the world by then, and I knew he would do the job wherever he went. But *especially* I felt he'd be suited to Newcastle. The people of that fine and friendly city have much in common with the folk from Malcolm Reilly's home territory, the north of England. They share the qualities of solidarity, of standing together in hard times. I felt very strongly that Malcolm would be a knockout success with Newcastle and its people.

So it was that I didn't feel *too* bad when the Knights came from the clouds in the final seconds to beat my Manly in the grand final of 1997. My disappointment was tempered by the fact that if we were going to lose such a game I couldn't imagine it going to a finer combination than Malcolm and his Newcastle team.

I am delighted that the Malcolm Reilly story has been told. He has been a major figure in world rugby league for the past 30 years, his superb achievements spanning seamlessly the league-playing countries of the two hemispheres. He has worked hard throughout it all, stuck to his principles and cared deeply for family and friends. I feel privileged to have played a part in such a career and am proud to call Mal Reilly a friend.

Ken Arthurson

Ken 'Arko' Arthurson AM was secretary of the Manly club 1963–83, chairman of Australian Rugby League 1983–97 and director general of the Rugby League International Board from 1985.

Introduction

Malcolm John Reilly OBE has been a household name in the world of rugby league for over 30 years, and in those three decades his presence has been immense as both a champion player and champion coach in England and Australia. Malcolm's awesome career has seen him span several distinct and contrasting eras in rugby league's evolution – beginning in those nostalgic days of the '60s when so many players, and Malcolm was one of them, would work at the pit during the week and emerge as a sporting hero on Saturday afternoons, and running right up to date in the new world of full-time professionalism and a summer Super League as the game heads towards a new millennium. In between, Malcolm Reilly has seen it all. I've followed his career since he first burst on the scene as a swashbuckling young loose-forward with Castleford, invariably with Alan Hardisty at his elbow waiting for the pass that would send the gold-shirted 'Classy Cas' to glory. Throughout those three decades I've observed and written about so many of rugby league's major events and historic moments from the sidelines whilst Malcolm Reilly has been right there in the middle of them – a history maker, a shaper of the game's destiny.

After two consecutive Wembley victories with Castleford, in the first of which Malcolm won the coveted Lance Todd Trophy at the tender age of 19, he played a key role in the last 'Great' British Lions tour. Controversy was never far away for Malcolm on that tour, but he emerged from it with a reputation as the most feared player in the game, the man the Australians respected more than all others as the Ashes were won by Great Britain for what has proved, with the passing of time, to be the last time this century. But it wasn't just the Ashes that Malcolm Reilly brought home to England in 1970. He returned with a burning desire to go back to Australia, having been entranced by its vast open spaces, its outdoor lifestyle and its pioneering spirit. I saw him play his last game for Castleford on a cold January afternoon at Whitehaven in 1971. A few days later, accompanied only by his suitcase and a morning newspaper and without any kind of contract or forwarding address, he set out from Leeds City station on the journey that was to change his life so dramatically. Waiting for him on arrival in Australia at Sydney's Mascot airport was Ken Arthurson, then secretary of the Manly–Warringah club. It was the start of a wonderful partnership and lifelong friendship, which Malcolm Reilly readily admits shaped the destiny of his life more than any other. He proved to be Manly's missing link in their long-held quest for a premiership, and in his five seasons with the club Reilly made an indelible mark on Australian rugby league. It was a time when the game was at its most brutal and Malcolm was at the centre of some of the most violent battles that have found their way into the game's folklore. But, always, Malcolm Reilly was both the broadsword and the rapier, that mixture of beauty and brutality that created so many of rugby league's legends and ignited so many passions. Alongside that unquestionable hard edge that laid low many an opponent and shook the confidence of entire teams, stood his array of subtle and spectacular skills – the chip over, the high kick (Reilly perfected the 'bomb' long before the towering attacking kick was given that tag), the deft pass. Australians have no doubts that he was the greatest English player of his time and arguably the most outstanding of the last 30 years.

Sadly, British audiences never saw the very best of Malcolm Reilly; that was a privilege enjoyed by the football fans of Sydney. He played in just eight internationals for Great Britain – all in one year, 1970 – yet his impact was immense. A chronic knee injury persuaded him in 1975 that the time was right to head home from the cauldron of Sydney rugby league to the softer grounds of England, and that's when that wily old negotiator, Castleford chairman Phil Brunt, brought him home to be player–coach at Wheldon Road and a resident of the beautiful Yorkshire village of Ledsham. Reilly the pioneer soon made an impact on the British game, introducing what were then regarded as revolutionary training methods aimed at improving the physical preparation of his players. When the knee injury finally proved too much, if Malcolm Reilly had finally hung up his boots and never gone near a football field again, he would have been remembered as one of the greats of the game – in both England and Australia. Instead, he drew a line on one discipline (playing) and moved immediately into another (coaching). There, astonishingly, he mirrored almost exactly the success he had gained as a player – a Challenge Cup final win at Wembley with Castleford, and later an Australian grand final win with Newcastle. And, most of all, he brought the same steely edge and pride to his coaching of the Great Britain national team as he had as a player back on that famous 1970 Lions tour.

Unfortunately for Malcolm, the Test arena didn't quite bring him the same glory and achievement as he attained as a player. The quest for the

Ashes went unfulfilled, but only just. After several years of humiliation against the Australians, it was Malcolm Reilly who moulded Great Britain into a truly competitive force again in the most demanding sporting arena in the world. Only one missed goalkick stands between Reilly and perfect symmetry in his long career; it was in the second Test of the 1990 series at Old Trafford. A late, kickable conversion shot would almost certainly have clinched the Ashes for the Reilly-coached British team, but at 10-all it was missed and the Aussies came back for a famous last-gasp victory thanks to Ricky Stuart's break and Mal Meninga's shoulder charge. Almost ten years on, Malcolm still remembers those events clearly, and still doesn't allow emotion to cloud his memory or his assessment of the situation. There is just the sheer professionalism of a man who always set the highest standards himself, and saw others fall down slightly on the job he expected of them. Malcolm Reilly is never a man to make excuses. The Aussies went on to win the third Test that year and clinch the series. Despite the way Reilly rebuilt the competitiveness and toughness of the Great Britain team, always the ultimate prize just eluded him as he duelled with his great friend and ex-Manly team-mate Bob Fulton. When Malcolm returned to Australia to coach Newcastle Knights, he was to finally finish on the winning side against 'Bozo' after the most thrilling grand final in the history of the game in 1997.

Malcolm's time with Newcastle added another major, and fascinating, adventure to his life in rugby league. Caught slap in the middle of the Super League war on his arrival in Australia, Reilly admits to being very fortunate to be in the 'right place at the right time' when the megabucks were flying around in the battle for control of the game. What he discovered in Newcastle was a people so loyal to and enthusiastic about their Knights club, who took this Englishman to their hearts and they to his. It's when he talks about Newcastle and the sheer passion of the people and the loyalty of the friends he made there that Malcolm's infamous cold steel eyes start to show the faintest signs of misting over. Reilly dismisses the theory that the 'fear' factor, based on his own reputation as a player, is an element in his coaching. But that he is a 'hard man' still is beyond doubt. At the age of 51 he still competes in a number of disciplines at the same high level as his players, as he did throughout his years as Great Britain coach and at the Newcastle Knights. At 92 kilos he weighs exactly what he did when he was playing. Softly spoken and slightly distant, there is a quality about him which has been described as 'quietly menacing'.

But Malcolm Reilly has always been one of those men in rugby league who you could depend on to be straight, and he expected you to be straight with him. In years gone by I've heard other highly respected rugby league men who've worked alongside Malcolm confirm that view of his tremendous dedication, his attention to detail, his loyalty, his immense personal pride in rising to all challenges, and his sheer enjoyment of playing and coaching the game – men like John Sheridan, Ron Willey, Frank Stanton, Phil Lowe and, of course, Ken Arthurson.

For those who know only Malcolm's intense professionalism as a coach, or who still picture him at the centre of those bruising encounters of yesteryear, his story may bring some surprises as he talks of his love of nature and wildlife, the inspirational messages he has taken from the Bible and Christian martyrs, and the genuine emotion he found stirred up by the many letters and messages he received from supporters of the Newcastle Knights. His story also reveals many of his philosophies on coaching and the preparation of footballers, and the enthusiasm he still thrives on when he sees young players displaying the keenness to learn and improve that he had over 30 years ago as a teenager at Castleford.

The life of Reilly has unquestionably been something very special. Malcolm's mixture of talent and toughness, his love for his chosen sport and his relentless commitment to excellence – set alongside his unquestionable loyalty to family and friends – has made his life in rugby league an inspirational one.

As I helped Malcolm put the finishing touches to this book he was fighting some of the toughest battles of his career as the Huddersfield Giants struggled against some overwhelming odds. It all seemed such a far cry from those glory days at Wembley and the Sydney Cricket Ground, or the moment Darren Albert skipped over for *that* try for the Knights and tears of joyful emotion flowed on the sidelines between coach Reilly and captain 'Chief' Harragon – two of the toughest men in any sport, anywhere in the world.

Malcolm Reilly's story was originally written in association with Ian Heads in Australia, and Ian's work forms the basis of this telling of Malcolm's life in rugby league, for which I express due acknowledgement and grateful thanks.

Harry Edgar, August 1999

Harry Edgar was the founder of *Open Rugby* magazine and for 22 years as its editor/publisher became established as one of the most knowledgeable writers on international affairs in rugby league. He now acts as consultant editor to the magazine's successor *Rugby League World*, and has published two books – *Super League: The Official Fans' Guide 1997*, and *Chocolate, Blue and Gold, 50 Years of Whitehaven RLFC* – as well as contributing to numerous annuals and anthologies, including *XIII Winters* and *XIII Worlds*.

ONE

In the Beginning

The story of this football life which has taken me around the world has its beginning in the Yorkshire village of Preston, where I was born in the heart of a rugby league season, on 19 January 1948. When I was about four the family moved to Kippax and it was there that I did my primary schooling. It was a great part of the world for a growing kid; there was still much open countryside around and it seemed we were always out in the woods or the fields. My memory is that I was forever walking or running. The school was at the top of the hill, half a mile from home, and I'd run there twice a day – in the morning, and after lunch. It was a steep hill too, great for building general fitness even at an early age. My parents were Robert and Annie Reilly. My father worked in the mine, in the boilerhouses in earlier years, then down in the colliery. There are two Reilly kids, myself and my sister Jennifer, who is a year and four months younger than me.

Preston is a pit village – well, it used to be. The pit was at Allerton Bywater and there was another pit, older still, at Bowers Row, but that was not operable even when I was a boy. There was a further pit at nearby Ledston Luck, so the area of my boyhood was a heavily saturated mining community. My earliest memory is of my grandad wheeling me along in my pushchair. I was three or four. Things were changing, even back then; a lot of the woods were outcropped and open-cast mined and much of the countryside was progressively devastated.

My dad was from Preston and my mum was from Allerton Bywater, neighbouring villages. That cliché of parents not wanting their children to go down the mine certainly was a fact of life in our house. My mum never wanted me to . . . nor dad for that matter. But as is the way of things in such communities I eventually *did* go to the pit – to Ledston Luck Colliery, where at 15 years of age I started off an apprenticeship at William Pepper's, a plant hire company, and a busy place at that time when the pits were thriving. I spent two years working through an apprenticeship in Mechanics, City and Guilds, Engineering, and then when I was 17 I moved on to Smith and Robinson's, working on their heavy commercial vehicles and from there, a year later, to South Yorkshire

Motors at Pontefract. Before I made the big move to Australia in 1971 I was back at Ledston Luck – basically because there was more money in the work there – fitting and welding.

The thing I remember most about all those four jobs in my early adult life was the tremendous atmosphere that existed in the working environments. It's something I can't identify or find in today's society. I don't know why. But I know this: I thoroughly enjoyed it and won't ever forget the wonderful camaraderie of the workplace in those years.

I was a soccer player from when I first started school at four or five. It was the only game we played and we had all the necessary facilities laid on. Right outside the Reilly house were the Kippax Welfare recreation grounds, two big fields for football (soccer) and cricket. I enjoyed my football. I was never very big but even from my earliest days I was always very competitive.

Dad wasn't a rugby league fan, and I didn't really stumble across league until I went to Ashton Road Secondary Modern School at Castleford when I was 11. Roy Close was a maths teacher and sports master there and the school was renowned for producing good rugby league players. Alan Hardisty and Keith Hepworth had both gone there; so too had Bill Bryant, Johnny Ward, Clive Dickinson and plenty of other players. Roy played rugby union for Old Pontefricians. I think he had captained the Pontefract Firsts in his serious playing days. He was a fitness fanatic and he encouraged me to try my hand at league; he taught me a lot of skills. Roy Close was also one of those old-fashioned teachers who could teach young fellas like me a lot about the way life works. I remember a morning when Roy sprang a mental arithmetic test on us, consisting of 20 questions. Now, if sport was my strength at school, it's just as certain that maths was my weak spot. During the test I was gazing around, and, I admit, looking over the shoulder of the boy in front of me as I struggled to come up with the answers. Out front, Roy took note. 'Malcolm, come out here and sit next to me,' he said. So I went and sat next to the teacher who was also working his way through the test. To my surprise, Roy gave me a nod and a wink that I could copy off his paper – which I did. 'How good is this?' I thought. Finally, Roy called time and set about writing the correct answers on the blackboard. I got 3 right out of 20! Afterwards, he called me to one side, 'Let that be a lesson to you, Malcolm,' he said. 'If you're going to do anything in life, do it yourself.' I never forgot the message. He was a wonderful man and this a lesson well learnt.

The breeding ground for so many players was a 20 yard by 80 yard playground on which there would be a game of touch and pass played at every dinner and play break. As it turned out, the game of rugby league was ideally suited for my personality, if not my size.

I was playing mainly at stand-off in the district schools side at inter-mediate level for 13- to 14-year-olds. I played alongside Roger Millward. I remember Roger playing scrum-half against Hull one afternoon. He got knocked out and I finished up going to half-back, to number seven, a position I'd hardly ever played in before. Six was basically my position through my school years. I have no doubt that the skills I acquired then, being close to the action, helped a great deal later on when I did eventually grow.

When I left school at 15 I was still only five foot four tall and weighed in at eight stone four, something of a midget really. As a little fella, I got sick of being knocked out. I was concussed on numerous occasions and it wasn't a great feeling.

Then after I left school I stopped playing rugby league and went back to soccer, playing for the local Kippax Welfare Club in the premier West Yorkshire Division. The switch back to league, which was ultimately to change and shape my life, came completely by accident. As a late teenager I was very involved in my soccer, happy with the game I was playing. However, on a winter's afternoon in 1966 both Kippax district teams – soccer and league, open-age West Yorkshire and Under-19s rugby league – met, as usual, at the Kippax Monument. The weather was atrocious and the news came through that the soccer game had been cancelled because the ground was waterlogged; the rugby league game, however, was to go ahead. On the league team were a lot of the guys whom I'd played with at school and they invited me to join them. That afternoon at Hunslet I played loose-forward, and in 80 minutes the die was cast.

The match was not without incident. They had a big second-rower named Richardson who at one point grabbed me in what is known colloquially as a 'Christmas hold'. I waited my opportunity to get square, eventually burrowing through a late scrum to get at him. In the confusion the ref identified our hooker Graham Tyreman as the culprit – and sent him off! I enjoyed the game so much that on the following Tuesday at training I turned right to the rugby league dressing-room instead of left to the soccer room, and trained on the bottom pitch instead of the top one. I had made a decision that turned out to be for life. I had chosen my game.

I'm sure now that all the clattering I got as a not very big half-back when I was younger hardened me up. I think it comes down to this: if you think you can tough it out when you're eight stone four and still come back for more, then when you're 14 and a half stone, still with the same ball skills and determination, you've really got something going for you. Strength can come out of weakness.

My parents just let me get on with it. In fact they became terrific supporters. Mum was always pretty fanatical and I know Dad was embarrassed to sit with her at times. You know what mums are like when they're cheering for their own sons – they can really go beserk. Dad didn't say anything but I know for sure that he didn't want to sit there when she was shouting and hollering. Mum still gives me a word of advice when I ring her up before a big match all these years later. 'Tell them to do plenty of tackling,' she'll say. Sadly, when my life became rugby league Mum and Dad never came out to Australia, as my mum wouldn't fly.

The game came really naturally to me, and I don't know why. I hadn't set myself any particular goals apart from the fact that I knew I would love to play with men as good as Alan Hardisty and Keith Hepworth, who I read of so often in the local papers. The sort of credibility they had achieved already in their lives through football was very appealing. My career moved with some speed. From signing on with Castleford (Cas) from Kippax Under-19s, where I'd shared in some success via the winning of two local finals plus a Sevens competition (I signed on 15 May 1967 after just six games with Kippax), it was only half a dozen or so second-team games before I was thrown in at centre for a first-team game against Hunslet, away, at the famous old Parkside ground.

My very first taste of first grade, however, was pretty much unforgettable, owing to an incident or two, and the quality of the players I found myself confronting. I was given my chance in a benefit match at Craven Park, Hull, against a Hull Kingston Rovers side which included the likes of Roger Millward, already an international by then, the legendary Arthur Beetson and Jim Hall, in recent years the head of the NRL Judiciary in Australia. I recall Roger, who I had known for years of course, rubbing my face in the mud (of which there was plenty that day!) by way of a friendly greeting to first grade. Later in the game I had a brush with Big Artie which ended in him grabbing me by the jersey-front. The jersey stretched about four feet as I receded, at some speed!

My signing for Cas was a big event, carried out at the Reilly house with Len Garbett, club secretary, and Ron Simpson, the chairman, in attendance. The signing-on fee was two hundred pounds, which was a lot of money in those days. I was elated. There wasn't much negotiation: 'We've got the two hundred quid, lad, does tha' want to sign?' That was about it, there were no negotiation stances. And I did. Winning and losing money was something like fourteen and six or sixteen and eight pounds. For Cup matches the fee was a little more. But at that time sixteen pounds was a full week's wage for a forty-hour week in most places.

I remember my début League match at Hunslet well; considering all the years (and the matches) since, you'll understand why. I played left-centre, opposite a guy named Phil Evans, who was about my age. I scored a try and performed quite soundly in general play. 'As a whole he played as well as, if not better than, some of the other players with much more experience,' said the local paper on my contribution. Keith Hepworth was the captain that day in Alan Hardisty's absence through injury, and during the game our goalkicker, Ron Hill, suffered a broken jaw and was taken from the field. Near the end, at 10–5 to Hunslet, Johnny Walker scored for us, to make the score 10–8. Remember, it was my first game in the first team, but Hepworth threw me the ball with the accompanying words: 'Kick the goal.' The conversion attempt was from about 12 yards to one side of the posts, and honestly, I just didn't handle it. I missed. And all Keith could say to me was, 'You dozy bastard, do you realise how much you've cost us?' He'd calculated how much the total bonus would have been for an away draw if I'd kicked the goal, and divided by 15. I think the difference was about eight pounds apiece. He just rubbished me with the words, 'This is what you've cost us.'

It was the sort of start to a career that a young player wouldn't ever forget, and was probably a lesson of what a hard game rugby league can be. However, even that first afternoon, nerves were not a big problem for me. I was always fairly comfortable about my football, and any game I ever played was a personal challenge for me. I was anxious at times, and sometimes the fear of failure was a reality. I remember well the Challenge Cup semi-final with Cas against Wakefield in 1969, the first year we got to Wembley. They put on a couple of early tries at Headingley, and we were down 10–0. 'That's it.' My mind raced with doubts about whether we could win the game. But then Alan Hardisty scored a try, Mick Redfearn kicked the goal and on the way back up the field I said to Alan, 'Do you really think we can still win this?' He was genuinely amazed at the question. We were only 20 minutes into the game, down only 10–5 and here was this young bloke asking if we could win! He told me in no uncertain terms to get positive. Alan had no doubts, none at all. And we did win. That experience was another early lesson for me; the truth that confidence is such a determining factor in sport. The more you have of it, the more likelihood you have of winning.

In fact we ended up winning that game on the back of the best goalkick I've ever seen, and I've seen some good ones over the years. But this one was just remarkable. A near blizzard was howling up Headingley that day, and we were running into the teeth of it. The kick that Mick Redfearn, who happened to be Alan Hardisty's brother-in-law, took was from right on the touch-line, into and across the gale. Remember that it was to win a semi-final and get a much coveted place at Wembley – this was a *big* pressure kick. And Mick kicked it, the ball swinging back seven or eight yards like a duck-hook at golf, to find its way between the posts.

Incidentally, Mick was an old-fashioned toe-kicker; you don't see them any more.

I remember a few years later, in 1973, Graham Eadie as a teenager kicking a series of wonderful goals in a similar Headingley gale to win Australia the second Test and level the series in which they went on to regain the Ashes we had won so memorably in 1970. The Wombat. What a player he was – big, strong, fast, determined, with a good sidestep and tremendous hands. He could run over the top of defenders or he had the pace to run around them – take your pick. I have a memory of him sitting in the reception area outside Ken Arthurson's office at Manly the day he came down to sign with Manly. Just a big kid from Woy Woy.

Alan Hardisty was a guiding light for me in those early Castleford days. He often spoke to me before games and advised me to pace myself, not to get involved as much as I probably would have liked to have done. Share the workload, he said. And I can always remember our front-row man, Johnny Ward, telling me to piss off out of the way and let the front row get on with the hard work. He used to rollock me if I got involved too much up front. Big Dennis Hartley (our other prop) took me under his wing and did his best to look after me. For a 19-year-old, playing first-team football – which could be mighty rough at times and not short of characters who would be quite happy to take your head off – to have Dennis as some sort of 'minder' was appreciated. Hardisty had wonderful anticipation, and he was years ahead of his time in the way he prepared for games and looked after himself.

In that heady first year at Castleford I had my first experience of the men in green and gold who would go on to become such a focal point in my career in the game, both as player and coach. I was in the Cas side that played the Kangaroos at Wheldon Road on the afternoon of 9 November 1967. The match had been scheduled as a mid-weeker but was called off because of fog. Back in those days they used to give the kids the afternoon off school in Cas when the Aussies were in town. It was the year of the famous 'Bowler Hat' tour, and the Kangaroos, led by Reg Gasnier, took home the Ashes. However, that afternoon in Castleford, we whipped them. The score was 22–3 and the *Daily Express* headline told the story: AUSSIES HIT ROCK BOTTOM. When I look back down the avenue of my career it always reminds me of what a thrill it was to have played against the likes of Langlands, Irvine and Sattler that day – and come home a winner. I was 19. It was the heaviest defeat inflicted on an Australian touring team for 11 years. We were a very good side – but most likely they underestimated us.

Bob McCarthy, who was to become a much respected opponent in later years, was at the match as a spectator (he was controversially left out of that 1967 touring team) and described Cas as 'one of the greatest rugby league teams I have ever seen'. Wrote McCarthy: 'I saw three forwards who could easily be in the Great Britain side – Ward, Bryant and the most impressive 19-year-old lock Reilly. He played like a seasoned campaigner and if I was picking the Swinton Test team he would definitely be in.'

Even 15,000 miles away and many years on, as I began collecting my memories for this book whilst the coach of Newcastle Knights in Australia, I could still recall the sights and sounds of Wheldon Road, Castleford, my home ground for so many years. Back then, the Wheldon Colliery sat at one end of the ground, the railway yards adjoining. The colliery is all wrapped up now, as most of them are. It's where Roger Millward worked for a number of years, as did various other team-mates of mine. The ground hasn't changed very much over the years, although things moved ahead a bit in the '80s when David Poulter, a local builder, came on to the board of the club and then became chairman. David did a terrific job, going around the ground with his men and gradually upgrading the place. Outsiders, certainly most Aussie fans, wouldn't see it as anything extravagant, but I can tell you the atmosphere was extraordinary at Wheldon Road on big days. The ground held around 15,000 people, every one of them close to the action on the field and the noise would be enough to send a rumble through the town.

A man named George Clinton was my first coach in top-grade football. He was an engineer at Glasshoughton Colliery and the coaching was straightforward and basic, as was the way at that time. The big changes that revolutionised coaching (and the game) had not really started then. Derek 'Rocky' Turner came the following year and it was in his first season that we went to Wembley. 'Rocky' had a legendary reputation as a hard man, and what he instilled in the side was a determination in defence, a sense of real urgency. He built in us a real pride in our defensive performances. Under Turner our record in defence was excellent; with the ball we had plenty of players, like Alan Hardisty, who could capitalise on opportunities. The balance was good. However, training was fairly basic compared with the way things are today. There was a lot of running, some ball skills, a few scrums . . . very basic stuff, and definitely no weights. I don't think anyone was doing weights at that stage. What strength players had was natural strength, largely gained through the jobs they did.

Right from the beginning I did a lot of training by myself. Near where I lived at Kippax the woods ran up to a big open field, probably three-quarters of a mile around. I'd go up there at least two nights a week to do interval work, jogging 400 metres then sprinting 100 metres. I spent quite a lot of time in that field. There was not much training in strength work, just push-ups and pull-ups and exercises like that. I didn't start doing weights until I got out to Australia. At Castleford, we relied very much on our front row, on the ball-playing abilities of Johnny Ward, on Dennis Hartley being able to offload in tackles, and on Brian Lockwood, later bound for a career in Sydney club football like myself, who was also a very proficient ball player.

I built a terrific understanding with our stand-off Alan Hardisty. From the base of the scrum we would often work quite sophisticated moves that I wish I could get players to do these days. Alan never used to look where he passed the ball because he knew I was always there; we'd performed the play again and again in training and perfected it. Even in those days you got out of football what you put into it. We did a lot of rehearsing. This was the practice of nearly all teams in those days. Small relationships would develop between players and an understanding was created; from that comes team understanding, and it's no different today.

I got some nice write-ups in the local paper, but it never occurred to me to really stop and think I could be someone special in the game I was playing, even when I was picked as a 'shadow' forward for Great Britain against France near the end of that first season. I was only 19, and less than a year before I had been playing local soccer with the prospect of a trial with Huddersfield Town. It was remarkable how quickly my sporting life had changed. After that there was talk of me being selected for the Great Britain team that was going to contest the World Cup in Australia in 1968, but I missed out as the selectors chose to go with some older, more experienced forwards. An early interview with a journalist named Jim Greenfield gave one or two insights into me and my philosophy about playing rugby league. 'Whatever I'm doing, I've got to keep having a go,' I said. 'I can't even bear to lose a friendly argument in the pub with my mates. I hate pain – but once the game's in motion, I'll tackle anything. You just don't think about getting hurt.' In each game I just went out and tried to compete to the best of my ability. For me, the motivation was the personal challenge and pride in my performance. I also felt very strongly that I didn't ever want my opposite number to outplay me. Very early on I started setting myself goals.

The end of my initial season in the Castleford team, 1967–68, was the first time I was interested enough to go down to London and watch a Wembley final. I travelled down with some friends from Featherstone, for Leeds versus Wakefield Trinity, the infamous watersplash final of '68. I still remember how the hairs on the back of my neck stood up when the teams walked so proudly on to the field. The atmosphere was so electric I just couldn't believe it, and straight away I knew it was something I desperately wanted to do in my own career. Next season, remarkably, I was there, out in the middle at Wembley. But we had some success in that 1967–68 season too – the win over the Kangaroos, and victory over Alex Murphy's Leigh side in the Floodlit Trophy final at Headingley.

How well I remember it: Wembley 1969, Castleford against Salford, at the end of a notable season for me. That season I had broken into representative football, with Yorkshire, and that meant a lot to me. I made my Yorkshire début in a 23–10 win over Cumberland up at Whitehaven in September 1968, a match in which I found myself playing on the same side for the first time in professional football as my former schoolboy colleague Roger Millward. The honour of playing for my county was something very special to me as a young player, and I know my parents were very proud; plus there was an added bonus alongside my first county cap because my agreement with Castleford when I first joined them was that I would get three hundred pounds if I played for Yorkshire – more than I got for signing on! We went on to beat Lancashire 10–5 at Hull KR's ground and won the old county championship for Yorkshire for the first time in five years. In the Challenge Cup with Castleford, having survived tough, close games against Wigan, Leeds and Wakefield in the earlier rounds, we won through to Wembley. We headed south on the Wednesday before the final to Crystal Palace, where we stayed. These were a superb few days for this team, with its great, close spirit. Training went very well and we also had some fun, larking around in the indoor pool and diving off the top tower. The players were very dedicated and focused, but the night before the final I couldn't sleep for thinking about the game to come and what a big occasion it was. Castleford had last been to Wembley as long ago as 1935, and it meant so much to the people of the district for us to be back there again in '69. However, if the night before the game was long and endless, the game itself just seemed to flash by.

Of all the things that have happened in my career, I still recall the walk up the tunnel that afternoon as the most vivid experience I have ever had. I felt ten feet tall. Even though I've represented Great Britain in an Ashes-winning side and played in grand finals in Australia, I have never felt as privileged as I did that day in 1969. It was like a dream: to go from hardly being involved in the game to running out at Wembley in this most famous of games, a member of an outstanding and close-knit team. By that time at Cas the understanding between Hardisty, the forwards – between all of us – was superb. There was a terrific team spirit and camaraderie and I knew it would see us through against Salford. Despite that, it was a tough, tight match against a very good side, which included excellent players such as Colin Dixon, David Watkins and Chris Hesketh.

My own contribution? Well, I just enjoyed putting myself about, I think. All of it flashed by so quickly; although the second-half try that Alan Hardisty scored still burns in my mind. It would probably rate as the best I was involved in throughout my career. It came 13 minutes after half-time, with the score 4–3 to Salford, off a Hardisty pass, a short ball. I think I was second man out, or it may have been from a scrum. As I went through, their half-back Jackie Brennan sort of half-tackled me but I managed to shrug him off and keep going another 20 yards or so and suddenly Alan was by my side – the *other* side from where he'd given me the ball. His call was everything. I heard him and just reacted and let the ball go. Alan didn't miss opportunities like that; he snapped it up, sped through and put it down under the sticks. It was like lightning. We won 11–6, and took the Challenge Cup back to Castleford.

Many things stay in my mind: winning the Lance Todd Trophy as player of the match, of course; the wonderful enjoyment of the Castleford fans afterwards; the colour and splendour of the whole afternoon. But it was the spirit of the event that made the most impression, that unstoppable will to win. Soho was the venue afterwards, and we visited various bars. I can remember being passed over the top in one place. It was so crammed with Castleford fans there was no chance of getting to the front, so they just picked me up and passed me over the crowd. It was a good night followed by a party in one of the players' rooms. Next morning it was straight back to Castleford, and a big reception. My head was still spinning with the Wembley win and the fact that my name was engraved on the Lance Todd honour roll, alongside the likes of Gerry Helme, Ernest Ward, Ces Mountford, Alan Prescott, Neil Fox and Brian McTigue. Then life resumed and it was straight back to work at Ledston Luck Colliery. It was such a different world for rugby league players then, and there was no way that football was allowed to interfere too much with your work. For a midweek away game you might need an hour or so off, and that was about it.

When I worked at Ledston Luck Colliery as a fitter and welder, things were a little easier when it came to concessions being made for my football. I was on the surface, but also spent plenty of time working down the mine. I remember one occasion when I was down doing some work on gearheads, and some fitting. The manager of the mine at the time was Granville Craven, who happened to be a fanatical Castleford fan. On one particular day when Mr Craven came down to inspect some aspects of the underground workings, the crew I was with were having a break. I was training hard with Cas at the time and would take every opportunity to rest and sleep. Now, sleeping in collieries is a sackable offence because there is a need to be alert at all times. However, Mr Craven came upon our crew when I was laid out having a kip. 'Who's that over there sleeping?' he asked. Then he realised. 'Oh, it's Malcolm. Well, leave him alone – he's playing tomorrow night.' He was very good to me. At the colliery we used to have a certain amount of rest days each year. Mr Craven allowed me to take mine in half-days, so when we were playing on a Friday night – which we often were – I would work eight to twelve and then go home and have a meal and a sleep and prepare for the game. The collieries are gone now; the town of Castleford is a different place.

After my second season with Cas – and what memories there are of that for me, including Wembley and also being in the Yorkshire team which won the county championship – Derek Turner moved across to Leeds as coach. He made it very clear that he wanted me to go with him to Headingley. We spent quite a lot of time talking about it, driving around in his car. Derek told me how keen the members of the Leeds board were, and how much they wanted to get me there. Undecided about my future, I was out of football for six weeks or so, as Leeds courted me and Cas waited for answers. Meanwhile Tommy Smales had joined Castleford as coach. I hadn't had much to do with him, but he was a smashing fellow, a good tactician and he talked a lot of sense. 'I feel we can double up at Wembley, that we've got the players to do it,' he said. By then Castleford had added the big Cumbrian second-rower Bill Kirkbride to an already formidable pack. After that, said Tommy, there's a tour to Australia. If you *really* want to earn some money, that's what you should aim for. 'Look, Malcolm, you don't want to be going to Leeds. Your best prospect if you want to make a future in the game is to play in Australia.' Tommy Smales knew what he was talking about. In 1967 he'd been over to play a part season with North Sydney. He knew about Australian football, and he had contacts in Sydney. 'I'll give you some good contacts over there,' he said. Tommy delivered – and especially so when he handed me the name and telephone number of a Sydney-based solicitor, Jim Comans, a man who was to help me in various ways in the years ahead. 'Make sure you look him up,' said Tom. I'm glad I did.

So I stayed on at Castleford and we went to Wembley for the second year in a row, just as Tommy Smales suggested we might. But, to be honest, I shouldn't have played in that year's Challenge Cup final (against Wigan). I was down with flu and on the night before the game some of the club directors were out and about in London trying to find an all-night chemist to get me something that might help. I couldn't train the day before the final and spent it in bed. By night-time I was running a hot fever. But by next morning I'd improved a little, enough to go ahead and take the field anyhow. The decision didn't prove to be a great mistake for the team, although obviously my energy level was limited. I hadn't been eating well and I just didn't have my natural energy store. In the end, I enjoyed the game, despite some people describing it as 'the drabbest of Wembley finals'. We won 7–2, with just one try being scored by our winger Alan Lowndes, and I was pleased to come out on the winning side against a Wigan side whose back three were all internationals, Bill Ashurst, Dave Robinson and Doug Laughton.

I remember 1969–70 with special affection, not just because of Wembley, but also because it was in that season I made my début for England. It was in February 1970, and we beat Wales 26–7 at Headingley. The results of that day, later followed by Cas completing the 'double' at Wembley, pretty much assured that I would soon be Australia bound.

TWO

The Last Great Tour

Dreams of Australia and the possibilities that existed there occupied my mind in the late 1960s. However, that move was a little bit down the track, and there were many stepping stones along the path. In fact, my first full international experience overseas was for England against France, in March 1970. And I'll never forget *that*. My opposite number that day in Toulouse was the experienced Jean-Pierre Clar – a tough nut with a beaten-up face and a disposition to match. I spent most of the game chasing him, owing to the fact that in the opening minutes of the game he caught me square, right on the nose. He just stood back and walloped me, breaking my nose and sitting me on my arse. Try as I might I couldn't catch him to get square, in fact I didn't even get close. He refused point blank to take the ball up and I finished the game frustrated, and with a sore nose. I thought him a bit of a French coward at the time. To make matters worse, we lost the match.

Brian Lockwood had just made the international side as well and he was on the bench that day. The other Cas players in the Great Britain team knew it was worth three hundred pounds to Brian if he got on the field, so Johnny Ward and I worked out that one of us would have to go off at some stage to give Brian his chance. In the end it was Johnny who departed early. Maybe he'd negotiated a commission.

There was an incident in that Test in Toulouse that reflected the qualities of Huddersfield referee Billy Thompson. One of the French touch-judges had given an outrageous decision, ruling that a French kick which was out on the full by at least three metres had in fact bounced inside the line. For the resultant scrum in a tight game it meant that we had the feed – but they had the head. And if you had the head in those days – well, literally, you had a head start. I think Roger (Millward) was the half-back that day and he was appealing vigorously. 'Billy, Billy . . . it was three yards outside the line,' he pleaded.

Billy Thompson knew *exactly* what had happened. 'Pipe down and feed the scrum!' he bellowed at Roger. So Roger did – illegally – and we won the ball. It was a funny moment. The French couldn't understand a word

Billy said and no doubt reckoned they'd conned him. He was a referee who knew how it worked.

Referees like Billy Thompson and, before him, the somewhat notorious 'Sergeant Major' Eric Clay, really knew their stuff. Billy was a yarn-spinner and a character and a damned good referee. 'Sergeant Major' Eric Clay was a big beefy bloke who would most probably be left panting far behind in the wake of today's players, considering the overall pace of the modern game. But (and I know some of my Australian mates won't agree with me on this) Clay was a very good referee, a man who really knew football. Players respected him — and he respected the way the game worked. If someone had given an opponent a short arm or something, Clay would file it away in his mind. If there was a square-up ten minutes later, he'd haul both players out. 'OK, that's it,' he would say. 'You're all square now. If you do it again . . . off!'

One morning in April 1970 there was a knocking on the front door of the Reilly house in Kippax. I knew the team selection for the Lions tour to Australia and New Zealand was pending and when I opened the door to Roger Millward and Johnny Ward I asked, 'Have you heard?'

'Congratulations,' came the reply. 'You've been picked for the tour.'

The feeling that morning was just superb — and it was even better when I learned that a total of five Castleford players had been named for the campaign 'Down Under': Johnny, Dennis Hartley, Keith Hepworth, Derek Edwards — and me.

The great adventure began at Manchester airport in May. They numbered the players one to 26. I got 25 and the other loose-forward, Doug Laughton, was 26. We sat together on the long flight over, Dougie the older hand, several years my senior, and me. Early in the journey Doug asked me, 'How are you going to fancy playing in the second row?'

I answered, 'I don't think I'll have to.' And as a matter of fact that was the way it turned out. That was Dougie all the way down the line, a brash, confident sort of person. He obviously didn't know me, and if he had, he wouldn't have said what he did. It just added to my resolve to succeed, to be the number one loose-forward on tour. Not that I needed any more incentive; I was quite confident in my own ability at that stage.

The tour began in tropical Darwin, with a match played on the evening of our arrival. We landed on a steamy Northern Territory morning and played that night at half past seven in temperatures of 28 degrees. It was all a bit of a shock to the system: a swim on arrival, a couple of sandwiches, a sleep in the afternoon, up at five o'clock, a bite of tea, a quick check of boots and kit — then on the bus and off to a game of football. Despite that preparation, we won easily enough, and the campaign was under way.

I liked Australia straight away. I remember thinking on the trek down from the Northern Territory through Queensland how big the anthills were! But I felt in tune with the place immediately. I liked the active, outdoor feel that Australia had, and I sensed from very early in the tour that the country was going to be part of my life long after the battles of 1970 were over. In that amazingly balmy northern Australian winter we trekked down through Townsville, Rockhampton and Wondai to a meeting with the Queensland state side in Brisbane, which we won 32–7. At that stage we had scored 165 points against 48 in five games and everything, on the surface at least, was going sweetly. But in reality the 'easy' start to the tour hadn't done us too much good, because we hadn't really toughed it out at all by the time the opening Test came around.

The question was still unanswered: who was going to front up when the going got hard? Under-prepared, and with the 'wrong' team on the paddock – missing people like Dennis Hartley and the tough-tackling second-rower Jimmy Thompson – we took a hammering in the first Test at Lang Park, 37–15 in a fierce game in which we won the fight, but took a beating in the football department. We definitely picked the wrong side. The full-back, Terry Price, a former Welsh rugby union international, was a nice footballer, but far too slow. And Dave Chisnall at prop – he was a decent player at club level, but was not Test material.

In fact it was Chisnall who caused the famous blue between rival props Cliff Watson and Jimmy Morgan. I happened to be in the thick of that when Chisnall was under fire after lashing out with his boot. Morgan retaliated to what Chisnall had done, then Cliffy ran in and Jimmy just headbutted him. I was right next to Cliff – and the expression on his face at that moment was one of amazement, not pain. He looked at the Australian front-rower somewhat quizzically as if to say: 'What was *that*?' Then Cliff grabbed Morgan; he didn't project his body at him at all, but just pulled Morgan towards him at some speed. He really smashed him – you could hear the sound of bones being crushed – and Jimmy was left with his nose spread all over his face. The subsequent photo became quite famous, the result of one of the most infamous moments in Test football, of Jim Morgan sitting bemused and bloodstained on the floor of the Australian dressing-room, looking rather less than handsome.

The Australians had a fine side with legends like Arthur Beetson, Graeme Langlands, Billy Smith and Ron Coote who really taught us a lesson. The match in Brisbane that day snapped the tour to life; it reminded us of what we had to do and of the changes that had to be made if we wanted to regain the Ashes.

*

29

It was in Brisbane before the Test that I had my first spot of bother on tour, via an incident at a party put on by some air hostesses we had met on the flight down to Brisbane. At the party a man whose name was to haunt me for some time – a Brisbane football coach and businessman called John Ryan – was giving everybody a lot of abuse, and directing a fair bit of it towards me. 'Pommy bastard' was about the least of it. I don't go looking for trouble, but in such situations I tend to have quite a short fuse. Eventually, sick of it, I took some direct action and, unfortunately, as a result of it he spent some time in hospital and quite a lot of time off work. I was young and naïve, and the profile that rugby league has in Australia hadn't really sunk it. If the incident had happened in Castleford or Featherstone nothing would have been said or done. But this was a Great Britain touring side in a major sport, and the troubles that night hit the headlines and were to haunt me for some time to come. Obviously, I know it was the wrong thing to do, whatever the circumstances. I had fallen down in my responsibilities to the tour. At 21, and on my first Lions tour, I didn't feel great about that.

In Brisbane I was visited by police at the team hotel, and I also saw Ryan at Brisbane hospital where I told him, 'I regret this happening, and I am very sorry it finished like this.'

He replied, 'It is now a matter for my solicitor and I will not discuss it.'

As with most things in life, no matter how serious, there were some funny elements in what unfolded. Ryan took action against me – for sixty thousand dollars – and for some days they attempted to serve me with a Supreme Court writ. When we played Queensland a man was at the ground trying to serve me with the papers. He got as far as the dressing-room door, and no further. As we ran out on to the field the players actually made a tunnel for me so nobody could get to me. At half-time there was a similar huddle to whisk me off the field. It became a battle of tactics. When we left Queensland to fly to Sydney, Ryan's people had organised a very nice-looking girl in a mini-skirt to serve the writ. And I nearly fell for it when she was asking for me at the airport. Sydney journalist Alan Clarkson was one who pleaded ignorance when the young lady asked for me. I was standing almost alongside him at the time. Fortunately, Dennis Hartley grabbed me. 'Get on the plane,' he said. So I did, donning a pair of sunglasses and grabbing a window seat. While I was sitting there, stewing over what I had started, a message came over the PA: 'Would Mr Reilly please press his call button, we have a lady here who wishes to speak to him.' There was a brief moment of quiet – then a call button went on, and another, and another. Suddenly the plane was lighting up like a Christmas tree. Every player in the party had pressed his button. The young lass just shook her head and walked off the plane.

They got me in Sydney in the end, at the hotel, and that's when solicitor Jim Comans came into the equation in my football life. I dug out Jim's number which had originally been given to me by Tommy Smales, and made contact. He readily agreed to act on my behalf. From there our discussions progressed to the matter of my desire to come back to Australia after the tour had concluded. 'Leave that with me,' he said. A Queen's Counsel was thrown into the fray on the Ryan matter, costing a lot of money, and eventually the thing was settled, having gone as far as the Supreme Court.

In court I told of Ryan's shouted taunt: 'Wait until Beetson gets you – you Pommy bastard!' I told how Ryan had come towards me again and looked as if he was going to throw a punch. It was then that I had struck him. Witnesses told how I had attempted to avoid Ryan, who seemed determined to follow me. My tour mates backed me all the way. With a total bill of more than nine hundred pounds they threw in thirty-five pounds each to help out.

Looking back, which I can do now with a little more comfort, there were some even funnier aspects which came out of that unfortunate affair. One of them was Johnny Ward's involvement in backing me up in court. In his evidence on the Ryan matter, Johnny went strongly in to bat for me, something he's never let me forget, backing me up on a fairly contentious part of the evidence. Later on the tour, when we were in New Zealand, he and I had a falling-out – one of those things that can happen when there's a bit of alcohol around. In Auckland one night Johnny came barging into my hotel room. I won't give you all the reasons, but I was quite annoyed with him and a little later I went down to his room, where Jimmy Thompson, Bob Irving and a couple of the other guys had gathered. Johnny was lying on his bed when I barged in, really cross, and tipped him off and onto the floor. Unfortunately he cracked his head on the wardrobe and opened up a cut. 'You bastard,' he said. 'I committed perjury for you!' So began a few days of a big freeze, with Johnny Ward refusing to talk to me. Anyhow, we headed on to a match in a very wet and gloomy Greymouth, with both Johnny and I in the squad. Dougie Laughton and I were on the substitutes' bench on a horrible, freezing, miserable, wet day. Both of us were keen to get on the field to try and stay warm. Finally someone got injured and I virtually sprinted down from the stand to get into the match. About ten minutes in I was fortunate enough to take a good ball and make a bust down the side. One of Johnny Ward's great attributes as a footballer was his support play and as soon as I busted he was up on my shoulder shouting, 'Malcolm! Malcolm!' I glanced across. 'Get lost, you're not talking to me,' I said. He screamed back, 'I will, I will!' So I gave him the ball – and the big freeze was over.

Johnny Ward was a terrific player, a sort of Arthur Beetson without the size. He was very, very skilful, with a great ability to manoeuvre players in the defensive line. He would walk into a defender and hold him at arm's length, then somehow shake away from him. Like Beetson he was really astute at offloading, getting the short balls away. At Castleford he and Dennis Hartley were very protective of me when I first came into the side. They'd growl at me if I got involved in 'their' work in close.

There was a time on that 1970 tour when I wasn't far off being sent home. Manager Jack Harding and coach Johnny Whiteley were obviously – and rightly – upset with me over the Brisbane incident and all the trouble it had caused. Then in Sydney, against everyone's wishes – and especially mine – I found myself in hot water again.

One night I went to Souths Leagues Club with a few of the guys. It was soon after all the publicity had hit the papers about my problem in Brisbane. As the night wore on, the players gradually drifted away and I was left with a man and a couple of other friends. At the end of the night things started to get a bid edgy. I had ordered a last drink – and no way were they going to let me drink it. I'm sure the bouncers knew who I was and had read the stories of the trouble up in Queensland. They were doing their best to provoke me, just baiting me to have a go; but I realised that, having been in trouble so recently, there was no way I should risk another public 'incident'. I relented on the question of the drink, told them it wasn't important, and walked out.

However, also in the club that night was Kevin Longbottom, the big full-back who played for Souths. He'd obviously seen what was going on and followed me out into the street where he was baiting me from a few paces behind. I did my best to ignore him, and in fact hopped in the back of a Mini, ready to go. But Kevin walked by and couldn't resist one parting shot. I just snapped. I leapt out of the car and there in front of the club started a fight with him. Unfortunately, Longbottom had to go to hospital as a result of our little disagreement. I did have a short fuse in those days.

I went back to the team hotel and the first person I saw was big Dennis Hartley. 'Dennis,' I said. 'I've done it again.'

I was really depressed then, accepting the fact that there was every chance I would be sent home. The incident hit the papers very quickly, the next day when we were playing a match in Queanbeyan, near Canberra. Jack Harding, our team manager, Frank Myler, our skipper, and Cliff Watson, as a senior player, pulled me in and read the riot act. The prospects of me being sent home were definitely real, and I would have suffered the shame of being the first ever Great Britain Lion to be so punished. But Jack Harding was a compassionate man and settled for a fine of seventy-five pounds. I accepted the penalty, but told the media:

'Apparently it is all right for people to abuse us and call us filthy names, but there must not be the slightest sign of retaliation.' The newspapers reported that I had been barred from Souths Leagues Club as a result of the incident. All these years on I can live with it now and can even manage a laugh, but it was deadly serious then. It was a major issue and I wish it hadn't happened.

It actually got to the stage where my problems became a bit of joke within the team, providing some light relief. The players used to rib me, ask me where I was going at night. I'd tell them and they'd say, 'OK, good. We'll be going somewhere else.'

It was a difficult time, although I was still able to focus on the job at hand and play some good football. For a while I got quite homesick because of the hounding by the media. Notwithstanding all that, the enjoyment of the tour far overshadowed everything else. Before the second Test in Sydney we stayed at the Olympic Hotel, right across the road from the famous Sydney Cricket Ground (SCG) and all morning on the day of the match, from almost first light, we watched the people streaming in, filling the famous Hill and the stands. The atmosphere on that ground on those Test match days was superb. Of course the crowd were hostile towards us – 'useless Pommies' and 'Pommy bastards' were just some of the insults they flung – but there was also a lot of affection and respect in it. Day by day we met a lot of lovely Australian people. The barracking of the crowds didn't put me off at all.

The second and third Tests of that tour were among the most special days of my career. To play them both on that famous ground (the SCG) and to win them both – and the Ashes – was just a dream, something very special. Who would have predicted back then in 1970, that as I write this 30 years later on the eve of a new millennium, Great Britain would still be waiting for its next Ashes win?

By that stage of the tour we had the 'mix' right in our team. Only half a dozen of us survived from the first Test team: Atkinson, Myler, Hepworth, Watson, Laughton and me. Roger Millward was in and so too was a hard man at hooker, Tony Fisher replacing 'Flash' Flanagan. As the name suggests, 'Flash' was flash, Fisher, was hard and uncompromising. The second Test, squaring the series, was Roger Millward's day: a mighty hand from the 'Dodger', 20 points from two tries and seven goals as we won clearly, 28–7. The third and deciding Test, two weeks later, was closer on the scoreboard, but not in reality. We had their measure, and scored five tries to one. But their late replacement full-back, Allan McKean, kept potting penalties from the many blasts of referee Don Lancashire's whistle and with a scrambled try near the end (by Bob McCarthy) featuring blatant offside play, the Aussies got to within a point at 18–17. It would have been a traversty of justice if we had lost that game and, thankfully, two minutes from time I managed to put Doug Laughton (playing second row!) through a gap and Roger was on the end of it to run clear and score the winning try. We had won the Ashes – a big relief because there was so much at stake.

It was a nice touch, Roger Millward and me having a hand in the try that clinched the Ashes. We had known each other since we were knee high. Come to think of it, Roger was *still* knee high! We had played school representative football together when we were 13 or 14. Roger was a great talent. He was a Wheldon Lane kid, from Castleford. I used to see quite a lot of him later on when he was courting Carol Bailey, who lived opposite my mum's house in Helena Street. They've been married now for the best part of 27 or 28 years. Roger was a bit of a legend almost as soon as he started playing rugby league. He was playing Test football at 17 and I thought, 'Gee, he's done well for himself.' I was a late starter.

The going was never easy in Australia in 1970, and nor should it be on an Ashes tour. I recall that after the third Test and the long, late celebrations that followed, we had to back up and play Southern New South Wales (NSW) at Wollongong the next day. They set out to give us a real hard send-off, putting on the biff from the start. They didn't want to play football; they just wanted to fight. But we had put out a very strong forward-orientated side – eight or nine forwards in the thirteen, Phil Lowe on the wing, Bob Irving in the centres – and they came off worst. We did well to get a side on the paddock at all; I still have the image in my mind of one of our forwards sitting on the pavement outside the team hotel at five o'clock that morning, very much the worse for wear. I backed up and played – and got a bout of concussion for my troubles – but I don't think we were feeling too much pain. In fact afterwards I felt quite sorry for the other team because they looked a real battered outfit. Every one of them had cuts and bangs. I got my knock in the early part of the game when someone belted me. I remember Roger telling me afterwards that I'd kicked somebody up the backside on one occasion. I didn't realise I'd done it; I was on automatic pilot. It was a funny occasion, resulting in a 24–11 victory, which left us with just one loss in the whole tour of Australia.

Going on and beating New Zealand was the icing on the cake. We played three Tests over there and the Kiwis were never really a threat because, by that time, our side was so strong and confident. We started slowly in each of the three Tests but just *knew* we could do what we had to do to win. Mid-winter New Zealand came as a bit of a shock after

Australia. I remember Greymouth; how low I was in spirits there, posted in a room by myself in a gloomy, wet town in which there wasn't a light to be seen after half past six at night. And Wellington, so windy and wet. And soggy Carlaw Park . . . I think it's better now, but it used to be a real quagmire back then, a tidal ground where the mud stuck like glue.

I remember one time heading back in to Greymouth on the train late at night after a match. Back at the hotel the bar closed at midnight and some of the players bribed the driver: 'We want to get back quickly, before twelve o'clock.' After a while I went up into the cabin with the driver. That was terrific; there was a lot of wildlife close to the tracks as the train's lights cut through the night, possums and other animals. I took a can of New Zealand lager with me. The driver, though, had a *flagon* planted there, from which he'd take a large swig every now and then. 'What's that you're drinking?' he asked me. I told him, and his response was to grab the can and fling it out the cabin window. 'This is much better . . . we'll share this,' he said. I'm still not sure what it was, but here we were on this blackest of nights, speeding along, me and the train driver, swigging some concoction.

Eventually nature took its course. 'Listen, I'm going to have go to the toilet,' I said. 'I'll go back.'

'Don't bother,' he said. And with that he pulled the brakes on, stopped the train and opened the door! It was hilarious. Everybody thought there was some drama, or we'd run over an animal or something. We never did get back for midnight and last drinks, despite the driver's best intentions. At one stage we were going so fast that Jack Harding came up front. 'For Christ's sake slow down,' he said to the driver. 'We want to get back in one piece.'

That 1970 tour was something very, very special to me, as I'm sure it was for every member of the Great Britain party. I was young and full of fun, and visiting Australia for the first time really opened my eyes – the sheer vastness of the place was something that never left me. The camaraderie between everybody in the squad was tremendous; every day was fun. Training was fun, but all the players were competitive among ourselves because we were all fighting for a place in the Test team. I loved that atmosphere and it brought the best out of me. All the players had full-time jobs at home, several like me had to go down the mines, so to go on a three-month tour, staying in hotels and living the life of a full-time professional player was like a dream come true. You couldn't get any more professional than we were, training every day, sometimes twice or three times a day. I used to get up every morning and go for a three-mile run before breakfast with the coach, Johnny Whiteley. The result was I was fitter than I had ever been in my life. And it was the same for every player in the Lions team, whilst we were away on tour everyone was making the same progress in their fitness, so you didn't fully realise the improvements you were making individually. It was only when I got back to Castleford after the tour and started training with the other guys that I realised just how far I'd moved on. I was two or three metres quicker, and much more confident mentally, than I had been before I went away on tour. When you win a Test series against the best (which invariably means the Australians in the world of rugby league), psychologically you make a great step forward.

THREE

Manly Man

Back in Sydney, before we said our farewells to Australia and its people during their 1970 season, I had done important business. A day or two before we left I had visited Jim Comans in his Macquarie Street office. 'Yes, there are clubs interested in you coming back,' he told me. The front runners were Manly and St George. We left it at that; any further business could wait until I got home. I had the utmost faith in Comans, a sincere, genuine person who knew football and footballers. Later he seemed the perfect choice as head of the NSW Rugby League Judiciary when the game in Australia was going through something of a crisis.

Not so long after we got home, I went to the Castleford boardroom and explained to the directors that I intended emigrating to Australia. They didn't believe me. I'm sure they thought I was just bluffing to get more money out of them. Their response was: 'Well, you can't. We won't let you go.' So I left it at that; I just didn't reply. By then I had already taken the necessary first steps, got all the details sewn up, and organised the ten pounds' passage. The final decision that the club I would be joining was almost certainly going to be Manly came during the World Cup in November (more of that later), when I met up with Manly secretary Ken Arthurson, who was managing the Australian team. Ken advised: 'Just hop on a plane and come out to Australia. I'll sort it out with Castleford then.'

I played for Cas in the first-round game of the 1971 Challenge Cup, against Whitehaven, then bought my ticket. It was only then that they realised I was deadly serious. The fee Cas placed on my head, and much aired in the press, was twenty thousand pounds – an astronomical figure in those days.

Not surprisingly, the press were not slow in reminding me of the problems I'd had in Australia during the Lions tour, but it was something I was ready for. Before going I told the *Daily Mail*'s Brian Batty: 'I realise I could well be provoked again out there, but I am determined to ignore it. I realise where I went wrong – I won't make the same mistakes again. I am not just going for the rugby. I like Australia and the life out there, and this is a real adventure, for I have no club or job yet.'

I left from Leeds City railway station on an overnight sleeper to London in January 1971, just me and my bags and a morning paper – and with no one from the club there to say goodbye. The farewell party was a small one, my mum and dad, their next-door neighbour Brian Norden, and Sue Sault, who had recently become my fiancée and who was to join me in Sydney later that year. There was no contract with Castleford to concern me, although there was much to be worked out. In those days you just signed on and that was for a lifetime, unless you negotiated a transfer to another club. So I sort of jumped out of the situation and said, 'Look, we'll negotiate that at a later stage. I'm gone, I'm of no value to you. I'm in Australia.'

I remember there was a mail strike on at the time and I got no more than a brief message through that I was arriving on a particular flight. I landed late on a Sydney summer's night, and was greeted by Jim Comans and Ken Arthurson, and some media people. Even though I'd been in Australia the previous year I still had trouble coming to terms with the enormous media interest in rugby league, and anything vaguely involved with the game. Almost 30 years on, nothing has changed; the attention paid by the media to the game, especially in New South Wales and Queensland, is unfailingly generous and extensive. In 1970 it was quite a revelation for a boy used only to the *Pontefract Express* and the *Yorkshire Post*. After some interviews on that night of my arrival, Ken Arthurson eventually whisked me across the Harbour Bridge and down the peninsula to Manly – and to my new life. It was one place I hadn't been to on the tour, and I was very impressed, gazing out over the waves from the Manly Pacific Hotel, where I was better looked after than ever before in my life.

The Australians were back on top of the league world by then – or thought they were. They had beaten us in the final of the World Cup at Headingley in November 1970 in another one of those 'most brutal games we've ever seen'. The match gained much notoriety as the years went by and became known as 'the Battle of Leeds'. It was a hard enough game all right, although no harder than some others I have played. In the end I felt a certain responsibility for the fact that we lost it (12–7). We had beaten the Aussies convincingly, 11–4, in the lead-up game and that, added to the events of the previous Australian winter on their home soil when we were clearly superior, had Great Britain as hot favourites. With hindsight, I think a little arrogance had crept into the side because we had won the lead-up games convincingly, whilst the Aussies had been beaten by France at Bradford's Odsal Stadium. We were a little below strength for the World Cup final, with Roger Millward out injured, but it was a game we were thoroughly capable of winning.

We fell for the thimble and pea a bit; we got tangled up in the rough stuff and lost our way. I think the Australian tactics were just right. They knew they were up against a good football team. I'm sure their thinking was that if they could preoccupy us with the physical stuff they had enough very good players themselves to have a real chance. I cost us a try, charging into Ron Coote with the intention of hurting him – which is what you did in internationals of that era – and had the ball jarred out of my hands. They picked it up and on the next play winger Lionel Williamson scored. We failed to take some available chances – one being when John Atkinson had a clear opportunity to score a try on the left wing in the first half, but turned back inside instead of going for the corner. I believe he would have scored. It was a tough, intense game, although perhaps not living up to its subsequent legendary status of infamy.

All the international games in those days were tough uncompromising battles and I don't remember that day being any more vicious than any of the others. However, there was certainly some over-the-top stuff. I remember one instance, down the right-hand side when big Mark Harris was chasing our centre Syd Hynes. Syd had done something to Billy Smith off the ball. At times it was like there were two games going: one involving the football and the other more to do with players pursuing players *off* the ball. I remember one thing very well: an Aussie player biting me hard in the middle of the back as he made a tackle – just sinking his teeth in. I know who it was, but it's all long ago and far away now and we won't worry about that. I have teased him a little about it in the years since.

To be honest, we didn't play much football in that World Cup final. Towards the end the frustration was creeping in, and the more frustrated we got, the more confident the Australians became. I know I did a few things in that game that I'm not proud of. For example, I did a silly thing to a bloke who was to become a team-mate at Manly later – John 'Lurch' O'Neill. I jumped on him at one stage when he was on the floor. It wasn't malicious, more a frustration thing. A gentle tap with the foot. 'Lurch' had a big game that day, a huge game. He was playing against a very solid pack – we still had Dennis Hartley, Tony Fisher and Cliff Watson in the front row – and he really stood up to be counted. Bobby Fulton had a big game too; every time he got the ball the danger signals were flashing for us. It certainly ended in some drama with John Atkinson giving Eric Simms a 'love tap' on full-time when Simms came in to shake hands. Then they went into it and Cliffy Watson sailed in to get involved. It's a strange thing, but I became very good mates with a number of the Aussies who played that afternoon. That's football.

*

The natural advantages of a good climate and an abundance of good food became apparent in my early days in Australia after I made the big move. I remember an early, informal training run in Manly which gave me quite a jolt on the subject of fitness. Manly coach Ron Willey arrived on the morning of the second day after my arrival to take me for a gallop. We had a run with Ken Arthurson and some other guys; around the front, and around the harbourside of Manly. I was 23 at the time and considered myself fairly fit, having come straight out of the English season. Some of the guys I was running with this day must have been in their late fifties or early sixties, and I thought to myself, 'I'm going to be waiting around for these old fellas.' Anyhow, we took off – and they finished up waiting for *me*. I was (and am) one of those people who try very hard to compete, but back then I just didn't have the aerobic fitness level that they had. It really got me thinking. I mean, some of these blokes were 40 years older than me, yet they left me behind. And when we got there – I think the run was about five miles, it seemed a lot longer (maybe I was suffering jet-lag) – we went through 15 minutes of callisthetics, sit-ups, push-ups and various other exercises. Then they said, 'C'mon, we're going to run back now.' Oh no!

It was an incredible environment to be in. Gazing out over the Pacific I thought, All this and they pay you as well! All this time the negotiations were proceeding, with Jim Comans at the helm. St George made an offer to Castleford of twelve and a half thousand pounds, which was a lot of money in those days, but Manly eventually topped it with a record fifteen thousand, and some toing and froing over whether we were talking *dollars* or *pounds*. It was really no contest, even if the money had been the same. Ken Arthurson had done the right thing by me and I was already halfway to being a Manly player. It would have taken something extraordinary for me to leave there and go to St George. Apart from that, it was the right choice for other reasons: St George seemed on their way down after so many great years (11 premierships straight from 1956 to 1966!) and the Manly team was in a building phase. I signed for five years. The press guessed the contract at fifty thousand dollars and were close enough to the mark.

On 5 March 1971 I played my second club game in Australia, a pre-season fixture against Wests at Brookvale Oval watched by 8,000 people, scored a try and – guess what? – got sent off! I really fell for the thimble and pea trick. The Wests forwards baited me, and I retaliated and got marched. It cost me a week out of football. 'I have learned my lesson early in the piece and you can go ahead with all the niggling in the world,' I told the Sydney media. In fact I was sent off again a few weeks later, but I rated myself unlucky this time. Canterbury prop Bill Noonan ran into my elbow at some speed, doing him very little good. The incident came in the last minutes of the match; it looked very ugly, but it was also purely accidental. The Judiciary took a different view and suspended me for three weeks.

My Sydney premiership début came against Parramatta at Brookvale and brought a 38–9 victory for Manly. It was a nice way to start. The critics were kind: 'I was startled by lock Mal Reilly's form,' wrote former Australian hooker and captain Ian Walsh. 'He's as good as I've seen. In fact I can't remember when I saw an English forward get through so much work in a game.'

The early match against Wests set the tone for what I came to expect and had to adjust to in Sydney football. I had arrived with something of a reputation and everyone was hell-bent on fixing me up. The game was survival, a matter of looking after yourself. I have always found the best avenue of defence was attack – getting the ground rules square to start off with. Looking back now, some of the things that went on in those days make me shudder. No way could it happen in the modern game; nowadays, it's just not on. The game has changed a lot and I don't condone many of the things that happened then; really it was dog eat dog. Back then I never really knew exactly what would be coming at me on any Saturday or Sunday afternoon. More than once I was spat on, something that's especially hard to take. My own methods were direct. It wasn't as if I had a quiet way with some of the things I did, it was blatant. I could defend myself just as well carrying the ball as the other way, and there's no doubt I did some damage 'offensively'. Likewise, in defence, it was just a split second reaction thing. To the referees it wasn't such an obvious foul. However, as they became accustomed to my game – and also to the stuff thrown at me – I think they did become aware of the situation. At Manly some of the players nicknamed me 'Kiss', as in 'Liverpool Kiss'.

That first afternoon against Wests was fairly typical. One of their forwards in particular antagonised me, and I reacted. From that first day I knew the way it was going to be. The referees were all right with me; I don't think I was singled out. In fact, they were quite fair. In five years in Australia I was sent off and suspended on seven or eight occasions, of which I'm not too proud. I got to know Dick Dunn, head of the Judiciary, quite well. I remember him saying to me one night, 'Malcolm, you really don't have to do this. You don't have to be involved in this kind of play at all. You've got enough skill to get by without being over-aggressive.' And Jim Comans would tell me the same thing; as well as being my legal advisor he became a good friend, a man I much respected. Jim did his best to steer me on the right track – but occasionally I veered.

*

My fitness was up to the level of the rest of the Manly team by the time that first season of 1971 got under way. I was a keen trainer anyway and within a month or so of training with the squad I was on par with most of them, apart from exceptions like Allan Thomson, a nuggetty second-row forward who played Test football for Australia and toured with the Kangaroos in '67. He had limited ball-handling ability but defensively he never stopped working in a match. Allan was a ferocious trainer. He was always at the ground three-quarters of an hour before we trained, doing interval work, full lengths of the field. He was absolutely, superbly, fit.

We missed out that first year in the build-up to the premiership that seemed inevitably headed Manly's way, finishing third after being pipped by St George 15–12 in the preliminary final. The year left me with a permanent legacy I could well have done without. In the seventh-round game against Eastern Suburbs at the SCG on 26 June, I did my right knee in – thanks to the big, fast wingman Bill Mullins, who hit me side on and seriously damaged the lateral ligaments. It was my own fault because I left myself in his way. Effectively I was to struggle for the rest of my career with that knee which became quite famous via the Sydney media. Part of the senovial membrane was trapped in the joint and it would be OK for a while and then collapse on me. For three minutes or so I would be – almost literally – legless; then I would get going again.

Ken Arthurson delights now in telling the story of how sick he would get of the Reilly knee; how he would walk into the Manly dressing-room at training to be greeted by the sight of a cluster of medical blokes, with the knee poking up somewhere in the middle of them. I had an operation at the end of that first season in which they removed the cartilage, but mainly had a bit of a look around, with no further repairs. Many Sydney newspaper articles focused on 'the knee'. The *Daily Telegraph* columnist, Mike Gibson, contributed the most famous – a mock interview with my knee, which spoke with a Yorkshire accent! Next season, and the next, I struggled with it and it wasn't until I went back to England in 1976 that I had a second operation – a Macintosh reconstruction. It is still not too good, and the other one's not all that hot either.

I was in pain every time I played. Training was difficult, as was main-taining my level of fitness. And two or three times in any game I would be in agony – periods that would last for a few minutes before I got back to a more 'normal' level. I'd hobble around for a while, and then I'd be OK. At times, when I was going through bad periods with the knee, I had to amend my game to get through matches. Now and then I copped flak in the media because of it. *Rugby League Week* of 22 April 1972 reported: 'Malcolm Reilly seems to have lost all inclination to run with the ball. He is completely overplaying the role of ball-distributor; he is not busting the defence as he did last season.' The truth is, I was struggling. I was never again free from injury after that knock in 1971. The off-season became increasingly important to me as I spent the time working hard to get the knee into at least reasonable shape. Inevitably, though, three or four games into any new season, I would be in trouble again.

How I wish the technology available now was available back then. In recent times I had a cartilage out of the other knee. It was incredible; within half an hour of coming back from the operating theatre, I was walking. And they'd not just taken the cartilage out but done some repairs on one of the joints as well. Years ago you'd have been completely immobilised for a week or so before physiotherapy started. I finished my career, of course, playing at number ten (front row), where much of what I did was directing the ball around the park.

For me, 1971 was a settling-in year at Manly. I was homesick at times, and missed the social side of things back home. In a story that appeared in the papers in England I listed the drawbacks as 'missing my parents, my home, my mates and my two Kippax locals, in that order'. But never did I doubt I had done the right thing. I went into lodgings with a family called Hardings, nice people who made me feel very much at home. Susan arrived mid-season and eventually we moved into our own apartment at Little Manly. I loved the natural things about the Australian lifestyle. I was mad about surfing and scuba diving. I was one of those crazy Poms who'd be straight into the seas in the middle of June when the Aussies are wrapped up shivering with the cold. There was so much to do in Australia.

I have probably always thought of Sydney as something of a 'resort'. It's a beautiful city. I remember one of the first times I visited Sydney Opera House, which was opened by the Queen in my second year with Manly. I had won a contest for 'best try' in the pre-season competition, and they made the presentation at the Opera House. A brand new Leyland car!

Manly's dreams of a quarter of a century came true in the second year I was in Sydney, 1972, a year in which I captained the side briefly – too soon – before the job was handed back to our crusty hooker Freddie Jones. A team captain has to be someone who is strategically and tactically strong. With some players the extra responsibility can detract from their individual performance. Brad Fittler (Sydney City and the Australian captain in 1999) is perhaps a case in point in my view, although he is maturing well. I certainly was a bit 'green' for the job back then. As a matter of fact when they appointed me captain over the incumbent, Fred Jones, I said to him, 'It doesn't matter whether I'm captain or not Freddie; you're still the gaffer.' And that's how I felt.

At that stage of my career, the captaincy impaired my performance and after three of four games they came to me and said, 'Malcolm, your performance hasn't quite been up to scratch, so we're going to take this burden off you.' Fred Jones, a figurehead at the club, was the perfect man for the job, and it was on him that a very significant honour fell several months later. Fred was also a great character, a guy with a deep thirst, a dry wit and a fabulous commitment to the Manly cause. When Phil Lowe came to Manly, both Ron Willey, our coach, and the media raised the question about Phil's tackling. And it was Fred who went up to big Phil one day and said to him, 'You must be Harry Lowe!'

'What do you mean – *Harry* Lowe?' responded Phil.

'Well, you surely can't be *Phil* Lowe,' said Fred. 'You must be his brother Harry.' And from that day Phil Lowe was known to all and sundry as 'Harry'.

In '72 the Sea Eagles, under Freddie Jones, won the premiership – the prize they had been chasing since the day the club came into the competition in 1947. We beat a quality opponent, Eastern Suburbs, which boasted the likes of Ron Coote, a guy I'd come up against on a regular basis in international football and whom I much respected, the great front-rower Arthur Beetson, the big centre Mark Harris and the man who later became the chief executive officer of the Australian and New South Wales Leagues, John Quayle. We beat them in the grand final 19–14 after getting away to 19–4 before they came back at us with two tries in the last ten minutes.

The feeling of elation after the game was just tremendous. Manly have for so long been the bridesmaids of the competition. Now they had done it at last. In later years there has been a strong perception among Aussie league fans of Manly being the flash gits from the wealthy suburbs – the silvertails. But I don't think this was the case during my time with the club, although Manly certainly had a reputation as a big spender, a club which would target top players to achieve its ambitions. I think the 'silvertail' thing gained much more strength in the late '70s, particularly after the Manly raids on 'the fibros', Western Suburbs, which saw players like Les Boyd, Ray Brown and John Dorahy enticed across town to Manly. In more recent years you could equate Manly with Wigan back home.

The grand final was a wonderful experience, which was made even better because it was played on the Sydney Cricket Ground where so much of the city's sporting tradition lies. The build-up, however, wasn't as colourful or as intense as before Wembley. We had no special preparation, no hotel camps or anything like that. It wasn't like England before the Cup final. We came from home on the day of the match, met at the club and went to the SCG by coach if memory serves me correctly. I still remember so well, however, the run down the steps of the old Members' Stand – and out on to that huge, open field, with over 60,000 fans packed around.

Getting to grounds in Sydney was a problem for me now and then in those early days as I struggled to get to know the city. We used to make our own way to matches, by car. I remember that on one of the first times I went to Belmore (Canterbury's home ground) I had planned to follow one of the other players. However, in the morning there was a phone call: he had to leave early as he was meeting someone. 'You'll find it easily,' he said. 'There are loads of supporters going over.' I thought I knew basically where it was so I just took off. My colleague was right; there were plenty of Manly cars heading that way, ribbons and flags fluttering. I picked one out and trailed behind, thinking 'this is going to be easy'. And wouldn't you know – he was the one Manly fan who *wasn't* going to the game, despite the flags streaming out of the car window. I must have gone 15 miles out of my way following this guy before I realised there was something wrong. I finished up getting to the ground only 35 minutes before the kick-off. I just sped into the car park and jumped out, leaving Susan to park the car. When I offered my apologies and explanations, everyone just laughed.

We went back to the Manly Leagues Club on the night of the grand final win, and it was a very, very emotional occasion for everyone. The whole district was over the moon. We all got up on the stage and said a few words and the supporters cheered themselves hoarse. They were so swept up in the emotion of it all; I'm sure they would have cheered if I'd read them selections from the Sydney telephone book! I didn't stay too long; I just had a couple of drinks, then left. We had won Manly a grand final for the first time in the club's history, but I was in bed before ten o'clock, absolutely drained. I slept for a few hours, then got up again at half past two, headed down to the club and rejoined the celebrations. When it comes to the Aussie premiership it really is true what people say about players and supporters being drunk for a week after a grand final. I went back down to the Leagues Club that Monday afternoon and some of the boys had *still* not been home since Saturday night. The celebrations were still in full swing.

The club took us all to Fiji as a reward for winning the grand final and it turned out to be quite an experience, owing to a spot of bother that erupted one night at a nightclub in Nandi. A bunch of us got into some trouble – and how – and I'm not even sure whether I should tell the tale, even now. However, after all these years . . .

What happened was this. At this particular nightclub on this particular night there was an increasing friction with some of the local men who were showing understandable resentment at the interest women in the bar were showing in the Manly players. The blokes kept thumping us on the back and telling us they were our friends, but my ears pricked up when I heard Bobby Moses say, 'If one of those bastards hits me again, that's it, the ball's over the wall.' Nothing happened, however, until we left the club and were standing at a nearby taxi rank. There were only five of us by then: Bob Fulton, Fred Jones, Bobby Moses, Peter Peters and me. The others had already gone back to the hotel. Suddenly a big bunch of Fijians appeared and it was on.

Things got so fast and furious that at one stage I swung round and hit Freddie Jones square on the chin. Fred reckoned later that he was going all right until I knocked him on his arse – but at that stage you were just hitting anything that moved, and Freddie was a bit slow to react. Fred had been smart. Realising what was about to happen when the Fijians appeared he had taken out his false teeth and put them in his back pocket for safekeeping. Unfortunately, he got knocked down and there were also a few blokes around him kicking him viciously. When Fred did eventually come round his teeth were all in pieces. The only fortunate part about it was they weren't in his mouth when they broke!

Peter Peters played a starring role in the incident. He made a quick exit from the scene when he saw the trouble brewing, headed straight to the police station, and commandeered a Land-rover which he brought roaring down the street, lights flashing, bells ringing. Thankfully the Fijian blokes all ran off when they saw it coming. By then we were in a pretty bad way. Our captain, Freddie, was down, and he and Bob Moses ended up in hospital – which, as it happened, was a maternity hospital. Those of us who were still standing went back to the police station, where I caught one of the guys who had been involved in the fight and gave him a really hard time, interrogating him.

Had the story of this 'international' blue involving rugby league's premier team got out, it would have made banner headlines in Australia. But somehow the club managed to hush it up and in the public domain at least it has remained an untold story . . . until now. One of the players was all for calling the Australian consul to make a formal complaint, but had second thoughts.

Winning our second grand final the following year (1973) had much less impact, they always do second time around. There was a lot more pre-match newspaper hype with the second one, however, because it involved a clash between Englishmen – Cliff Watson and Tommy Bishop on one side (Cronulla) and me on the other. There was a lot of press talk about what they were going to do to me. Cronulla were in the same position that Manly had been in the year before; they were hungry, had never won the premiership. All the talk was that it would be a very fiery game.

And so it was. The first half was pretty close to a continuous brawl from start to finish under the benevolent refereeing of Keith Page. In one of the all-in brawls, at one stage Cliff Watson and I suddenly found ourselves face to face. In the same instant we both turned away and found someone else to sort out. Being tour friends creates a powerful bond, and that sort of camaraderie doesn't snap easily, especially when you're both far away in another country. I think if we'd have been in England then we would probably have tested the water with each other, but when you're playing the game away from home, well, it's all Pommies together. Little Tommy Bishop, though, was an exception to that unwritten rule. Tommy was bloody infuriating, a hornet who would intimidate and niggle if he thought the tactics could add a winning edge. In that grand final I can see him nipping in aggravating and straight away, back to the outskirts, snapping away behind his pack of forwards. Then he'd be in the referee's ear, or back behind the forwards, shouting abuse.

There was very little football played in the grand final of 1973 and most of what there was came from Bob Fulton, who won the game for us. Manly's win was not in any way a single-handed performance, but the two tries we scored were both brilliant individual efforts by Bob. I don't believe anyone else in rugby league could have scored them. One in particular was unbelievable; he must have run 120 metres. He ran from right to left, gained about five metres, then ran left to right, did a 90-degree turn and went around the defence – and scored under the posts. 'Bozo' had so much going for him: the change of pace, the speed, the strength. But, you know, much of it came down to preparation. He was ten years in front of a lot of the guys in his preparation and that, allied with a very special natural talent, is what made him so great.

My own grand final was short and painful, the match a somewhat strange memory for me considering that we won the premiership. I had little involvement, getting smashed out of it soon after the start. It was very early in the game and they were moving up quickly in defence, leaving opportunities at the back. I chipped over the top and followed the kick. I had said to our half-back, Johnny Mayes: 'Follow me through, I'm going to chip over.' As I did, Ron Turner, the Cronulla hooker and an opponent in the World Cup final in 1970, came in from the left, well after the ball had gone, and caught me full force with his knees right on the point of the pelvis. This was payback time. Turner had had his fair share of stick from me in previous games, including a whack in the mouth that needed 27 stitches to repair. To put it simply, I got my comeuppance. What goes around comes around. It was one of the worst injuries I had during my career and effectively it knocked me out of the grand final. I left the field to have painkilling shots, but even that made little difference. I was hobbling and useless, and the match had finished for me almost before it began. I don't hold anything against Ron Turner; that was the way football was played then.

We won the grand final 10–7, and now stood undisputed as kings of the league. Aussie journalist Geoff Prenter wrote in *Rugby League Week*: 'Call it vicious, call it great, call it anything you like – Manly are the 1973 Rugby League champions and they deserve the title.' Prenter wrote of 'wild, unrestrained punch-ups' – and in legend all these years later the grand final of '73 is remembered as the most violent ever in Australia. In winning, my club Manly had matched the achievement of my *former* club Castleford in winning back-to-back trophies – Cas, of course, had won the Challenge Cup at Wembley in both 1969 and '70.

Among all the hard stuff there were some wonderful skills in the game at that time, with the bitter Manly–Souths rivalry ebbing to an extent as the Rabbitohs went into decline in the '70s, and we Englishmen were able to make our contribution to the Australian game on that score, with men such as Bishop, Brian Lockwood, Mike Stephenson, Laughton and Bill Ashurst adding deft touches they had learned on playing fields far away. My own game, based on variety, was part of that too. It was in those early years of the limited tackle rule (four tackle from 1967, six tackle from 1971) that the high kick became a new (well, not so new really) and lethal weapon. There was debate about who could claim credit for the 'bomb', as the media soon tagged it. Its beginnings can probably be traced to the game's earliest years when oldtime players in their long shorts and ankle-high boots would hoist up-and-unders. John Peard (Easts and Parramatta) got credit in some quarters in Australia for 'inventing' it, and I probably received some similar acclaim. For my own part the fact was that I had used the kicking game from my earliest days in rugby league; it was really just an extension of my days as a soccer player. I recall that Ron Willey used to encourage me to use the kick when I first arrived in Australia, in 1971. There is no doubt that 'Bomber' Peard perfected the high punt in his years with the Roosters and especially during their premiership-winning years of 1974 and '75. But there is also no doubt that I was using the kick well before John did his 'perfecting'. I am not putting my hand up to claim that I invented the bomb; but I certainly utilised it to a high degree – and so did Easts under the coaching of Jack Gibson.

At Manly, we were quite happy to use it on the first tackle. Straight from a tap, too; we'd hoist the ball and there would be five or six chasers – with the poor full-back completely isolated back there. I have clear memories of that tactic back in 1971 and '72. In those days the full-back got very little help from his team-mates. Things are even more sophisticated with the boot these days – including the cross-kicks for the wingers, and the 'reverse swing' kick that Brad Fittler does so well, as Deryck Fox used to in England in the late '80s and early '90s.

My Great Britain team-mate Phil Lowe came to Manly as we prepared for the 1974 season and I had two enjoyable seasons with him. Phil had starred in the 1972 World Cup and '73 Test series against Australia in England, and Ken Arthurson moved swiftly to sign him and make Phil a Sea Eagle. It took Phil a while to settle in. For some time our coach Ron Willey, a genial man with a hard edge, didn't think Phil was up to scratch defensively, and the early weeks were tough for him. Phil was a devastating runner, though and once he had settled in he made a huge impact. A fellow back-rower, I regarded myself as possessing above average pace for a forward. However, when we were doing sprints Phil just used to make a joke of running alongside me. I'd be flat out and he'd be looking back over his shoulder, going at about 80 per cent of his top pace.

I took Phil under my wing when he first arrived in Sydney and showed him around. We got on really well and lived in each other's pockets for a long while; the friendship has lasted strongly up to now. We share the same birthday, 19 January, although I'm a couple of years younger than Phil.

I'm sure Phil found things just the way I did in Sydney – invigorating and thoroughly enjoyable, although the football that was at the heart of it all was unrelentingly hard.

The seasons that Phil Lowe and I played together belonged to a brilliant Eastern Suburbs side under the coaching of Jack Gibson, but they still brought a lot of success and consistent hope to Sea Eagles fans that we *might* win again. For me, the 1974 season included a couple of consecutive unwanted 'holidays', when I copped two weeks on a headbutting charge, then four weeks on a high-tackle charge after an incident which involved Australia's then Test half-back Tommy Raudonikis of Western Suburbs. In '74 we finished second to Easts on the ladder, scoring only one try less than a truly outstanding Tricolours outfit. But we went down 24–10 to Canterbury and then 23–20, after we had led 15–4 at half-time, to Wests in the semis – and were out of it.

In 1975, my last year with Manly, Frank Stanton, a man I respected a great deal, took over the coaching reins. His move from second- to first-team coach was the first step in what was to be a notable career, including being at the helm of the famous 'Invincible' Kangaroos who, in 1982, became the first Australian touring side to go through Europe undefeated. Again there was much success at Manly and the consistent production of quality attacking football; with 477 points scored, including 90 tries, we scored more points than any other team in the competition. But again we fell short come September. After losing to St George 10–3 in the first semi-final, we beat Parramatta 22–12 in the minor semi-final the following week. But by then, unfortunately, my season – and effectively my career with Manly – was over. My knee packed up in the finals and I became a spectator on the Hill as my team battled to try and add another premiership to the 1972 and '73 successes. In the end Easts beat us comfortably, 28–13, in the preliminary final, and that was that.

I struggled at times during that last year; including the previous off-season back at Castleford, I had played three straight seasons of football on a knee that really wasn't up to it. It was becoming obvious to others, and former Australian captain Keith Barnes, at that time a newspaper columnist in Sydney, took a look at me in June 1975 and wrote: 'I reckon Reilly is jaded – obviously feeling the strain from playing the off-season with Castleford . . . and I wouldn't be surprised if he was carrying an injury.' That just about summed it up. So, in October, with a heart both heavy and happy, I packed my things and got ready to drag my perpetually sore knee home to England.

FOUR

Worlds Apart: The Return Home

During the Australian off-season of 1974–75 I went back to England for a time and played ten games with Castleford. While I was there I was offered, and accepted, the player-coaching position at Cas for the following season (1975–76). I had an option for another season at Manly (1976) but a number of things made me feel it was time to go home. Maybe it would have been different had I managed to buy the piece of real estate in Cromer Heights that I had bid for. Perhaps with that sort of permanency I would have been more inclined to stay in Sydney.

The talks with Castleford had begun in early 1974, when the club chairman, Phil Brunt, came over to see me. We corresponded from that point and Phil tempted me with the lure of the coaching position at Cas, plus the prospects of securing a house in the quiet village of Ledsham, close to where he lived. There were reasons for making the move. The hard Aussie grounds were exacerbating the problems I was encountering with my knee, and Sue was missing home quite a bit. Summing it all up, I thought that it was time to go.

When it came to the departure, however, I was very, very sorry to be moving on. I can still remember the day at Sydney's Mascot airport very clearly. Frank Stanton, Ron Willey and Ken Arthurson were there, and for me it was a terribly sad occasion. There had been a few emotional partings at Manly, and there had been leaving parties for weeks, but when it eventually came to that final moment – of saying my goodbyes and getting on the plane – it was tough, I can tell you. My mind was racing with the thought that I was turning my back on some of the best years of my life.

By then there were three of us in the Reilly family. Sue and I had been married in England, in the All Saints Church, in 1972 at the time of the World Cup. Ken Arthurson and all the Manly players who were on tour with the 1972 Australian team came to the wedding: Dennis Ward, John O'Neill, Fred Jones, Ray Branighan and Bob Fulton, plus some others from the club and the mayor of Manly, David Hay. Bob Higham, who was the club doctor, was my best man. It was a great affair with them all being

51

over there. Our son Glen was born in Manly Hospital on 26 January 1974. Daughter Lyndsey came later, born in England on 24 May 1978.

There was a price to pay for my years with Manly. The step I took in leaving England to become a Sea Eagle meant that, in the end, I only played for Great Britain nine times. Five years away is a long time, and obviously there were many Tests played over those years. I remember especially the pangs of regret in 1974 when the Lions team came out to Australia and sitting in the stand were such players as Phil Lowe, Doug Laughton, Bill Ashurst, Mike Stephenson and myself. The international board rules of the time, which precluded us from playing for our country because we were with Aussie clubs, certainly didn't help the Great Britain cause. There was quite a lot of speculation that I would be included in the squad for the 1972 World Cup, which was played in France several weeks after the end of my season with Manly. Speculation increased because I had returned to England at that time for my wedding to Susan, and did not plan to return to Australia until the new year. At that time no overseas-based player had ever represented Great Britain before, but despite selector Harry Womersley stating publicly how much he wanted me in the team, I wasn't included. Mind you, the British boys did OK without me that year, winning the World Cup after an epic extra-time period in the final against Australia in the French city of Lyon. Yes, my Test count would have been much greater if I'd stayed on in England and obviously I have some regrets about that. But only a few. I would have loved to have captained my country. I missed some special times, some tours, winning the World Cup, some Tests against the old enemy Australia – events I would love to have been involved in. The 1970 tour of Australia remains as one of the great highlights of my life, and there have been occasional pangs of regret that I never got to play in another Ashes campaign. However, the best thing I ever did in my life in football was to make the decision to play in Sydney, and with Manly. Twenty years on I made the same decision again and went back to Australia – this time as a coach.

I packed a few mementoes in my bag when I left Sydney in 1975: a Manly jersey (I've still got it) and the premiership blazer from 1972 – a truly awful thing with wide lapels, in a sort of off-pink colour. I mean, you could never actually *wear* it. Unlike back home in England, they didn't give teams medals in Australia at that time, they gave blazers. When we won the comp again in 1973, we were instructed to go back to the same clothing shop. All the boys were getting fitted out for their blazers, but I said quietly to the guy at the counter, 'Listen – if you don't mind would you give me two pairs of slacks instead of a blazer?'

'No trouble at all,' he said.

So that's what I got for my part in winning the 1973 Sydney rugby league premiership – two pairs of trousers. At least I got some wear out of those!

The gap between Australian and English football had widened noticeably by the time I got back home in late 1975. Coming back after my five years with Manly, the difference in fitness levels in the two countries stood out a mile, with the Aussies way ahead. The first training session back at Cas sticks in my mind. I had been on holiday and hadn't played for two or three weeks, but I was as quick as the backs, even though I was a forward playing on a bung knee. I didn't realise how bad things were until I started chasing balls with them and then it became glaringly evident. My level of fitness had automatically increased with the intensity and general fitness level of the game in Australia. I know if I had stayed in England, my fitness would have stayed at the British level. That's human nature; you do as much as you need to do. I believe that the imbalance is still there today, although narrower now than it was 20 years ago.

At Castleford I began the process of change. We used tractor tyres for tackling practice and a weights machine. I was very aware by then that the physical side of the game had to be addressed. Some players saw the way immediately – but you can't make all the horses drink, even if you do lead them to the water. Some of the players were going along only half-heartedly, reluctant to change their ways. What made it harder was that the game was barely semi-pro; everything was being done in the evenings, after work. I progressively introduced a variety of training aids over the seasons: the 'Gauntlet' – pads mounted on springs with some 300 cwt of resistance; and 'sprint suits' – sort of cut-down wet suits with weights added to increase the resistance, and defence shields.

In later trips to the USA, via my Great Britain and then Newcastle Knights connections, I kept myself educated on the latest game-related equipment. I formed an affiliation with the Kansas City Chiefs and particularly with Al Saunders, head coach of the wide receivers. Visits to their off-season training camp at River Falls were a great learning experience.

It was a case of worlds apart; Castleford was so far removed from a glamour club like Manly it was almost like being in a different game. We had no star players at all; we bred our own. The club didn't go out and spend money on signings, because it couldn't afford to. The chairman, Phil Brunt, insisted on balancing the books, and if that was sometimes frustrating as we missed out on players for the want of a few extra pounds, I could also see that it made sound business sense. However, without the signings – the addition of extra talent – we were always struggling to compete on the field with the big spenders. Phil was the man who got me back to Cas, in late 1975. Neighbours at Ledsham, we were of like mind and very close. I would meet him two or three times a week in his office in the Potteries, in the industrial area of Castleford, and we would talk football through the afternoon and try and plot great deeds for our team. We didn't have much to spend, so we worked hard to try and buy the *right* players for the club. Phil was a cranky old fellow at times, but he was a terrific guy, and great for the club. He loved the place. Back home in Ledsham, I still see his widow June all the time, a lovely lady.

We lost three successive Challenge Cup semi-finals to Hull, who had bought Steve Norton from us along the way. A budding young star named Lee Crooks was coming through their ranks, and Garry Schofield was rising to prominence. Even more importantly, Hull later still unleashed the cheque book to sign the likes of Peter Sterling and John Muggleton from Australia alongside the Kiwi quartet of James Leuluai, Dane O'Hara, Gary Kemble and Fred Ah Kuoi. These were the people who turned games for them. It was frustrating for us at Cas, but that was the way of the world in rugby league. In that period we suffered a version of the 'North Sydney syndrome', which I got to know all about during my times in Australia – the syndrome of being up there in the big games with a chance, then stumbling at the penultimate hurdle.

I remember once coming back on the coach from a game at Headingley and I was just about ready to join the Foreign Legion, I was so fed up. I thought to myself, I'm going nowhere. It was just the way it was. Hull had the money – and spent it. We didn't. Our own overseas signings were at a significantly lower level, but effective all the same. In fact, at Castleford I was one of the first people to start bringing Aussies over because when I came back home, I brought players back with me. Big forward Paul Kahn joined for a time; later he played State of Origin for Queensland. We signed the tall running back-rower Brett Atkins and Steve Robinson, the St George stand-off. They all did well for us. But, with no disrespect, the calibre of players we were bringing over was not that of the Peter Sterlings – because we simply couldn't afford them.

Later on, when we had a little more money, we didn't always get full value from our Australian imports. We had problems with a few of them. I brought Chris Johns over one year, when he was only a young kid, and he started knocking about with one or two of the wrong people. One night he went to a nightclub in town, got involved in a bit of a fracas, and came training the next day with a broken hand. We were paying him decent money and as a result of the incident he missed nearly half the games that he should have been playing, which was a shame, because he was a sensational player. But Chris was a heck of a nice guy – and talented. I can picture him running in our Christmas sprint handicap at the club, off scratch – and winning the race, despite the plaster cast on his broken hand. He was quick and had very good leg speed. Johns went on to play for Australia.

Someone who was a big success was the 19-year-old New Zealand scrum-half Gary Freeman. I signed him long before he made his mark, and then spent the rest of my club coaching career trying to get him back! He originally came over to England to play for the short-lived Kent Invicta club. When we played them, he stood out a mile. So when we discovered that he wasn't very happy down there, I invited him up to Castleford and he eventually became a lifelong friend. I've been on the other side of the fence to Gary in a Test series and he was a very determined and competitive player – definitely one of the best scrum-halfs in recent years.

Queenslander Bob Lindner was another overseas signing. Bob and Ian French, who both played for Wynnum Manly (Brisbane), each had a spell at Castleford. They were different types of players, but in their day both extremely good. We got Bobby over for just one season; however, he was hampered by a few injuries and though he did fairly well, he wasn't outstanding. He came back a second time, after I had left Cas and Dave Sampson was coach, and I understand he didn't go down at all well that time. Ian French played for Castleford in a Challenge Cup final along with another Queenslander, Jamie Sandy.

That 1986 Wembley win over Hull Kingston Rovers, in which French and Sandy played big parts, was the highlight of my coaching career at Castleford. But there was always hope at Cas, plenty of enjoyment and certainly some success in the years I was there. In 1976–77 we reached our first Floodlit Trophy final since 1968, and repeated history when we beat Kevin Ashcroft's Leigh side. Then we won the John Player Trophy, beating Blackpool Borough in a highly entertaining final at Salford. That season I also made it back into the England jersey for the first time in six years. However, the match was no celebration; it was a miserable game, lost 6–2 to Wales. In 1977 we won the Yorkshire Cup, repeating the performance in 1981 in a season when I was edging towards retirement as a player.

People who visited both camps during the week of the 1986 Wembley final told me they were sure Cas were going to win, because when they went to see Cas training there was such a buzz about them, whereas everybody at Hull KR seemed a bit flat. I was just as confident, because the preparation had been absolutely spot on. We were a confident team and we were ready. In the hotel on the eve of the match I had nothing on my mind but the game. Preparation is the science of success, and I knew we were well prepared. I filled in my time writing my speech for the after-match function. Call it arrogance, or whatever you like, but that's how confident I was.

People at Hull KR would probably say, 'Oh, if Gavin Miller [the club's ace Aussie import] had been fully fit, it would have been a different story,' but in fact the score – 15–14 (after we had led 15–6) – flattered them, because we let in a couple of late tries. They scored with about 12 minutes remaining and then scored again virtually on the final hooter. If John Dorahy had kicked the touchline conversion in injury time they would have won – and that would have been an absolute travesty. There is a photo of me on the bench in those last few minutes at Wembley and the expression on my face seems to be saying, 'Here, what's happening? It's getting away from us.'

It was a truly wonderful day. I was then in my eleventh season coaching at Cas, and that's a lot of years to be knocking on the door waiting to win the big prize. We hadn't won the Challenge Cup since 1970, and there were elements of what we achieved in '86 that made it very special indeed. Former Castleford chairman Phil Brunt was ailing at the time, but managed to make it to Wembley, and I know what a great lift it was for him. In the final days before Phil finally succumbed to the cancer he had been battling, I know that the victory of 1986 would have been a ray of sunshine for him. For me, just to be there brought the memories flooding back – back to '69 when I won the Lance Todd Trophy, and to 1970, when we won again. This year the famous trophy awarded to the man of the match went to one half of our famous pair of twins, our scrum-half Bob Beardmore. After the match my son Glen, then 12, joined me in the dressing-room, and that made the occasion even more special.

The welcome home to Castleford was something grand. Times had been especially hard in the town due to the effect of the long miners' strike, factory closures and huge unemployment. However, Castleford was dressed to kill, awash with yellow and black, and thousands of people waited to greet the team as we travelled to the Civic Centre aboard an open-topped double-decker bus. It was a great example of what sport can do for a community.

The Challenge Cup was the shining achievement of my years with Cas. I stayed only one more season as coach, stepping down after I was appointed as Great Britain coach in 1987. Things may well have been more bountiful at Cas if we had had the money for one or two big signings, but we didn't, and we worked with what we had. The Castleford lads were as fit and well organised as any in the league. As soon as I took over, I brought some of my own weights to the club and eventually they built a gymnasium. I encouraged players to work with weights as often as I possibly could.

Kevin Ward was one of the best examples of the benefits of that encouragement. We had signed Ward from a soccer club and an Under-19s rugby league team, where he played as a centre, and he finished up as one of the finest front-row forwards in the game. He became so powerful through his weights programme that it was difficult for opponents – even Australian forwards – to compete with him. When Kevin was in Australia, playing for my old Manly club in 1987, he was fairly close to being the top front-rower in the world – a hugely powerful lad, competing with the Aussies at their own game. I'm told that his performance for Manly in helping them win the 1987 grand final was sensational. Just 24 hours off the plane from England he walked into heatwave conditions at the Sydney Cricket Ground – the match was played in temperatures above 30 degrees – and was rated by many as the outstanding player on the field.

Ignoring the reality, a lot of people in England continued to be complacent about the strength of the British game, until the all-conquering 1982 Kangaroos finally opened their eyes to the way things were. Frankly I had been of the belief there was going to be an ever-widening gap since the Great Britain tour of Australia in 1970. Back then, every Saturday and Sunday the playing fields around the Sydney metropolitan area were full of youngsters playing rugby league. Every field you passed was covered in young footballers. The game was growing so fast, it seemed to be almost running away with itself. From that quantity, I knew there would eventually come the *quality* at the highest level.

Added to that, the drain of top talent was all in one direction – from England to Australia. Apart from myself, others such as Brian Lockwood, Cliff Watson, Tommy Bishop, Phil Lowe, Bill Ashurst and Mike Stephenson all gave up their UK careers to join Sydney clubs. At one stage we had a full pack of international forwards playing in the NSW premiership, none of whom were eligible for the British team because of the way the rules were at that time. The signs of things to come were there for anyone who cared to read them.

However, there didn't seem to be any great interest in learning from my Australian experience when I got back to England. There was no path beaten to my door, and I wasn't the kind of guy to go out and start writing in newspapers about my exploits. Maybe I could have played a bit more for Great Britain after I came back, but due to the reality of my knee problem I had just about given up that sort of ambition by then. I wasn't chasing international football any more, although the opportunity was still there. Eric Ashton, who was Great Britain's team coach for the 1979 tour Down Under, asked me to captain the side – before Dougie Laughton was appointed. I told Eric I couldn't do it, because my leg was no good, which it wasn't. I needed an off-season's rest to get it right and I knew if I was going to go out to Australia it would have been a huge struggle. I didn't think it fair to the team.

In my 'second career' back in England, to start with, of course, I was a player–coach, a dual role that I didn't find too difficult. However, I have the most serious doubts that I could have possibly handled it in the modern era. In the early stages of my move into coaching, it was not much more than an extension of what I was doing out on the field anyway. It was a matter of being able to transform the team by giving on-field direction; a lot of my initial coaching success was built simply on my ability as a player. Being out on the field I could help shape the game from our point of view. Rugby league has advanced in giant strides since then. My view is that at the highest level it would be impossible for a player–coach to look after his own fitness and the demands of playing and still direct, motivate and encourage his players, and bring the best out of them. Coaching has become much more of a science; it would just not be possible for a coach to assess physically and mentally what is required as he battled his own fatigue and took care of his own obligations on the field.

A positive aspect of my new role at Cas was that there had been a five-year gap since I had been a player at Castleford. I didn't have to face the difficult transition from being one of the lads one day to being the coach the next. That situation can sometimes be very tricky. My strong belief is that there does need to be space between a coach and his players – some distance.

There was no video analysis of matches when I was playing at Manly or when I started coaching at Castleford. That extra string to the bow of the modern coach came later. Naturally, though, the players were thoroughly aware of key opponents. The profile of the game in Australia was so high that you knew the playing traits of players such as Ron Coote or Arthur Beetson very well indeed. In my view there is far too much video analysis nowadays. Although a coach must make his players aware of the opposition's traits and style, it is still a fact that the good sides concentrate more on their *own* game and let the other team do the worrying about them. There is a happy medium somewhere; my own preference has always been to create a good understanding with my own side and let the opposition worry about chasing *us* about. Players can be affected if there is too much focus on the opposition and too great an emphasis on stopping them playing rather than concentrating on how you intend to dictate and shape the game.

My struggles without major stars, without major influential match-winning players, made me realise the value of the Peter Sterlings and Wally Lewises of the world to a football team. In a Challenge Cup semi-final against Hull at Leeds in 1985, in which we were leading by four points with about 12 minutes to go, Sterling put a kick up on the last tackle. Gary Hyde, our left-centre at the time, elected to wait for the ball to come to him instead of going up to meet it. Sterling, who was only a little bloke, beat him to the punch and before he'd landed, the ball was already on its way to the support player, his brother-in-law John Muggleton, who had been 'bludging' on the blind side. Muggleton went 15 metres then threw a pass back inside that was never really on. And who do you think was there to take it? Sterling, of course – and over he went for the try as my head descended into my hands. Oh shit, I thought. We were playing very well at the time but by sitting back and waiting on that last tackle kick – sweating on the turnover – we had been caught out by a champion. The Peter Sterling try turned the game on its head. Instead of winning it, as we were poised to, we drew, bound for a replay – which we lost. Those sort of players can do those sort of things to you – and generally do.

We bred a lot of good juniors at Castleford, like the identical Beardmore twins Robert and Kevin, who were both extremely talented footballers, and Barry Johnson, who pushed for international honours and played for Yorkshire. We blended these younger players with some older heads such as full-back Geoff Wraith, who we got at a cut-price rate. At one stage we had my old 1970 Lions colleague, hooker Tony Fisher, in the front row with the local Alan Dickinson and John Burke, whom we signed from Keighley. However, there were always limitations on what we could spend and who we could buy. I don't think I ever spent any more than ten thousand pounds on any one player, whereas teams such as Leeds, Wigan, St Helens and the two Hull clubs shopped freely, unchecked by any financial restrictions. Phil Brunt would sell players to balance the books, which is not particularly good for the coach.

It was rather ironic that having spent my whole coaching career at Castleford – 13 years – under that ever-present constraint, with no money available to buy players, when I finally left and a new coach came in they suddenly started spending. Before long there came a time when there were news reports that my old club had tumbled more than four hundred thousand pounds into the red. Perhaps Phil Brunt's 'old ways' were best after all.

My development as a football coach began at Manly, under Ron Willey. Ron virtually gave me a free hand to organise set pieces and was happy to just let things revolve around me, giving me a free rein. As a result, I started thinking about other people's games as well as my own. I went from there. It was when I came back from Australia for my off-season with Cas and played about nine games when Dave Cox was in charge that I realised I had something to offer as a coach. I'd been coached by a number of decent coaches: George Clinton, who was in the old style, but knew the game; and Derek Turner, who added a dimension of aggression and certainly gave me a great deal of confidence in my early days. 'Rocky' was also the sort of person you wanted to do well for. If you didn't, then going back to the dressing-room afterwards was not a pleasant experience. The intimidation factor was certainly part of the way he operated. Then there was Tommy Smales who took us to Wembley in 1969–70, and Johnny Whiteley, such a success with Great Britain on the 1970 tour of Australia and New Zealand.

In Australia I was coached by Willey, who I thought was a fairly astute coach, and then by Frank Stanton, a man I admire and like a great deal, who went on to coach the Australian side of 1978 and the 'Invincibles' of 1982. I always got on really well with him and although one nickname he carried was 'Cranky Franky' I never found him that way at all. In fact he was, and is, a really mild and pleasant person. However, if things weren't going well football-wise, Frank could really spit the dummy in the dressing-room and get stuck in. He's not the only coach like that; it's almost an expectation of the job. I remember a day in 1978 when my Castleford team lost a match to Bramley. It was a dreadful afternoon; Brian Lockwood, one of our key men, had not produced any form at all and the whole team had played extremely poorly. At full-time I stormed into the sheds and knocked all the cups of tea off the rubbing table. Our full-back, George Claughton, who was already in, saw my reaction, and promptly hurled his cup on to the floor.

Under Castleford's tight financial structure the realisation gradually dawned that the only real choice I had was to develop the talent available. I had a good eye for players myself, but I was supported greatly by people like John Sheridan, who was a good judge of footballers, and I left a lot of the junior signings to him. We never had any problem in finding good young players; for example, Steve Norton had already signed for Cas at that time. Our problem was always in *keeping* them. We could have won a lot more honours if we had been able to hold on to players like Steve and Gary Stephens, but we couldn't.

People often drew similarities between 'Knocker' Norton and myself, but I could never see it, although, of course, our career patterns were very similar – Castleford and Manly. Steve had football skills well beyond his years from the outset, and was a terrifically skilful and elusive player, but I honestly didn't see him as being as tough a competitor as I was. The competitive edge just wasn't there to the same extent in Steve; we were two different animals altogether.

Kevin Ward is a great example of the sort of progress a player can make in a career – physically and mentally. In no way did Kevin 'burst' on to the scene; rather, he developed over a period of time. I have no doubt he was held back initially because of reservations about his own ability. Astonishing as it may be to those who played against Kevin in his prime, he was not naturally aggressive. In fact he was very short of confidence in that area until he started pushing heavy weights. After that he just needed occasional reassurance. Deep down he wasn't a very aggressive person at all, but he built up such a powerful physical strength base that no one could compete with him. Working hard, Kevin grew in stature, bulking up from 14 stone 10 pounds to well over 17 stone, and without much fat. It was a natural progression for him – from centre, to back row, to number 8. It was there that he became the cornerstone of the Castleford, Manly and Great Britain packs.

Looking at the British rugby league scene now in 1999, as I recall such talents who came through the ranks like Steve Norton, Gary Stephens, John Joyner or Kevin Ward, it is obvious that the steady production line of junior talent to clubs like Castleford is no longer as strong as it once was. Over the years the decline of the coal industry and the other traditional northern heavy industries has cut deep into rugby league's base. It represents a threat to the future of the game well beyond towns like Castleford, for the junior game is nowhere near as widespread as it used to be. In almost every area where the game has traditonally been powerfully based, the population has declined.

Perhaps the switch to summer football will eventually halt the slide and bring rugby league a new audience, and new players. When the decision to move to summer was taken, I was 15,000 miles away at Newcastle in Australia, but I watched developments with great interest. A check of newspaper libraries would reveal that as far back as 1976 I went on record saying that, because of our tough northern England winter climate, we should contemplate the possibility of summer football. When it actually happened, I looked on with a slight twinge of envy from a coach's point of view. Now that I'm back home and actually involved full-time in the summer game, I look around at rugby league and have mixed emotions. Obviously the jury still remains out on the experiment.

FIVE

Coach and Country

I was invited to help with the coaching of the Great Britain side against the 'Invincibles' in 1982, mainly because I think the men at the top realised far too late just how important the series was – and involved Roger Millward and myself. I didn't have much responsibility. I just helped to try and give the forwards some sort of sense of pattern. As it turned out, the British squad got ripped to pieces along the way and I can still visualise those big, fit Aussies – Craig Young, Max Krilich, Les Boyd, Wayne Pearce, Rod Reddy and the others – destroying us up front in the matches of that one-sided Ashes campaign.

For a time in 1982 (and '83) I was trying to juggle various strands of my working life: the involvement with the GB squad, coaching Cas and doing my best as mine host of a pub in Castleford. That was a hard life, the pub life at the Pointer. The hours were long and the demands constant. It was an old place, and at night after closing there always seemed to be noises. I'd be walking around half the night, thinking someone was trying to break in. In 1982, though, my life probably wasn't *quite* as tough as that of the British players who found themselves up against Australian opposition which Alex Murphy colourfully described as being 'from another planet'.

Things were better for British league, but not that much better, when we met the Aussies again in 1984 and 1986. These were false dawns in which we finished up clutching at straws, saying things like: 'It's getting better, we aren't losing by as many points.' In the '86 home series, although Great Britain had some reasonable players, we were well beaten. Maurice Bamford coached the side, with Les Bettinson as team manager. Les was, and is, a real gentleman. We toured together in 1988 and the contribution from Les and fellow manager David Howes was immense. I don't know Maurice Bamford very well, but after the first Test which Britain lost by a lot (38–16), I have no doubt he made a big mistake in the dressing-room directly after the game by announcing an unchanged team for the next Test. I could understand the motive – Maurice was trying to get something positive out of the loss – but it was not a good move. On reflection I am sure that he would admit now that he would have been far better sitting down and watching the video in the cold light of day, thoroughly analysing the game and looking at different options for positions. Maurice Bamford perhaps put some pride back into the Great Britain players that day, but I felt that he allowed his emotions to influence his decisions. The Kangaroos went on to win both the second and third Tests – and thus repeat the clean sweep of 1982.

It was the overseas influence that really kick-started the turnaround in English league. Overseas coaches such as Graham Lowe and John Monie made a big impact in the late 1980s, but it was the guest players through the '80s who made the most significant difference. The British players could see for themselves in week-by-week competition that the Australians and New Zealanders were far better physically prepared. I've been criticised in England for dwelling too much on physical preparation; however, the fact is that if you don't get that physical side of the game right, no matter how well coached, motivated and mentally tough a team is, you'll just never get there. Fatigue will set in, deficiencies in strength and power will be evident. The important qualities of motivation, passion and emotion – no matter how strong – are just not good enough to over-come that.

The Australians reckoned that they could just about guarantee that the British would play well for 20 minutes or half an hour. After that a pattern would unfold: the less fit forwards would start to tire, and the ones who *were* fit would have to work harder and harder, covering for their team-mates. Inevitably they would start to tire as well.

In addition to the example they set by their physical preparation, players such as Peter Sterling had a tremendous influence on the British players around them, just by the standard they set, match after match. Sterling, of course, would have a big influence on any team he was associated with at any time in the game's history. He'd come through the Parramatta ranks in great years for the club and had been associated closely with Jack Gibson, a coach who had developed strong moral values about the game and life in general. Jack had been a regular visitor to America to study American football techniques, focusing in great detail on every aspect of the American approach to their game. He was (and no doubt still is) a great teacher of the game of rugby league – and Peter Sterling was a brilliant pupil. 'Sterlo' had a lot of natural ability and, even though physically he wasn't the quickest or the strongest player around, his awareness and vision were outstanding. I don't think I've ever seen a player contribute more to a team performance than he did. He was a coach's dream. Gibson himself said that Sterling would make the right decision more times, more often, than other player he had ever seen and I would have to agree with that. His awareness of the options available to him was second to none, plus he was brave, clever and relentless.

I wanted Sterling at Leeds when I was coaching there in 1988–89. We even negotiated terms for him to come over later, in 1988, in the twilight of his career. Sadly, he damaged his Achilles tendon in the last game of the Aussie season, playing for Parramatta against Manly, and in the end he had to pull out. I had tried to attract both Peter and New Zealand's Hugh McGahan to Leeds; if those two had come our expectations of success would have been very high indeed.

In the 1984-85 season, whilst he was playing for Hull, Peter and I were involved in quite a dust-up, although it's long finished now and we are good mates. We shook hands at the Sydney Cricket Ground one day in 1988, and that was that. In a semi-final replay between Castleford and Hull in 1985, just one game away from Wembley, I put myself on the bench. I was very much a senior player on failing knees then, virtually retired. We had drawn 10-all in the first playing of the semi, with Lee Crooks booting a late sideline goal to get them out of gaol. With their money and their class players, Hull always seemed to have the wood on us at that time and in a tough, close replay I substituted myself into the match just before half-time. I put myself in at loose-forward and I went in quite hard on 'Sterlo' when they won the ball from a scrum. I missed him with a high shot, but I did give his face a massage on the ground. It was nothing too dramatic or intentional – more a play to intimidate him.

After the match, which we lost 22–16, all hell broke loose. 'Sterlo' obviously thought I had intentionally tried to gouge him, which I hadn't. My arm did come into contact with his face, but in no way was there any intent to gouge him. Subsequently I secured a clear video of the incident, which certainly didn't suggest there had been any gouging.

Next morning my neighbour at Ledsham, Phil Brunt – the Castleford chairman – came knocking on my door, early. 'Malcolm, have you seen this?' he asked. 'This is scandalous – a real slur on your name.' He thrust a copy of the *Yorkshire Post* at me. The paper carried a strong story on how I had 'gouged' Sterling. 'If I were you, I wouldn't let this ride,' said Phil. So on his advice I *did* go on with it, taking action against the newspaper, which eventually made a settlement out of court. As far as Peter and I were concerned, the incident washed over quite quickly and the relationship between us is now good.

My playing career sort of stuttered to its ending rather than finishing abruptly, with one or two late, unexpected appearances such as that game against Hull. My memory tells me that my last game as a rugby league player was in the Castleford second team in a match at Wheldon Road, probably that same year (1985), in which I had not the slightest intention of playing. I had gone down the lane that afternoon to watch the A team in a Yorkshire Senior Competition final against Hull Kingston Rovers. When I got to the ground our coach John Sheridan said to me, 'Malcolm, you won't believe what they've done – they've put Casey in the side.' (Len Casey was a hard head and then current international.)

'What do you want me to do, John?' I asked – and I volunteered to play. The match was important to the club, and my boots were always at the ground. So I got stripped, put the boots back on, and went out with the sole intention of making sure that Casey didn't have a good game. He certainly didn't, and we won the game. That done with, I could get back to coaching and to the eventual progress towards the goal I had now set my sights on: to become Great Britain coach.

In 1986 Britain went into the series against Australia with a public declaration of high expectations; however, the outcome was another hammering, although the third Test at Wigan brought elements of hope. In the wake of the series I made the point that I believed Benny Hill could have coached Australia to victory on the 1982 and '86 campaigns. There was no disrespect intended to anyone involved, I just believed that the gap in standards between the two countries was that wide. Soon afterwards, for personal reasons, Maurice Bamford resigned as Great Britain coach. I didn't apply for the job, but one morning I took a phone call from David Howes, the Rugby League's PR man. 'Malcolm, can you come up to Rugby League headquarters?' he said. 'They want you to do the job.'

I had been interviewed for the GB job before the 1984 tour, when they appointed Frank Myler, and again before Maurice Bamford got the appointment in '85. This time there was no formal interview; they just told me that if I wanted it, the job was mine. I didn't hesitate. In fact, I was thrilled. Obviously I had some reservations; it was not something you take on lightly. If I was going to be associated with the Great Britain team, I wanted a level of success. That's not as simple a matter as just winning or losing; they are the measuring sticks of the fans. In coaching you can actually lose a game and be successful; you must have some means of measuring the degree of success that you've achieved – even in defeat.

On the day I became Great Britain coach, I did a BBC radio interview with Harry Gration. He asked me the simple question: 'What can you provide for the team that Maurice Bamford couldn't, Malcolm?'

My reply was simple and in no way intended to be 'smart': 'I've got to get the players to believe they can beat these Australians. Unfortunately at the moment they don't think they stand a chance.' I told him that I felt that the British players were at a constant psychological disadvantage in their battles with Australia, because they did not really believe that they could win. A lot of Britain's problems were to do with physical preparation, but a great deal were also in the realm of the mind. All I wanted to do, more than anything else, was convince the British players that they could beat the Australians. Once they started believing that, I was fairly sure that they *actually* would be able to beat them. Success breeds success; my mission was to try and breed the air of confidence that had been such a factor in the victorious 1970 side. However, I did have some reservations about the quality of players available, and there was only so much I could do in isolation.

The Australian international side has been influenced by its domestic game, and Britain was in exactly the same situation. Before we could think seriously about improving the Test side, we had to make headway in the preparation of our club sides. It is absolutely no coincidence that the majority of British international players in the past few years have come from Wigan, the club which attracted and developed players who really did want to succeed; players who took personal pride in their performance, players willing to strive for goals. The revival of Great Britain and the rise of Wigan were interlinked, and nor was it all one-way traffic. To a large degree it was Maurice Lindsay who assembled the bulk of the Wigan players – the core group contributing to national team success. Maurice had a keen eye for a footballer, and Wigan had the resources. It became the way that the Wigan players would take things back from a Great Britain session that would benefit the club, just as their dedication and professionalism benefited the Great Britain side.

When I started the building process, I concentrated the operation around a handful of players, headed by men such as Ellery Hanley and Kevin Ward, players already at the level that we needed. It was the only way. We had Andy Gregory at scrum-half, Shaun Edwards waiting in the wings, and Kevin Beardmore at hooker, forming a natural club-based combination with the strongman Ward. In the three-quarter line Garry Schofield was an important part of the team and when Martin Offiah arrived on the scene (signed by Widnes but soon off to Wigan) I was determined to involve him from the start. There were people who said to me, 'You can't pick him, he's straight out of rugby union and far too raw.' But I only had to look at what Offiah had to offer to realise that he had to be included in the team as soon as possible. Athletes like him are rare, bringing with them the potential to have an enormous influence on the outcome of any game they play. Martin was never the bravest of players, but he could sure score a try.

Taking the Great Britain reins full-time in the 1987–88 season, I didn't have too much opportunity to prepare for the 1988 tour to Australia. We had only three international matches – two against France and one against Papua New Guinea – to use as a springboard. Given the limited preparation time, there wasn't really a lot I could do with the squad before leaving England. All I could really do was to try and identify the players I knew I could work with on the '88 tour. I was confident about some of them – Hanley, Ward, Beardmore, Gregory, Schofield, Edwards, Offiah and Andy Platt – but others in the party had to be taken on trust. International football is the territory of the unknown, raising the perennial question of how players will react to the additional pressure and competition of the game at that level. Some players will grow in stature, others will disintegrate.

We assembled at Wigan before undertaking the great challenge of 1988 and, after all the goodbyes to wives and families and girlfriends, finally headed off. A mile down the road, I stopped the coach. There were some things I needed to say. I reminded the players that we had to create a good impression wherever we went, because we were not just representing ourselves, but our country. I told them that we were there to work, and laid down the ground rules that would build team spirit and ensure good discipline. I also threw down a challenge to the players: that anyone of them who didn't believe in his heart of hearts that we could beat the Australians would be well advised to get off the coach right then. I wanted no negativity, no losing mentality.

We flew to Papua New Guinea, a long and gruelling trek of 32 hours via Bombay, Singapore and Sydney. We had done our best to be ready; Forbes McKenzie, the team doctor, had handed out sleeping pills during the flight, adjusting our sleeping patterns to the time zone of our destination. But there was nothing that could possibly have readied us in advance for the impact of the heat and humidity on arrival in Port Moresby. Coming down the steps of the plane, the heat hit me like a wall. At that moment it was hard to imagine how we would be able to play rugby league. The temperature was in the thirties, the humidity nineties. Despite that, I was determined to get the team working straight away. The first Test against Australia in Sydney was only four weeks away and, in that time, I had to try and get these players fitter than most of them had ever been in their lives. Almost as soon as their feet touched the foyer of our hotel, I had them off for a three-mile training run.

The early omens were not promising. Our first formal training session was a shambles, with the players really struggling to cope with the heat and humidity. Worse than that, many of them just didn't seem to understand what was needed. Concentration on and awareness of what we were trying to achieve seemed to be completely lacking, although I realised some of that could be blamed on the conditions. Following that first session I was very worried, but we met immediately afterwards to discuss the team's objectives and the second session in steamy Port Moresby showed a remarkably big improvement. Already a strong team spirit was starting to emerge and the training sessions progressively improved as the players became more used to the heat.

Frankly, Port Moresby is one of the last places on earth I would choose to go for a holiday, but as a training base for a touring football team, it has its advantages. We stayed at a four-star hotel, the Travelodge, but the security situation in Papua New Guinea was so worrying at the time that we were virtually marooned in the hotel. The streets were hostile and we were strongly advised not to venture out. The hotel employed an army of security men who patrolled the foyer and the street outside and were unbelievably ruthless with their own people, hurling them down the stone steps and hitting them over the head with baseball bats. It was in no way a relaxing experience, but the lack of alternative diversions forced the players to concentrate even more on the job at hand. The existing feeling of 'us against the world' over there also strengthened the developing team spirit. We fostered that spirit by trying to keep the players together, taking them as a group to safe areas where we could relax with some snorkelling and white water rafting.

As the players grew more acclimatised we stepped up the training to two tough physical sessions a day. Many of the players were suffering from blisters and we had problems with the food and with bouts of gastroenteritis, but that was only in line with the law of averages. The players' diets were also monitored very carefully, with lots of fresh fruit, protein supplements and large fluid intakes. Notwithstanding, we still encountered some problems. With a party of 30, chances are that some would be off colour, no matter where you were. Grass burns from the hard, hot grounds also became something of a problem, exacerbated by infections picked up in the hotel swimming pool. The grass burns and other cuts and abrasions were inevitable, considering the grounds were like concrete and often littered with small rocks, while the grass itself was more like sandpaper – coarse, wiry and sharp-bladed.

Heat exhaustion was our continual worry whilst on tour in Papua New Guinea, and it wasn't always the biggest guys who suffered the worst from the heat. With the help of the medical staff, headed by Forbes McKenzie, we worked hard to counter that and also the ever-present risk of dehydration. The players were told to keep themselves topped up with fluids in the approach to every game. We would send four or five runners on with water bottles at every break in play in matches, and at half-time and full-time we had iced, wet towels in which to drape the players, bringing down their body temperatures as quickly as possible. Because of the hard work and the preparation, we got through without major medical problems caused by the heat, although there were times when some players were badly disoriented at the end of the game.

We had our share of injuries, and it wasn't long before the theme of the tour was established. Shaun Edwards was injured a few minutes into the Test against PNG and didn't play again on tour, being invalided home after being flown to Sydney for a specialist examination. It was a real body blow to the team, depriving us of one of our Test-class half-backs before we had even reached Australia.

By half-time in the Port Moresby Test, it was 28–6 in our favour, but the heat and humidity sapped our players badly and late in the game the Kumuls fought back to 28–22, placing it in the balance. Ellery Hanley was outstanding in that late period, saving two certain tries. Also Garry Schofield – our man of the match – helping us weather the storm, and then with a late strike to extend the lead. In the end it was a comfortable win, but only after some dodgy moments.

We played a provincial game in Lae a few days later, and another recurring theme of that tour – the weakness of the midweek team – quickly became apparent. On that tour of 1988, our lack of strength in depth was appalling for a professional international squad. It became very clear from the outset that beyond the first-choice team of 15 or 16 players, the rest were simply not up to it. The skill level was very poor, and when we picked up injuries to first-choice players, the replacements coming in were generally of a far lower standard. It sort of summed up the state of the entire British game at that time; I didn't feel anybody was left at home who should have been there. We took on tour what I felt confident was the strongest available squad.

Injuries did their best to wreck that tour. We had so many of them, several of them serious ones, resulting in no less than six players being sent home during the campaign and replacements flown out. We lost such people as Andy Platt, Paul Dixon, Shaun Edwards and Garry Schofield with injury, and with due respect to the replacements, they were nowhere near the same calibre. The one thing we had going for us was team spirit, which was terrific throughout. I have no doubt the choice of our home base in Sydney was a big factor in that. The players were thrilled with the Manly Pacific Hotel just across from the beach – the very same place I had stayed when I first arrived to join Manly in 1971. The training ground was just around the corner and up the road was an excellent gym at the Harbord Diggers' Club. It couldn't have been better.

If the facilities were great, the itinerary, however, was something less than that. The toughest challenges in the 'minor' matches always seemed to come in the week before Tests. The two things that stuck most in the minds of the Australian public were defeats by a Northern Division side at Tamworth and by my old club Manly at Brookvale. After the game at Tamworth I locked myself in the dressing-room with the team for 20 minutes and let them have it. It was an appalling loss against a team we should have thrashed and it once again identified the lack of depth in the squad. Obviously, Manly were far tougher, but even so, a 30 points to nil hammering, in which a young schoolboy named Geoff Toovey – who was destined for far bigger things – made a terrific début, was a miserable result. It left me distraught. The match came just four days before the first Test, so I couldn't have risked my Test players, yet it exposed all the weaknesses in our squad, the gap between the top side and the others.

We blew it in the second Test of the series at Lang Park, but apart from that we were very competitive in the fight for the Ashes in 1988; much more competitive, I think, than most people expected us to be. In the first Test at the brand new Sydney Football Stadium we led 6-0 at half-time, thanks to a typical and quite outstanding solo try from Ellery Hanley as he crabbed across the field. This was the Centenary Test between the two major league nations yet, for whatever reasons, the Australian Rugby League (ARL) declined to promote any major celebration of the event. After that excellent first 40 minutes our kicking game went to pot and the Aussies came back and got us in the second half, despite an injury which hampered Peter Sterling, the team's co-playmaker with Wally Lewis. In the end it was 17–6 to Australia after a hard contest – and we had taken a step down the track towards restoring the credibility of the tour.

I blame myself for some of the circumstances of the way we threw it all away in Brisbane in the second Test. As a relative rookie (international) coach, I went over the top with motivation and got the players in the wrong mood for what Lang Park had to offer. We were just too steamed up and gave away penalties from which the Aussies punished us. It was a Test in which the whole weight of the game seemed to go against us. In our own kicking game it seemed that we were always on the defensive, clearing the ball and just trying to escape from our own territory. They always seemed to have the better field position, although Martin Offiah's long, late try gave a hint of what might have been. At the siren it was 34–14, and Great Britain had slipped to its fifteenth successive loss in Tests against Australia.

It was a tough battle just like that Test I had played at Lang Park myself back in 1970; however, I took offence at Australian suggestions that some of the heavy-handed British tactics that night in Brisbane were 'premeditated' or that I had told my players to 'take heads off'. Gavin Miller, a genuine star in both England and Australia, was one who made such suggestions. I thought that what he had to say was right out of order

– and I said so. I was also angry at a published statement from ARL general manager Bob Abbott that there was a lack of promotion of the tour (which there certainly was) because pushing Great Britain was like 'flogging a dead horse', I found that humiliating and unfair. My own anger and determination was certainly reflected through the team, although we were in dire straits with injuries, with nine players now lost from the original tour squad. My view of the second Test was that emotion took over from logic on our part; it wasn't as if Australia had played champagne football, more that they had taken advantage of our ill-discipline. I talked to my players about the need to restore pride and respect in their performances – collectively and individually – in the third Test.

To nobody's surprise, the Aussie press wrote us off completely before that Test. Some of the tabloid writers didn't spare our feelings in their comments, and even in the more sober *Sydney Morning Herald* their correspondent John McDonald, using a horse-racing analogy as Aussies often do, wrote on the day of the match: 'If Great Britain were to win today it would be the biggest upset since Spear Chief beat Ajax, which was 40/1 on, in the Rawson Stakes at Rosehill in 1939.'

I was somewhat more optimistic, telling McDonald: 'We can match them man for man along the line – it all depends on how we combine.'

As it turned out, the third Test, 9 July 1988, was an amazing day for us and the start of the long haul back for Great Britain as a credible and competing rugby league nation. Against the odds, and with a string of players unavailable through injury, we gave Australia a pasting, 26–12, before a small but very vocal crowd – after which delighted British fans danced with joy. They looked on with wild excitement, and I daresay some disbelief, as we wrapped up the game with a scorching try by the crowd-pleasing winger Henderson Gill and then the sight of second-rower Mike Gregory galloping fully 75 yards to score off an Andy Gregory pass. I had encouraged Andy to run in that match, rather than restrict himself to a distribution role. He was strong and smart, able to take defenders on, and he did it that day in Sydney. In this match we stuck rigidly to a formula of intelligent, cool-headed football – vastly different from the ill-discipline of Brisbane. Under the circumstances it was an enormously pleasing win. In his book *The Struggle for the Ashes*, author and historian Robert Gate has written that the match 'symbolically restored the pride to British rugby league . . . a decade of misery and humiliation had ended for the Brits. Hallelujah!'

And that was the way I felt too. We had lost the Ashes, but now we had something we could build on – which was exactly what I wanted to do.

SIX

Coach on the Move: Leeds, Halifax

As a coach now in the summer game that rugby league in England has become, I remember only too well my own earlier frozen, wet, foggy winter days and nights as a player and coach in my native land. Probably the toughest of it weather-wise was in my time at Halifax (1993–94) high up on the approach to the Pennines. Thrum Hall was a cold place for sure, guaranteed to get its share of snow any winter. At Halifax you're talking a couple of degrees colder than anywhere else in Yorkshire, and if it's going to snow you can bet it will snow in Halifax before anywhere else. That meant we did a lot of improvising in training during the winter at Halifax; when the snow came we'd road run or use indoor school facilities. When I was at Castleford we'd used an indoor equestrian centre at Ledston, a small village close to my home, for some skills and speed work, or head out on a road run once the roads had been cleared by the council. It was a bitter place at times. There were plenty of nights when we all came in with rosy cheeks, and more than enough training nights when I hit the hot showers with hands so frozen and stiff that I couldn't hold the soap.

After leaving Castleford in 1987 I had a year away from the club scene, wrestling with my new challenges as Great Britain coach, and especially those posed by the 1988 campaign in Australia and New Zealand. But before going on tour we had journeyed to Leeds one day to be fitted for our travelling gear and there the Leeds club chairman, Bernard Coulby, and one of the other directors had approached me. Would I be interested in coaching their club the following season? I told them I would consider it, and in fact made a commitment to them for the 1988–89 season before I went on tour for the Ashes campaign. By then my feet were getting a little itchy because I was missing the day-to-day challenge of club coaching. And so it was that I came back after the tour to coach one of the most famous clubs in the English game.

Always regarded as a 'wealthy' club, Leeds had the purse strings still not fully unleashed at that stage. I think our highest-paid players were Lee Crooks and Garry Schofield on seventeen thousand pounds each. I remember very well how hard we chased Bradford's international front-rower Kelvin Skerrett, who was a free agent carrying no transfer fee, a unique situation at the time akin to Australian players coming to England. We were talking to Skerrett of a deal worth around twenty-five thousand pounds. Wigan offered him something like seventy-five thousand pounds – and of course he went there. It was the way things were in British rugby league at that time; Wigan just jacked up player costs unbelievably, introducing unprecedented inflation into the game. In those days at Wigan, when they had Lydon, Hanley, Edwards, Gregory, Goodway, Betts and plenty more, I am led to believe they had ten players on, or around, one hundred thousand pounds a year. They captured top players with ruthless efficiency; they bought success.

They also won me some money one season in the early 1990s. I'm not sure how ethical this was, but one year I backed Wigan to win the Regal Trophy, the Championship and Wembley before a single round had been played. I was having a beer with a bookie I knew one day and I asked him what price he'd give me on the treble. He offered twenty-fives. 'Give me thirty to one and I'll have a hundred pounds on it,' I said. So he fielded the bet – and I ended up winning three thousand pounds.

Wigan definitely cornered the market on quality players in the country, with Maurice Lindsay being the driving force. Maurice was an astute judge of a footballer. He and Jackie Edwards, Shaun's father, used to spend a lot of time together – and they won plenty on the weekly rugby league coupons through their combined expertise and knowledge of players and the game. And Maurice certainly made it hard for other clubs with his single-minded building of Wigan in those years.

My year with Leeds was challenging to say the least. I still worked for the John Smith's brewery then, and was trying to juggle three different jobs: Leeds coach, Great Britain coach and my day job. It took some planning, I can tell you. We had plenty of successes at Leeds and were always up there among the front-runners, but the biggest prizes continued to evade us. We did, however, come home with the Yorkshire Cup, an achievement that stood as the last piece of silverware that Leeds were to win in over a decade – until the Wembley triumph in 1999 – despite their expensive recruitment programmes and all their chopping and changing of coaches and players. That was a grand match, in front of a 23,000 crowd at Elland Road, bringing a 33–12 win over – guess who? – my old club Castleford. There were a few mixed feelings for me there, but it was lovely to win. Cliff Lyons, such a talent and such an enduring figure in the Australian game with my old Manly club, played a starring role for Leeds that day. Cliff, Andrew Ettingshausen and big Sam Backo were our Aussie imports that year. We finished joint second with St Helens on the ladder in the league that year, contenders all the way.

However, those achievements were not enough to satisfy the expectations of the club and its supporters. I found myself pretty unpopular when I started to put the cleaners through the Leeds playing ranks and began unloading a player or two. The decision to do that with Paul Medley, a player who had been in my 1988 Great Britain touring party, caused quite a storm. Paul was an explosive impact player, a man I found who couldn't do the job for the full 80 minutes, but who could be most effective off the bench. He had come home early from the '88 tour, partly because of injury, partly because I felt he wasn't quite up to it. Back at Leeds he let me down when I tried him for 80 minutes in matches, but he could be a real 'plus' off the bench. Anyhow, I made the decision to sell him to Halifax, effectively swapping him for Paul Dixon, a tough, uncompromising back-row forward. Dixon went on to become a cornerstone of the Leeds pack for years, but I copped plenty of flak for the decision, and especially from the *Yorkshire Evening Post* sports editor who was a keen Leeds fan. He should have pulled his head in, not let it get that personal. I knew *plenty* about both men, knew how tough they were physically and mentally. My judgement was made on what I knew.

I can stand criticism when it is warranted, but during this period at Leeds there was some pretty unfair stuff going around. I thought to myself, I don't really need this job; I've got two other commitments (Great Britain coach and the brewery job). Realistically I was probably only firing at about 75 per cent on all three jobs anyway. I was spreading myself too thin.

In September 1989 we lost our first game of the season, to Bradford Northern. The following week at home we beat Salford 34–28, and straight after the match I announced my retirement as Leeds coach. David Ward followed me, then Doug Laughton, then Dean Bell as Leeds chased that elusive butterfly – success. It only started to come almost ten years later after they brought Graham Murray over from Australia to take charge at Headingley. As for me, I didn't coach at club level for the next four seasons.

I moved to Halifax in January 1993 in somewhat awkward circumstances. The man I replaced as coach, Roger Millward, had been a friend for so long, and I felt some initial resentment from him. To be honest, I felt a bit guilty at the time, although in reality it was no more than a club declaring a vacancy, and me making a decision to go for it. There was no question of disloyalty to an old and valued friend. Soon enough it was water under the bridge, and things are fine now between myself and Roger.

Maurice Lindsay, and then Tony Gartland (the Halifax chairman), had rung me in late 1992, well after I had come home from the Lions tour to Australia. Halifax were struggling mid-table. Maurice made the first call to alert me that Halifax were interested in talking to me, then Tony rang with the news that Roger was going to finish at the club and the question: would I contemplate taking over the reins? By then I had left the brewery job at John Smith's and had been appointed full-time Great Britain coach, so I went back to them, and we worked out an arrangement.

We had a pretty fair side at Halifax, and wonderful, fanatical backing from the people at Thrum Hall. We cast a fairly wide net in our team-building programme and came up with players such as Michael Jackson, Michael Hagan, David Boyd, John Schuster, Gary Lord and Steve Hampson, whom Wigan let go. We were building a side – but we missed the guy who could have made all the difference. Bobbie Goulding was living in Leeds then; he was such a creative half-back, albeit a bit troubled now and then off the field. We were just five thousand pounds off securing him. The Halifax chairman, Tony Gartland, was a man who wouldn't compromise. He was a man of his word. He financed the club out of his own pocket. He was smart, astute and I respected his judgement.

When we were close to getting Goulding, Tony said to me one day, 'What's this fellow worth?'

I replied, 'What we've offered is what he's worth – but if we're going to get him we're going to have to pay a bit more.'

'No, that's it,' said Tony. 'We'll not go above the figure we've offered.'

St Helens threw in a block of land and a house at cost price and Bobbie, being something of a negotiator, took the deal, via his agent David McKnight. How ironic it was when I returned to England at the end of 1998 and took up the coaching reins at Huddersfield, who should I find as my new team's key player but the very same Bobbie Goulding.

SEVEN

One Kick from Glory

Memories of the first Test of the 1990 series against the Kangaroos will stay with me for ever. The famous Wembley stadium has rarely looked or sounded better. The crowd was a big one, 54,569, and the noise was extraordinary. A choir broke out into 'Land of Hope and Glory' as we came out of the tunnel and with the crowd joining in, the sound was awesome. The wonderful reception only served to further reinforce a Great Britain team that was very, very ready. We were all so preoccupied with the task at hand, and yet the stirring sounds of support washed over all of us like a wave. It was a day when we had what we needed in full measure: spirit, will to win and talent.

And if the build-up to the match was extraordinary, the game itself was even better. I was full of anticipation; I knew the lads were ready for the game – although you're never quite sure which way it's going to go against teams as strong and confident as Australia. If you can get all the basic things right, leaving a little bit to chance, there's always the real possibility of something coming off. Any side is vulnerable if sufficient pressure is put on them via weapons such as the high 'bomb'. You just have to make sure that you are subjecting your opponents to pressure, giving yourself that element of chance.

The theory worked out beautifully at Wembley. Kicking featured quite heavily in the victory that came our way that afternoon – particularly the chip-kick over the top, my own trademark when I was playing. Ellery Hanley did that for one of the tries, and then used his strength to get up and make a quick play-the-ball, enabling Daryl Powell to put Paul Eastwood over in the corner. The second try came from a 'bomb', with Ellery timing his challenge on Gary Belcher perfectly and Martin Offiah collecting the loose ball on the half-volley – a truly superb pick-up – to score. The third try came from another chip-and-regather, this time by Garry Schofield, with 'Barnie' Eastwood crashing over for his second try. Barnie's goalkicking had been a worry, in fact goalkicking was a problem throughout the entire seven years I was Great Britain coach – eased only once when Jonathan Davies came in as a late replacement against a depleted French team at Headingley in 1993 and belted over ten conversions as we ran up a record Test score.

That day at Wembley Eastwood, after missing a couple of early kicks which could have been crucial, saw his confidence grow as he started belting them over and he made sure of the win with a fine goal from wide out to convert his own try.

When the final hooter went, at 19–12, it was as sweet a moment as 1988 had been in Sydney. This time there could be no excuses for the Australians. In '88 there was muttering that we had won only because it was a 'dead rubber' Test. This time it was the first Test of a brand new series, and we had beaten them fair and square. We had beaten them twice in a row in fact, which must have jolted the Aussies a little bit.

Second Test, Old Trafford, Manchester. Up until half-time, the story was almost the same as in Wembley's Test. We had applied a lot of pressure, but had failed to convert it into points. Our only score of the half came when Paul Dixon scored a try off Garry Schofield's pass, regaining his feet after a tackle to crash over. In the second half the Australians rallied and came strongly into the game. We fell behind 10–6 but Paul Loughlin grabbed an interception off a long Ricky Stuart pass to level the scores, 10–10, with about ten minutes to go, reaching out a long left arm to drag the ball in. The conversion kick wasn't a difficult one, only about 15 metres to the left of the posts, the natural side for a right-foot kicker like Loughlin. In fact, he could have made the kick even easier because I had no doubts he was clear enough of the chasers to head to the posts when he scored his try. If only he had just pinned his ears back, but he kept straight on, making absolutely sure of staying ahead of the Australian cover coming across from the other wing. Laurie Daley just chased and chased in that regard, and in doing so probably saved the Ashes for Australia. A try which should have been scored near the posts was many yards wider than it should have been.

Having scored the try, Paul Loughlin wasn't keen on taking the kick. In my mind's eye I can still see him shaking his head 'no, no'. Right then, I should have sent out the message: 'Just compose yourself – and take it.' Instead, the left-footed Barnie Eastwood took the conversion kick, from his 'wrong' side, and missed by a metre or two. One solid, straight goalkick guiding the ball between the posts, and there is no way the Australians would have come back. Our blokes were tired, but taking the lead inside the last ten minutes with the Ashes Cup in reach for the first time in 20 years would have given them an enormous psychological lift, enough to get us through the last few minutes. Paul Loughlin should have taken that kick, but more importantly still he should have scored that try ten metres closer to the posts.

I've thought about this a lot since. One view is that if you're not confident about kicking the goal, then there's not much point lining it up. Under the pressure of the circumstances I think Loughlin probably thought: I don't want this. I've done my bit – I scored the try. He was frightened to fail, which is human enough, I suppose. It was never a matter of great discussion between us subsequently. We had another Test to go and sometimes, in a short time frame, it's not wise to bring up negatives. We did talk about it briefly over a beer one day and he just said to me, 'Oh, mate, I just didn't feel confident about it.'

Even without the conversion of that try, I thought we were in the driving seat. And as we neared the end of the 80 minutes, Garry Schofield put in a perfect kick – I couldn't have asked for a better one – right into the corner. We put on a big chase, and had them pinned in their own territory. I hunched forward on the bench, ready for our last set of six tackles, expecting us to regain the ball when the Aussies kicked on their last tackle then work our way back towards their line, with the chance of a drop-goal to clinch the game – and the Ashes.

Instead, on Australia's third tackle, an exhausted Lee Jackson took an outrageous dummy from Ricky Stuart in the middle of the field. Stuart had taken the ball from Cliff Lyons, veered right, past Jackson, and cut through into open space. Ellery would normally have picked Stuart up as soon as he broke the line, but he was so fatigued that he couldn't get to him. He already had something like 42 tackles on the sheet – an amazing effort in a Test match. Martin Offiah, the man who would *certainly* have snuffed out the danger with his speed, was off the field, injured. I have no doubt Martin would have closed it down within 10 to 20 metres. Carl Gibson came off the wing to tackle Stuart, but Mal Meninga just blocked him like an American Gridiron footballer. The French referee, Alain Sabrayolles, chose to ignore the illegality of Meninga obstructing Gibson, and although Carl recovered to make the tackle on Stuart close to our line, Meninga was in support by then to take the pass and score.

The look on Meninga's face as he stood up was not one of elation, but of relief. It said: We've done it – we've actually done it! The Australians knew they had got out of gaol, perhaps saved the Ashes, when just a few minutes before, as Eastwood lined up his kick, they looked lost. To be that close to glory and then see it snatched away was terrible for us. I don't think I have ever been so disappointed in my life. The Kangaroos had a very formidable line-up, but I had known before that second Test that they were there for the taking.

By the time the third Test came around, the whole momentum of the series had changed. They played their conservative power-game with battering-ram efficiency, grinding home 14–0 on a wet day at Elland

Road. In the end we were overpowered by Bozo's boys, but the lads did some stupid things as well. I remember Martin Offiah kicking on the first tackle, and then Schoey going for an interception and leaving a hole in the defensive line that they went straight through for a try. You don't win Test matches by making those sort of mistakes.

High-level international rugby league is very much about being patient. You just can't afford to give cheap chances to your opposition. When it happens there is a powerful negative effect on the team's morale and confidence. Concede a soft try – and you can see your opponents grow in stature. At Leeds that final afternoon of a highly competitive series, we fell short.

I could still mark that 1990 series as a big step forward from '88. We had competed all the way through and the margin between victory and defeat was wafer thin. Great Britain were still on a rising curve, but the Ashes were still in Australian hands and we were left yet again with the hollow consolation of 'what might have beens'. People consoled us. 'You were unlucky,' they said. But to me luck is the point at which preparation and opportunity meet. If you prepare yourself properly and the opportunity occurs then you are able to take it. Call it luck if you like, but what gets you in a position to be 'lucky' is hard work, not chance.

Even though I was pretty disappointed at the punchline that Elland Road provided, I had no thoughts of packing in the international job. I just wanted to keep on the building process, because the British game was progressing then, internationally and domestically, as a result of our performances. We were gathering growing recognition, and the media was responding very positively towards some of our achievements. I was itching at the thought of the next crack I would get at the Australians. It was a long way down the track though – two years away. I felt empty about that; finishing such a big series in which the adrenalin flowed so strongly, then facing a low-key international year with nothing but two Tests against France.

Andrew Clarke, the brother of Wigan and Great Britain loose-forward Phil Clarke, did a detailed analysis and comparison of the English and Australian games as part of his university degree, and his thesis came up with some very significant differences between the two. He pointed out, for example, that the 'Australian players sprint considerably more at the collision than the British players' – and he was not talking about marginal differences. It was 29 per cent as opposed to 5 per cent. In other words, the Australians sprinted at the collision nearly six times as often as the British. The Australian players were also significantly stronger in the upper and lower body than the British. That was demonstrated by the number of occasions that it took only one Australian defender to stop a British attacker, whereas it routinely took two or three British defenders to stop an Australian ball-carrier.

The yardage made by the Aussies carrying the ball averaged one or two yards more on each drive than the Brits. Multiply that by the number of drives in a game and you begin to understand why the Australians have been so dominant internationally. As I have identified elsewhere, it is a dominance built on the strength of their domestic game. Until we can match the physical preparation of the Australian players and match the intensity and quality of their domestic football, we will always be under a handicap when facing them at international level. The difference between the two countries in rugby league boils down largely to physical prepara- tion, with the Aussies still well in advance of the British at the moment, highlighted yet again in the 1997 series against the short-lived Australian Super League side, just as it was in the 1994 Ashes series and in the third Test in 1992 against my own team at Brisbane. The Australians' power that day enabled them to dominate territorially. We were always receiving kicks inside our own 20 metres and they were offensive, strategically placed tactical kicks – chips, grubbers, bombs. It seemed that again and again we were relieving a defensive situation, trying to get the ball as far downfield as possible.

In the period of my tenure as national team coach, I was never happy with the levels of physical preparation and basic skills possessed by players coming into the Great Britain squad. There was always scope for dramatic improvement, though it varied among the players from club to club. The specific assessment of individuals is so important in football today, and it is up to coaches to identify individual areas that players need to work on and then tailor a programme that is specific to their requirements. Skills training is also too often inadequate. Golfers go out and practise their swing every single day, whereas most rugby league players assume that they know the basic skills, such as how to tackle and pass the ball, and give no consideration to examining their technique, unless forced to do so by their coach.

It is a mark of how much room there was for improvement in the British game that even international players could go through their entire careers without ever learning certain skills. Scrum-half Andy Gregory, for example, could only throw a long pass to his left. To pass to the right, he had to turn completely around and pass with his back to the opposition. It obviously did not hamper him too much, because he was a world-class half-back, but I would catch Australians looking at Andy and saying, 'For heaven's sake, didn't this guy have *any* coaching?' The answer basically is, No, he didn't. If the English game is to flourish, there needs to be more focus on the basics, particularly with young players. Australia remains the role model: there, they have pursued coaching excellence, building a base on the perfection of fundamental skills and physical preparation.

It has been suggested that I am a coach who uses intimidation as part of what I do. I don't deny that if necessary I will confront anyone whom I feel is not pulling his weight for the team or who is undermining my authority. But intimidating players is not the way to get the best out of them, and it is not my way. Coaches who go into a dressing-room before a game, or at half-time, and rant, rave and scream at the players are wasting their breath. If the players have been harangued at half-time, the sure thing is they are not going to come out and do any better in the second half. What a coach must do instead is to make the discussion *positive*, identify areas that need improvement, but finish on a positive note – reinforcing to the players just how much better they are, individually and collectively, guiding them in how to succeed. My method is to be sure that I'm thoroughly aware of what has gone on during the first half of any match. A good stats man is a handy ally in that. My aim is always to focus on the positive things, and get the players out for the second half in a strong and positive frame of mind.

Vast contrasts exist between individual players in dressing-rooms. In the Great Britain room they ran the whole gamut, from someone like Andy Gregory, who was always talking a lot, joking and laughing, to Shaun Edwards, who wanted only to be on his own, pacing up and down and not talking to anyone. The main objective for each individual is to attain his IPS (ideal performance state) – to realise how to get there, and then to maintain it. Each player knows what is best for him; I just leave them to get on with it and do whatever is best for them.

The routine with a team on the day of a game does not vary much. Throughout the week leading up to the game, I will have been stressing areas of concern and areas where I want them to function. On match day we are looking to keep the players relaxed. A good breakfast and a pre-match meal are important – just fuelling up. I am a believer in the side having high-calibre nutrition so that they are fully energised. A team walk, even if only for half a mile, helps set the scene; it lets the players relax and talk about the game together. Along the way the coaching staff continue to talk to different individuals as well, reassuring them where necessary. Back from the walk, my usual programme is for a final team meeting at which I just get them to sit down and I explain one or two quick points. Then I'm out of it, leaving the players to do the final talking among themselves. It's the best way, this late player-to-player communication, because the reality is that out on the field, they *have* to communicate. I rate communication a key factor in any performance.

The captain has a very important role, and his personality is vital. I've been quite fortunate to have had some good ones during my time as a coach, with John Joyner, who led Castleford at Wembley in 1986, ranking high. Ellery Hanley and I worked soundly together with the national team for much of the time, although there were problems late in the piece. He was an inspiration to the other players and I based a lot of the motivational stuff around him. Mike Gregory, who led Great Britain on the 1990 tour, thrived in the role of captain, as did Garry Schofield, who always led the side well. Later, at Newcastle, Paul 'the Chief' Harragon was a natural leader, a strong brave player and a man looked up to by all his team-mates.

EIGHT

The Tear Gas Tour

When you consider the many dramatic things that have happened in rugby league, the game surely has *never* been the way it was in Papua New Guinea when I went there as coach of the Great Britain team on what has become known as the 'Tear Gas Tour'. The games at Lae and Goroka added up to a terrifying, unforgettable experience. At both places, police fired volleys of rifle shots and barrages of tear gas canisters to try and maintain crowd control. The atmosphere was just unbelievable. It was frightening all right, and I was out there right in the middle of it.

The trouble started at Lae, when we played a team from the northern Highlands Zone. Violent clashes between police and rioting fans locked outside the ground were the backdrop to the match. Shots rang out and the gas wafted over the ground. I went straight down on my knees and the players did the same. The police who were there seemed just as frightened by the situation as we were – they were carrying 303s, but seemed more on edge than the rioters. At Lae the growing drama with the tear gas assault was caused mainly by stupidity. The police were just incompetent; they threw the damn things anywhere. They were trying to stop people getting *into* the ground so they were firing off the tear gas canisters at the entrances. Then there were people desperate to get *out* of the ground, just trying to get out of the way. I can see them now, jumping on the stand roof and leaping from there, just to get away from the gas. It was incredible. Then one group ran on to the field; tear gas was thrown at the northern end of the field and the wind took it directly on to the playing area. Everyone dropped down to the floor. I thought to myself, 'This is madness, it's going to have to be abandoned.' Somehow, with sporadic rioting still in progress outside the ground, we managed to finish the game, winning 24–10, and we were happy to get out of there as fast as we could.

Goroka, scene of the first Test, wasn't quite as bad – but it was bad enough. Heading to the match in the team bus we got completely jammed up in a sea of humanity streaming towards the ground. We couldn't move, we were just stuck there with these hundreds of people peering through the windows. Eventually I got out and spoke as best I could to the people, asking could we get a clear passage so we could make our way to the game. A quarter of an hour into the Test the New Zealand referee, Dennis Hale, stopped play as police fired rifle shots and set off tear gas to try and dispel a furious mob of stone-throwing fans outside the ground. The match was delayed for several minutes as the gas drifted across the pitch. Right to the end, occasional gunfire and gas clouds provided the backdrop to one of most sensational Test matches ever played. We lost 20–18, after leading 18–8, faltering in the high-altitude conditions in the second half.

It was Garry Schofield's twenty-second Test and his first at stand-off, and it turned out to be a shocker for him. I had put Garry at number six with some confidence, but on that infamous day in Goroka he just didn't seem to know how to play the position. He would hold the ball, then throw long, ballooning passes out which either were picked off or gave our wings no chance. We had four or five opportunities to win the game and he just didn't know how to do it for us. Straight after the match I said to him, 'Mate, you frightened me to death. You've got to start exercising your options better. You've got three clear options: you either run at them with the ball, or put an early ball out finding your man before the defensive line has moved up, or hang on and hang on – and try and sell a dummy.' Garry went on to play the stand-off role brilliantly in New Zealand later on that tour. But, tear gas or not, we had no excuses after that shock defeat in Papua New Guinea, even though referee Hale gave us some bad calls. He was intimidated, I'm sure. Clearly some of the decisions he gave were one-sided, but we didn't deserve to win that game. The truth is that we were probably intimidated out of that one by the hostility of the crowd.

Papua New Guinea is an amazing country, such a mixture of things. I recall a night at our hotel in Goroka during which I had trouble sleeping. Hanging over the balcony in the warm tropical air, I witnessed a scene below in which it seemed certain one guy was going to kill another fellow with a hatchet. He didn't in the end – well, not there anyway – but I could barely believe what I was watching. The primitive nature of PNG really amazed me at times. There were places where they weren't selling the normal tourist things; instead they were selling bows and arrows, spears, hatchets and tomahawks – lethal weapons. The experiences of that tour also left us with a less than favourable impression of the administration of the Papua New Guinea Rugby League. I know our Great Britain manager Maurice Lindsay became exasperated on several occasions when he and several players had to man the gates to attempt to stem the flow of spectators forcing entry without paying, and when he sought assistance from the PNG officials he would find them in the bar, somewhat the worse for drink. In his tour report Maurice stressed that, whilst we should continue to play in PNG, we should do so 'on our terms and not theirs. We should play no more than two games, possibly three, over a space of no more than seven days . . . we must not be subjected to the intolerable conditions experienced manning the turnstiles. We must insist upon advance payments, with PNG welcome to keep any surplus – security is then their responsibility.' Happily, some of these views were taken on board and we had a much less stressful visit to PNG two years later in 1992.

However, amidst the tension and unease on that 1990 tour, we also had some terrific moments in Papua New Guinea. Local league men took us out on a couple of cruises. While we were in Lae, we headed to an island three or four miles out to go snorkelling. I took a few of the lads along after we organised some gear from a local sub-aqua place. The guy there gave me a tip: 'If you see any sea snakes while you're down there just give them a wide berth. Don't antagonise them because they're highly poisonous.' In the end I was the only one who used the snorkelling gear that day – the word had spread among the team about the sea snakes. But we had a great day with some swimming races, and a lot of fun. And we didn't see a single snake.

The prospect of this tour skirting around Australia to take in just Papua New Guinea and New Zealand was not greatly relished by some of the senior players back home in England. Many of them found reasons not to go. A number of players had committed themselves to go to Australia during that off-season, chasing the higher financial rewards. Frankly, I was disappointed at the attitude of some of them. Had the British Rugby League been blessed with the gift of hindsight, they would never have agreed to the tour in 1990. It proved to be little short of a financial disaster. Maurice Lindsay managed the team, after replacing Les Bettinson who had been such a valuable ally on the 1988 tour, and we headed off with what everyone considered to be a second-rate side. Martin Offiah was injured but joined us prior to the first New Zealand Test; Joe Lydon also joined the squad belatedly after missing the PNG leg of the tour. However, a string of top players did not tour at all – Ellery Hanley, Shaun Edwards, Andy Goodway, Andy Gregory, Steve Hampson and half a dozen others – all of them unavailable for various reasons. So it was that the Test team that faced New Zealand was unrecognisable from the one that had played and beaten them at home in England six months previously.

The absence of some of the more senior players – and some of the larger egos – did mean that the tour party was largely free of internal strife, however, and the one thing we did have going for us was a tremendous team spirit. The players really did work hard for each other and that inspirational spark and the team harmony made the tour. Deryck Fox was an outstanding figure on the whole campaign. The other scrum-half in the squad, Bobbie Goulding, and Deryck were two very similar players and Bobbie got the Test shirt. However, even though Deryck was not the first-choice half-back he did not let his disappointment affect his own form or his commitment to the team as a whole. He effectively ran the second-stringers and they built a tremendous sense of pride in their performances. On other tours of my experience down the years, the midweek team – the 'ham and eggers' – never had that kind of spirit. But on this tour it was something we worked very hard on achieving, and people like Deryck Fox were major contributors.

I remember a passage of play in a provincial match in New Zealand during which it was absolutely pelting with rain. I later extracted some motivation tapes from that game, because Deryck was so inspirational to the side that rainy day. We had this call – 'hit the beach' – and whenever it was made, the guys knew they had to take the game to the opposition as if they were troops coming out of a landing craft under enemy fire. The side we played that day – the New Zealand Maoris – had some big forwards, but when the call went out at a crucial point in the first half, Deryck put in four successive tackles, and each time the locals conceded ground. The sequence lifted the rest of the lads and they just drove them back in the tackle all day.

We were not expected to trouble the Kiwis in the Tests, but in fact we won the first two to take the series and were only a hair's breadth from completing a whitewash in the third. Martin Offiah's sheer pace was certainly the difference in the second Test. I can still see the winning try, late in the game at Auckland's Mount Smart Stadium, as clearly as if it had happened yesterday. Kelvin Skerrett made the bust up the middle and picked up Daryl Powell. He passed to Martin and away he flew – just beating Kevin Iro.

However, if Martin was a key figure (and he was), Garry Schofield was the man of the series by a mile. As the tour progressed he put his game together perfectly. The Kiwis simply couldn't handle him, especially his dummies. He kept selling them and selling them, putting people through gaps and scoring tries himself. He sold a dummy and scored a try in the first Test, which we won 11–10, and in the second the Kiwis were bang on him because they *knew* he was going to do it again. Yet there came a moment when he dummied – they held off – he dummied again, and they took it the second time. I just couldn't believe it, and he just hung on and hung on – and then sent Mike Gregory in for a try. I remember a New Zealand TV commentator hollering away behind me, 'Oh no, they're not going to buy that again, are they? . . . Yes, they are. Yes, they are!'

Schofield's tour just showed how one individual's confidence can blossom in the right circumstances. From stumbling through the first Test up in Papua New Guinea unable to take a right option that day even if his life had depended on it, he was transformed in New Zealand into the most dangerous and effective stand-off you could ever see – the man who won the series for Great Britain.

It was a fine Test series, intensely and closely fought. Even after we surprised them in the first Test at Palmerston North, I think the Kiwis firmly believed they would go on and win the trophy. But we got them again in Auckland in the second with that spectacular 75-metre Offiah try in the closing minutes. It finished up 16–14, and much to everyone's surprise we had wrapped up the series two-straight. But rugby league is a tough, demanding old game, as Martin Offiah was to find out in the third Test just a week later. A beautiful move engineered by Bobbie Goulding which covered some 80 metres of the field ended with Martin crossing the line and then attempting to make a one-handed touchdown between the posts. In the act of putting the ball down he fumbled it. And we lost the Test 21–18, despite scoring three tries to two.

Mistakes like Offiah's are real coach-killers. I suppose I took it hard enough that afternoon in New Zealand, but it wasn't the end of the world. The important thing is that people *learn* from it when they make mistakes. The thing about Martin is that he was such an entertainer that you knew that being flash was part of his game. To take that away from him, that gamesmanship, would be to take away a lot. I don't agree with some of the antics guys like Martin have got up to after scoring a try. It's more of a 'soccer thing' – the milking of the crowd, the playing up to the people – but it just happens to be part of Martin Offiah's make-up. Probably Martin was seen as an outsider in his early seasons in the game, the player from the south with the cultured voice. I am aware of those at Wigan who used to mildly take the piss out of him in the dressing-room on a regular basis. I think he tolerated quite a lot of them. But then again I think those same people also appreciated just what he could do in a game, how he could turn a game in an instant. Rugby league must cater for the differences of all its players; it must be big enough to make allowances.

It was in 1990 that scrum-half Bobbie Goulding got into hot water on tour, through an argument in a restaurant which spilled over into a fight. Goulding finished up being charged with assault and had to pay five hundred pounds compensation. What happened wasn't too bad, but we fined him, warned him and supported him. Bobbie is a guy with a short fuse, he was only 18 years old at the time and I think the whole thing was overplayed by the New Zealand media. After it happened I can remember listening to the radio one morning as we were getting ready to go to training. The radio station happened to be in a building right opposite us and the bloke was broadcasting: 'I think Bobbie Goulding's coming out, everyone better move!' He was really having a shot at him, making him out to be an animal. I had sympathy because I had been in the very same situation as Bobbie whilst on tour in Australia as a young fellow myself, many years before in 1970, and I gave the kid a lot of support. I knew what emotions he was going through. He'd got himself into some trouble a long way from home and he needed help. Maurice Lindsay handled it well; he understood, and provided support and positive advice.

Soon after returning home from that successful tour to New Zealand, the Aussies awaited us in the autumn of 1990 on a traditional Kangaroo tour. The big question being asked of me was whether I would stick with the players from the recent Lions touring team who had done us proud against the Kiwis, or would I bring the missing stars back in? The decision wasn't so tough really. While I appreciated greatly the efforts of the lads who had gone to Papua New Guinea and New Zealand, I had never been one who believed in cutting off my nose to spite my face. I knew very well that the players who chose not to go on that tour would now be regretting it because of the success we had gained. When we were out there winning they would have been thinking: 'Crikey, I wish I'd gone. I wish I had been part of that.' The fact is you can't buy memories. Those players had paid their own personal 'penalties'. When we did finally select the side to take on the Aussies then it was on the normal basis. There was no animosity.

One of the beauties of touring with a football team is that you come back fitter and more experienced. I know for a fact that when we came back from Australia after the '88 tour the fitness of the players was at least 20 per cent up on when they started out. On any tour, I believe it is the touring team that is in the driving seat because of the inbuilt improvement along the way. In 1990, we were back from New Zealand carrying the benefits of a testing campaign in southern waters. Conversely I knew the Aussies would gain momentum as their tour unfolded, but I was surer than ever that this Ashes series was going to be a close one – which it certainly was, as I have described elsewhere in this book.

Not long after that Ashes series, in 1991, as were walking down the path towards another tilt at the Australians, I was awarded an OBE for my contributions to the Great Britain 'cause'. It was a source of personal pride and also gave me a great deal of satisfaction for what the award meant to the game that had been my sporting life. Buckingham Palace was the venue – and I can tell you that the kid from Castleford was very proud that day.

The increasing pressures of football in technology's rapidly advancing years in the 1990s eventually pushed me into full-time coaching. In the build-up to the planned tour Down Under in 1992, I was still working with John Smith's as a regional manager, and they had been marvellous in allowing me to combine work with my football obligations. Shaping up for the 1992 trip, I knew that I was either going to have to approach them for time off (ten weeks) or consider a different direction. Ultimately it came down to the reality that it just wasn't fair to the company for me to keep things going the way they were. I explained my dilemma to the rugby league decision-makers; it went to the board of the RFL, and I was given a full-time appointment. My life in rugby league had changed again.

The '92 campaign in the southern hemisphere was hard business all the way – starting once again in Papua New Guinea, despite the great dramas of 1990. Happily, some of the lessons we learnt on that infamous 'Tear Gas Tour' were implemented, plus the political situation was more stable, so this time we got through trouble-free – dodging Lae, the main trouble spot in '90, and winning our three games in Goroka, Rabaul and Port Moresby. This was a streamlined schedule, much geared to the box office and minus the casual meander down through Queensland that once kick-started Great Britain tours to Australia – and which, as I discovered only too well back in 1970, can lure touring teams into a false sense of security before the Tests. We did start in Cairns (against Queensland Residents), but after that it was straight into top gear, with matches against five New South Wales Rugby League clubs dotted in among the three Tests. The overall strength of our squad had improved since the previous tour to Australia four years before, and I was confident we were in with a chance.

We competed so hard in the first Test before a capacity crowd in Sydney – a welcome upsurge in public interest compared to 1988 due, I am sure, to the way we tested the Aussies to the limits in the 1990 series – but took a real physical battering as the game unfolded, finally succumbing 22–6. It was a poor reward for a great effort. We sort of caught the Aussies on the hop very early in the game, moving the ball wide much quicker and sooner than they had expected. Twice Martin Offiah was just tipped a few millimetres into the touchline by Andrew Ettingshausen when he was away and looking certain to score. It was a premeditated plan against a well-drilled defence, a shock tactic if you like, and it so nearly worked. It was in this Test that Paul Harragon, later to be my captain at Newcastle, knocked our substitute forward Ian Lucas into dreamland, dispatching him to hospital with a questionable tackle. I can still see Lucas lying there three-quarters of an hour after the game. We couldn't get him around. The incident concerned me a good deal, and we were very worried for Lucas. From memory, Paul Harragon went in with the inside of his forearm and at the same time I think he was wearing padding. I was fairly concerned about the degree of padding, because I'd seen a similar situation in a Newcastle–Manly match when he flattened one of the Manly players, Martin Bella – turning out the lights on big Marty. There's something not quite right here, I thought.

I've never seen a dressing-room as bad as ours was after that Test match in 1992. Our blokes were like walking wounded, just battered. It had been such a physical encounter; the Aussies had really got into us. Players were strewn all over the place, there was ice everywhere. It was very difficult, because my players had given it their very best shot and all they'd come away with was pain and a four tries to one defeat. I didn't think we had played badly at all. The commitment had been good, although we had missed opportunities that could have made a difference. The Aussies, razor sharp after the intensity of their State of Origin series, had taken all their opportunities. I can remember how down everyone was in the dressing-room afterwards.

To get them back up from that and on to the triumph of Melbourne just two weeks later was something very special in my coaching career. Before that match there was a lot of paper talk about us getting even with Harragon for what he had done to Lucas. This was never a possibility; I mean my problem was finding somebody who could do such a job! In fact in the second Test our hooker Martin Dermott, one of Lucas's best mates, stood toe to toe with Harragon, jumping up, trying to get at 'the Chief'. If Paul had connected he probably would have knocked Martin out of the stadium.

The good thing about the team was that spirits were never down, despite the physical battering we had taken in Sydney. For Melbourne we were in good spirits, tactically ready, and very committed and determined. It was one of those nights when everything clicked. The atmosphere was electric, thanks to a travelling army of about 8,000 vocal British supporters in a crowd of 30,257. That was a tremendous statistic that rugby league could be very proud of. I don't think any other sport, including soccer, has ever been able to generate such an enormous number of fans travelling to support our national team, not just across the channel to the continent, but right to the other side of the world.

We played a brand of football that matched the occasion; we shifted the ball about and backed it with very sound defence. Once again that parallel between preparation and opportunity was so evident. People might say we were lucky because we scored four tries from kicks, which proved to be a killing weapon for us on the night, but the fact was we'd trained to do specific things like that, and to move the ball in various areas of the field.

It all worked marvellously and again the element of confidence increasingly played its part. The longer the game went on the more the lads grew in confidence. In the end it was 33–10, a record-equalling 23-points margin for Great Britain – and a fabulous night for British football.

I remember the game very fondly indeed. I had never before (or since!) felt comfortable at half-time in an international match against Australia. I mean, you never do. However, in Melbourne on the night of 26 June, we led 22–0, and I figured that was going to be sufficient breathing space for victory, whatever happened. It was a wonderfully exciting night, a coach's dream. The kicks we had tried at training came off; things we had worked for clicked into place. For a coach that is a mighty feeling; it is on those days or nights that you feel as if you have truly been a major contributor. I can still see Martin Offiah and Graham Steadman flying in for tries down the left-hand side, to wrap up the game for us in the final stages. We were never threatened.

A week later in a high-pressure third Test at Lang Park, the Aussies beat us 16–10 (two tries to one) and so held the Ashes. This was like the third Test of 1990 over again – the Aussies so big and physically strong, playing a highly structured brand of power football which did the job for them. The winning edge was not much, but it was enough. Again our problem was clear: matching them physically. They did nothing too flash, but were effective all the same in pinning us for too-long periods in our own 22-metre area, controlling the ruck and dominating field position with accurate kicking. Again it was a case of so near, yet . . .

The New Zealand Tests that followed on that tour provided a curious contrast. I have no doubt whatsoever that we should have won the first, which we let slip 15–14 after leading 14–6 with 20 minutes to go. In the second we were in desperate trouble, down 10–0 midway through the first half. But it was a mark of the character developed over a ten-week period that we were able to steady ourselves – and come back and win a thriller 19–16 to square the series.

The World Cup final at home ended that crowded and eventful year of 1992. But it was the same story as before: an Australian win by just a few points (10–6) before a world record international crowd of 73,361 at Wembley. Again it was as close as a single lapse of concentration. With 12 minutes left on the clock, we led 6–4, having matched the Aussies tackle for tackle, pass for pass. But when Alan Hunte knocked on and Australia won the scrum, the flying centre Steve Renouf was able to swerve past John Devereux, who had come into the match to replace an injured Gary Connolly, and speed away for the match-winning try. We gave them just one chance and they took it.

We struggled positionally in that match. We seemed short of middle-backs. I made a mistake pairing Deryck Fox and Shaun Edwards together as our halfs – two guys of similar ability. Frankly, Shaun just didn't perform at number six. It was a bad mistake playing him there; he was in the sin bin at one stage and just nothing much seemed to come from him that day. The cause wasn't helped when Gary Connolly was injured in the first half, ending his involvement in the match. Deryck Fox kicked extremely well and we contained them defensively, but we'd not much attacking flair out wide. It was a game in which we matched them in most departments, turned by just that one mistake – John Devereux's in the centres. Looking back it was probably why I played Garry Schofield out there in the centres (with Connolly), because I believed at that stage that Devereux was a little naïve defensively, still lacked a little awareness. He matured a lot more later. We were a bit thin in the centres actually, with both Daryl Powell and Paul Newlove out injured. Paul Loughlin was out too. So the Aussies got us again – by a whisker.

The credibility of our Great Britain team was long since restored, but a win in one of the really big ones against Australia would have been nice. 'Where does Malcolm Reilly go from here?' a reporter asked me in the Wembley dressing-room after the game. 'Back to the hotel,' I joked in reply. It raised a laugh, but – drained and disappointed as I was – it was genuinely about as far ahead as I was thinking at that time. And that World Cup final proved to be the last time I would be with a British side taking on the old enemy – the Aussies.

NINE

Knight Flight to Hong Kong

The circumstances of my decision to leave Halifax, and the Great Britain job, to return to Australian rugby league after a 20-year absence and coach the Newcastle Knights, had all the elements of a John Le Carré spy thriller. The story involved some chance meetings and quiet conversations between influential friends, as well as mystery flights and secret meetings in downtown Asia. There was also the element of a greater, guiding hand in the decision I finally reached.

Without ever knowing it Nigel Wright, the very promising young Wakefield stand-off, had a fair bit to do with what unfolded. There was a time at the end of 1993, during my first year as coach at Thrum Hall, when I was desperately trying to sign Wright for Halifax. The asking price was £140,000 – a lot of money. But I liked the look of him, and Tony Gartland – such a genuine and generous backer of the club – had offered the £140,000 out of his own pocket to clinch the deal when I made clear my enthusiasm for signing Wright. But there turned out to be a fly in the ointment. I went over to the Rugby League headquarters in Leeds to see Rodney Walker (later Sir Rodney), the Wakefield Trinity chairman, who was in a board meeting at Leeds that day, to try and clinch the deal. 'Rodney, I've come to make an offer for Nigel Wright,' I said. 'We are prepared to pay you £140,000 but we want to sign him immediately.'

Walker's answer was positive: 'I'll contact two of the board members – and we'll go from there.'

I left the meeting with the impression that Nigel Wright would very soon be a Halifax player. I am unsure of exactly what happened from there, but I do know that Maurice Lindsay – who was no longer involved with Wigan, but, of course, had been – somehow came into the equation. Next thing Wigan were in with a counter-bid, offering more money. A day later Wright signed with Wigan. I may be barking up the wrong tree . . . maybe Wakefield contacted Wigan themselves and asked for more money. I'll just say that the circumstances were most disappointing, and leave it at that.

Having missed Wright, I decided to make contact with Michael Hagan, the very skilful ex-Canterbury, then Newcastle, stand-off in Australia. Hagan, in the latter stages of an excellent career which had included a season as a teenager at Halifax in the mid '80s, had rung sometime earlier to express an interest in coming over to finish off his career in England. So it was that we signed Michael Hagan instead of Nigel Wright. In the course of conversation with him, I said, 'Look, we're in the market for a centre and a decent forward too.' Hagan put forward the names of David Boyd and the former All Black, John Schuster. Boyd was already interested in coming over, and Schuster was reportedly out of favour with the Knights' coach David Waite and there was a chance he was also interested. In the end we signed all three of them.

Schuster was the next link in the chain that led me back to Australia. Sometime in early '94 his manager, a man named Mike Tyler, joined him in the UK on a holiday trip from Australia. One night Schuster, Mike, myself and our wives had dinner in a restaurant high on the Pennines between Halifax and Huddersfield. During dinner Mike, with whom I was to become good friends, asked the question: 'Have you ever fancied coaching in Australia?' I told him it had been one of my goals for a long time, a deeply held ambition, but I didn't know when or where or if the opportunity would ever arise. The conversation moved on. The fact was that the distant prospect of one day going back to Australia had always been somewhere in the back of my mind. During the 1990 Test campaign in England I had told the experienced Australian journalist Alan Clarkson in an interview: 'I have thought seriously about going back to Australia to do some coaching, but the offers have not come along. I love coaching and would certainly enjoy the challenge of being involved with a Sydney club.'

The day after the dinner with John Schuster and Mike Tyler, Mike called in to Ledsham for coffee on his way to a day out in York. I showed him around the village and then he headed on. I didn't think too much more about it until the phone rang at home one night a few weeks later. It was Mike Tyler. 'Listen, I've had a word with Arko [Ken Arthurson],' he said. 'He thinks it's a good idea [me going back to Australia to coach] and he'll put some feelers out if you like. I can tell you there are a couple of clubs interested,' said Tyler. The thing was really moving now. Mike's next call brought me the news: 'Newcastle are very interested . . . Would you be prepared to meet them?'

This was June or July 1994, during our off-season. The prospects for Halifax seemed sound enough, but things were not progressing quite as I would have liked. We had missed out on a couple of signings, Bobbie Goulding among them, beaten for his signature by St Helens. The New-castle interest was a development from left field, something I had not anticipated, and I mulled over it for days. My initial reaction was: 'Well, it won't hurt to talk; I probably won't do it anyway.' Deep down I was greatly attracted. There had been some preliminary sparring with the wealthy Eastern Suburbs club in Sydney and I still held the view that the real test for a rugby league coach lay in Australia – where the pressure was on every week and where every result really counted. I had talked to people who had coached over there and thought to myself: I've got as good a knowledge of coaching and football as they have. Why not? Susan and I talked it over. Initially she wasn't keen. 'No, I'm not going back,' she said. 'I'm happy – I'm settled here. If you want to go back you'll have to go back by yourself.'

However, the talks with Mike Tyler had lit a fire which turned out to be unstoppable. 'Give me a couple of options,' I said. 'I'm prepared to meet you, but I can't afford the time to come out to Australia. How about meeting halfway somewhere?' Hong Kong was suggested. They talked to me about my schedule, then the message came straight back: 'We've booked your tickets.' It was now August 1994, pre-season at Halifax. One Friday night we had a training session planned and then some fun and games at a go-carting track. The next training session was scheduled for the following Sunday after a junior trial game.

Unbeknown to anyone but my wife, I jumped on a plane at Manchester on the Saturday morning and flew to Hong Kong. There at a hotel whose name escapes me I met Brad Mellen (general manager) and Terry Lawler (chairman) of the Knights over lunch, during which we discussed all the possibilities centred around me joining the club as successor to David Waite as coach: financial package, playing personnel, family arrangements, timing, accommodation, travel. By 10 p.m. that night Hong Kong time I was back on a plane, winging my way to Manchester, my mind racing with all that we had talked about. Mellen and Lawler were on their way too, heading home to Newcastle. I arrived back at Manchester airport at 7 a.m. on the Sunday morning and drove straight to training at Halifax. No one was ever the wiser.

At that stage I'd say my thoughts were about 80/20 on the side of taking the job. But this was a big step in my life – so much was involved. To say I was anxious was an understatement. I had a club commitment stretching two more years, and a commitment with Great Britain – in a season in which the Kangaroos were coming. Then, most concerning of all, was my family situation. My daughter Lyndsey was 16 and had just finished her GCSEs at school. She was going to have to change friends and environment, never easy at that age. Then there was the house in Ledsham; I certainly didn't want to sell that.

There seemed to be one giant step after another. The first of them was a family conference at which the message was a positive one: 'If this is what you want, we'll give it a go for a couple of years.' The next step was a meeting with Maurice Lindsay to inform him of my inclination to take the Newcastle job and so give up my position as Great Britain coach. By the time I saw Maurice my mind was already moving to faraway Newcastle; I was by then regularly watching videos of the Knights in action. I had individual profiles of the players sent over and I was actively preparing an off-season programme for them. My mind had already switched to the new challenge. Much as it hurt, I felt it would have been wrong for me to proceed with the Great Britain job, to take that on with a mind distracted by other things. Maurice was receptive and understanding. I had always had a good working relationship with him over the years, and he understands as well as anyone that things can change in a football life. 'Funny thing though: if at the eleventh hour they had summoned me with the message: 'Look, we really don't want you to go. We're kind of desperate,' it might well have changed my mind. I wouldn't have let them down. That's how unsure I was about the step I was taking.

My next port of call was Tony Gartland, chairman of Halifax, and he was devastated. Tony's support of Halifax had been little short of extraordinary. He had virtually been the instigator of any player-purchasing that had taken place and had done it out of his own money. Sometimes I had felt embarrassed when he had dug deep yet again to secure a player. His loyalty to Halifax was immeasurable and admirable. When I told him my news, at first he was stunned. 'Malcolm,' he said, 'you have a contract with *us* for the next two years.'

'I realise that, Tony,' I said, 'but this is something I have always wanted to do and now the chance has come up. Honestly, you don't really want someone coaching your team who doesn't want to be there, who would rather be somewhere else?'

Tony understood; he was a wonderful person. 'No, we wouldn't want that,' he said to me eventually. 'We'll find a way of getting around it.'

By then the story was starting to leak. With nothing finally in place I had no option but to fend off media enquiries linking me with Newcastle. 'I have been linked to Easts, Wests and now Newcastle in the last few months,' I told the newspapers. 'I would like to move to Australia one day and coach but not in the immediate future.'

Then, in my deep uncertainty, something happened which added to my own belief that there is a greater guiding hand in life. As I was wrestling with my own great dilemma (which was really not so great when put in perspective), a very close friend of ours, Jill Beaumont, died of cancer, finally losing a battle that had gone on for a long time. At a Sunday communion sometime after the funeral at the village church just around

The young warrior: 19 years old and *en route* to a first Wembley final and the Lance Todd Trophy in 1969.

BELOW

A teenaged Malcolm in his first season in pro football is about to be confronted by a legend of the game, Neil Fox. This was in March 1968 as Cas played at Wakefield in a Challenge Cup quarter-final. Malcolm has just released the ball to his famous team-mate, Alan Hardisty, whilst Bill Bryant is directly behind him.

RIGHT

Margaret and Sam Reilly, Malcolm's grand-
parents, outside their home in the Yorkshire
village of Preston. The close resemblance
between Malcolm and his grandad can be
seen in this photo. One of Malcolm's earliest memories is of his grandfather wheeling
him in a pushchair to the pithead.

BELOW

Malcolm and his mum on a day out to
Blackpool, 1950s.

OPPOSITE PAGE

They start them early in Castleford: a
youthful Malcolm Reilly gets a colourful
pre-Wembley send-off in 1969 from local
schoolchildren.

BELOW

Malcolm in action for Castleford against
Salford in that 1969 cup final at Wembley.
He was voted Man of the Match.

The infamous 1970 World Cup final at Headingley, Leeds. Reilly slips the ball to his Great Britain colleague Jimmy Thompson, despite the attentions of Australia's John O'Neill, Paul Sait and Bob O'Reilly. The referee is Fred Lindop.

Player-coach Reilly lifts the Yorkshire Cup for Castleford in 1977, chaired by teammates Geoff Wraith, Bob Spurr, Sammy Lloyd and John Joyner.

ABOVE

The warm glow of satisfaction: Malcolm enjoys the moment with assistant coach Phil Larder and business manager David Howes after Great Britain's Test win against Australia at the Sydney Football Stadium in 1988.

RIGHT

A mutual admiration society: Malcolm Reilly and Ken Arthurson, towering figures in rugby league's world over the last 30 years.

LEFT

Malcolm Reilly OBE at Buckingham Palace in 1991, a proud day in a great career.

BELOW

Coach at the top: Malcolm with the Challenge Cup in 1986 after his Castleford team had beaten Hull KR at Wembley.

ABOVE

Leading out the Great Britain team at Wembley for the 1992 World Cup final, with manager Maurice Lind and captain Garry Schofield. Opposite Malcolm on the Australian side is his old friend Bob Fulton.

BELOW

Strong-arm stuff: the coach takes on front-row strong man Tony Butterfield as Newcastle Knights colleag lay their bets.

the corner from where I live in Ledsham, I opened the Prayer Book and this tiny cutting fell out, a passage from the Bible:

> In heavenly love abiding, no change my heart shall fear;
> And safe is such confiding, for nothing changes here;
> The storm may roar without me, my heart may low be laid;
> But God is all around me, and can I be dismayed?
> Wherever He may guide me, no want shall turn me back,
> My shepherd is beside me, and nothing can I lack.

It was a small but profound event, immensely important to me in the decision I was about to make. Reading that passage conveyed many comforting messages to me: not to fear change; the message that nothing would change 'here' (at home). It was a case of a small, chance event providing comfort and the message of support and certainty that I needed at a difficult time. But was it really only chance? I still carry the message with me, a little use-worn now, but still saying those wonderful things.

So, I decided to return to Australia, 19 years after I had boarded the jet at Sydney's Mascot airport and flown home to England at the end of my time with Manly. The decision was firmly set now. I have to give it a go, I thought, otherwise I'll never know. My contract was for two years (extended by another two in February 1996). In an interview published in *Open Rugby* magazine, I stated: 'If you are *not* always ready for new challenges then it is time to pack it in. The structure and pressure on Australian league is so different.' Despite subsequent events it was not a decision made of financial grounds. The financial package I received at Newcastle was just about identical to the one I was getting in England via my dual roles as Halifax and Great Britain coach. I am unaware of the full details but I believe Newcastle paid Halifax a compensation fee for my transfer. The prospect of an Australian club turning to an English coach in 1994 may have caused surprise in some circles, but the Newcastle club was certainly right behind me; I learned that the Knights board vote for my appointment was eight to one. In Sydney the *Sun-Herald* commented: 'Reilly's appointment represents a huge financial gamble by a club that doesn't have a major sponsor and started this season $2 million in debt with accumulated losses of a further $1.5 million.'

In 1971 I had left, alone, from Leeds railway station on the first leg of the great adventure Down Under. This time Susan and Lyndsey were at my side, and we flew from Manchester airport, answering again the call from the land so far away. A quarter of a century on I left with emotions jangling: the old familiar mix of apprehension, expectation, excitement at the challenge that lay ahead, and a certain feeling of warmth too that I was once more heading back to my 'second home'. We holidayed in Thailand for a week before flying on to tackle whatever the city of Newcastle, and its football team, had to offer.

My son, Glen, didn't come out with us. He was quite settled at home in England back then, 21, with a girlfriend and a life he was enjoying, and playing some rugby league. He trekked out mid-year in 1995 with my nephew and some other friends, stayed about six weeks and loved it. He loved it so much in fact that he went back home, sold up all his possessions and came back to Australia to live. I doubt he'll come back to England. He's got a house in Newcastle, a good job, and the sort of love of Australian life that I first acquired way back in 1970.

The warmth of the greeting in Australia from people like Mike Tyler, Terry Lawler and Rod Harrison couldn't have been better. We were made to feel very welcome, very quickly. It was a difficult time, though; things were tough for Lyndsey, who deep down really didn't want to come. It was so hard and I agonised for her – there by herself, in a new country, with no friends. Human beings are adaptable creatures, however – and so it was with my daughter. Things changed to such an extent that when the time came to fly back home four years later, she wanted to stay in Australia. I wouldn't let her – just yet. She's a lovely lass with a heart of gold, but a little young for her age. She'd say to me: 'I'm coming back.'

'That's fine,' I told her, 'but you've got to come home for a time first.'

Lyndsey is quite an equestrienne, she just loves horses, and grew to love that part of her life in Australia, competing in cross-country events and show-jumping.

For Susan it proved easier this time too, despite her initial reluctance. She was very young in '71 when she first touched down in Australia. This time it was much more comfortable – and with a passing parade of visitors from home to show around. It seemed that we always had people staying at our house in Newcastle. Australia is like that – a place that people just want to visit and explore.

TEN

At the Eye of the Storm

I had no idea of the hurricane that awaited me in Australia. Its name was Super League. I had first heard the term on an afternoon in Leeds in the autumn of 1994. I had headed across to the Kangaroos' team hotel there to see an old and close pal, Bob 'Bozo' Fulton, who was at the helm as coach for a second successive Kangaroo campaign. The word in Leeds was that Ken Arthurson had flown home in some haste to counter the growing threat presented by this new 'Super League'.

In that unsettled Australian summer of 1994–95, the newspapers and the airwaves buzzed with speculation of a 'takeover' of rugby league, centred around the Rupert Murdoch-owned News Ltd. My first direct involvement came in early 1995 when I was asked by the Knights' CEO, Brad Mellen, to attend a board meeting, at which a representative of the Super League concept would be present. I wasn't privy to all the discussions but the matter on the table centred very much around the prospects of the Knights being part of the new deal. Later I met Brad, Malcolm Noad from News Ltd and Terry Lawler. Subsequently at a private meeting Noad talked about a contract for me, and gave me some figures for three key players, Andrew and Matthew Johns and Adam Muir, and a provisional offer for Robert Finch. The offers were substantial. 'This is the money we're talking – and we want to sign them on a three- or four-year deal,' he said. Would I consider looking after that? I told him I'd give it some thought.

I decided not to. Instead I met with Knights' football manager Robert Finch. 'This is what's happening,' I said to him. 'These people have been to see me, and I believe they're keen to see you. But I'm the coach here, not the football manager. They are proposing this sort of money for the players – and I don't believe it's my role to be conveying that. Will you speak to the players on their behalf?' And that's what happened. In the meantime there was contact from the Australian Rugby League (ARL), and a visit to one of our training sessions by Phil Gould, such a powerful advocate for the ARL cause. Gould addressed the players on an extraordinary night at the International Sports Centre in Newcastle, while Super

League representatives, Noad and Michael O'Connor, waited in a hotel room for the outcome of their offers to the players.

In that turbulent month of April '95, the whole thing rapidly shifted into overdrive. I quickly became aware that the club I had joined in this city that was to be my new home was seen as the jewel in the crown in the war between the game's two opposing forces. There was the now famous morning when 'the Chief', Paul Harragon, loaded the players into a minibus and drove them himself down to Sydney to talk to the ARL negotiators. Aboard the bus Mark Sargent took a call on his mobile from Knights' chairman Terry Lawler. 'Sarge' was one of Terry's favourite sons. My understanding is that the message was along the lines of: 'This is what's going on – and we want you to be a part of it [the Super League].' At Swansea, Mark Sargent got off the bus. That trip to Sydney by 'the Chief' and his men proved to be a significant event in the ARL 'holding' Newcastle. The club had been widely tipped to go 'Super League'. As Mike Colman reported in his book *Super League – The Inside Story*:

> It [Newcastle club] was one of the first to sign a confidentiality agreement with News Limited and one of the last to sign the ARL's loyalty contract. John Ribot and other Super League officials believed it was just a formality that the Knights would take up a Super League franchise . . . Super League believed it was a done deal.

Colman's book includes a telling claim from Super League chief Ribot:

> 'Their board was in it up to their eyeballs. They were at the meetings we held up to that stage, we thought all along they were with us. Terry Lawler certainly made us believe that. He talked tough, he just didn't have the ability to pull it off.'

These were unbelievable times, a rumour or a development with every phone call. Players were tugged this way and that by endless phone calls from the recruiters.

Progressively our core staff fell away as Knights officials were conscripted on substantially larger pay deals by the rival Super League Hunter Mariners. Brad Mellen left, headed for the Western Reds in Perth, and Keith Onslow and Neil Cadigan went to join the Mariners. At one stage there were only three of us left – me and two of the office girls. It was a club ripping and tearing itself apart internally. There's no doubt that at a high level of the Knights' administration the preference was to go over to Super League, because of the financial security offered to a significantly cash-strapped club. But the players, in the main, had chosen to stay ARL-loyal and so had I.

My own position, caught in the middle of it all, was extraordinarily difficult. I had uprooted my family, flown 15,000 miles to be part of the Knights' future, and now I was caught up in a civil war. I had arrived back in Australia relishing the thought of coaching people like the Johns brothers and Chief Harragon. Now the world was upside down. It was pretty frightening, I can tell you. If the whole club had chosen to go to Super League I would have had just two choices: to go with the flow, or to take a stand and say, 'Look, I don't believe in this.' My inclination was never, ever to go the Super League way, and my long and close association with Ken Arthurson was a factor in that. Eventually it was made easier for me when the players – or the bulk of them – decided that they were staying loyal to the ARL. I was comfortable with that. It was at that point I went to Sydney and met up with Bozo, who was fighting in the trenches for the ARL, a key spokesman for the cause. He set up a meeting with James Packer and Geoffrey Cousins of Optus, and I told them what sort of contract I had been offered by Super League. 'What sort of deal do you need to stay on with the Knights?' they asked me. We agreed on a figure.

I find it hard to describe the situation I found myself in at that time. 'Unreal' is a word that comes to mind. I had negotiated a fair contract, and suddenly, for reasons that had not a single thing to do with me, here I was negotiating a new deal at *three* times the value of what I had been on. If there was ever a classic case of a guy being in the right place at the right time, then it was me. Now and then in quieter moments I would shake my head in disbelief. I'm sure I wasn't the only one doing that in those mad times.

Yes, the 'loyalty' contract was a big one, and people took a stab at various figures. Journalists guessed as high as 2.3 million Australian dollars for the four-year agreement I signed with the ARL on 12 April 1995. There was speculation – and resentment too – in the fact that I had not long been there, and maybe also that I was an 'outsider' – an Englishman. On one Sydney radio station, breakfast show announcer Alan Jones had a real swipe at me, calling me a 'blow-in', and slamming the amount of money allegedly paid to me. Jones, the former Wallaby rugby union coach, had no idea of the circumstances and just shot his mouth off. I was not, and am not, interested in his views. Even a couple of years down the track I was still being asked questions about the deal they offered me, and about Jones's criticism. But I would tell sportswriters 'I don't want to talk about that – that's a long time ago. I never forget, but there is no use dragging up the past.'

Despite the rumours to the contrary that were put out now and then, I was never a great fan of Super League; I never fell for the rhetoric or the so-called vision. I was deeply disappointed that the English game succumbed, although I was well aware they were clutching at straws back home, with the game struggling constantly with its financial problems. Suddenly someone came along with countless millions of dollars and said: 'OK, we're prepared to put this into your game.' Not surprisingly, the English Rugby League took the bait. The thing I really hated about it was that the signing of England, New Zealand and the others was no more than a tactic – a device to isolate Australia, to bring the Aussies to heel and force them to fall in line with the Super League–Pay TV–World Vision scenario. It was divide and conquer at its very worst – and in a game whose world had always been relatively small, but close-knit and loyally bound since its very earliest days (1908) when England, Australia and New Zealand first got together to start playing international rugby league. I looked on at all that took place in 1995 and despaired – for the great traditions of the Tests and the history that underpinned the game. This was the people's game, always had been.

For much of the subsequent damage and tearing apart of the game in Australia, I blame the English administration for selling out so swiftly, so cheaply – and selling the *entire* game. And do you know the worst thing in the whole mess? It's this: if only the parties had taken a step back, a pause, and then come together to sit around a table, I'm sure they could have worked something out that would have benefited the *whole* game. But I knew what Super League knew, that their interest was never really much about the game. The motivation was purely commercial. Through it all I felt so much for Ken Arthurson, a loyal and valued friend to me throughout my career. I know the war that tore the game apart broke Ken's heart. To see and hear other people who had not contributed to the game an ounce of what Ken had over so many years, criticising him and his achievements with the ARL, was hard to take, very hard. Inevitably the circumstances led to a situation in which a sizeable gulf was created between myself and the English Rugby League boss, Maurice Lindsay, a man I had always worked well with. There were no great dramas or falling-outs between Maurice and myself, just a separation.

Financially it has been a devastatingly dumb exercise. The money spent – whether it's three or four hundred million dollars – will never be retrieved. The war of seasons 1995–96–97 left rugby league as a seriously diminished game, based on hugely inflated and unsustainable player payments. It will take vast amounts of intelligent, hard work to get it back.

At that fraught time in 1995 I spoke to the ARL on Robert Finch's behalf, and Robert was offered a contract. I had got on well with Robert, who had joined me in England in late 1994 to help plot the campaign that lay ahead for the Knights. I remember walking down to his office one morning and asking the question: 'Have you done anything about the ARL contract?' He told me he had lodged it with a solicitor and it was '95 per cent sure' he would be signing it on that day. In one of the many phone calls that punctuated the times, I was later told that Robert had been advised by Terry Lawler not to do anything until he had spoken to the property developer, Jeff McCloy, who went on to become chairman of the Hunter Mariners, and Bob Ferris from the Western Suburbs (Newcastle) Leagues Club. Next thing, Robert was gone, to become football manager of the Mariners. Their hope was for a 1996 kick-off in Super League's own competition, but the ARL's Federal Court victory in February '96 stymied that and placed the new club in limbo. Justice James Burchett's decision arrived with ironic timing, on 23 February, the very day the Hunter Mariners were officially launched at Newcastle Ferry Wharf. Not until the dust had finally settled on the long and immensely costly brawl which dragged through the courts did the Mariners get out of the starting blocks, in 1997.

In one of life's strange turns of fate I found, when I returned home to England in late 1998, that the Mariners' coach Graham Murray, who was one of the 'enemy camp' in that sometimes bitter battle for the city of Newcastle during the Super League war, had become one of my neighbours. After the Mariners were wound up after just one season, Graham became the successful coach of Leeds, and came to live in Ledsham during his time in Yorkshire.

But back in early '96, the whole situation of our club being drained of players – about a dozen went across to Super League – led to a rift between Robert Finch and me, and there were some broadsides between us in the press. As football manager he had come over to England before I left to do some reccy work, and we had got on pretty well. We had toured around a fair bit, looking for players, interviewing players – to Fiji, to New Zealand – and the working relationship had been a good one.

I took offence at suggestions that (a) I had 'abandoned' my English club Halifax and (b) that I was all set at one stage to jump to Super League. Robert had a crack at me in the media on those grounds in early 1996. 'He talks about loyalty. I worked closely with Malcolm and take it from me his initial judgement was to go to Super League,' said Finch. In those angry times as the war raged I saw it as no more than an attempt at character assassination; it was bullshit. On the first point: yes, I made a tough and awkward decision to leave both Halifax and my Great Britain commitments. But I can tell you I left on the very best of terms with both Maurice Lindsay and Tony Gartland, the boss of Halifax. They didn't want me to go, but they understood. It was total rubbish to question my loyalty because I gave them (Great Britain and Halifax) a month's notice after I made the toughest decision of my life. The truth is that despite my inclination to cut free, if they had asked me to, I would have stayed and done the Ashes series. On the other score, I helped Steve Simms, the new Halifax coach, for two weeks to settle him in. The club received compensation from the Knights for the time left on my contract. It was an immensely difficult time for me but I am satisfied the business side of things was handled ethically and honourably. Finch's remark, questioning my loyalty, was totally untrue, although certainly consistent with Super League's tactics at that time.

As for Finch's remarks on me and Super League, I have pretty much explained my situation already. Sure, I had a close look at what they had to offer; I would have been crazy not to. I had no idea in the early stages which way the club, and the players, were going. Via my meeting with Malcolm Noad, and the questions I asked, I was fully aware of what Super League were proposing. In April 1995 I told the *Newcastle Herald*: 'I've got to make a decision. I've had a [Super League] offer made to me and I'm giving it consideration . . . whatever the players and the club are proposing to do, I won't be doing anything other than that.' A week later I informed Newcastle officials that I was staying with the ARL, and I called a press conference to let the media know. I can tell you now that for reasons far removed from any financial aspects, I was very happy to stay with the ARL. Later, reinforcing my belief in the Knights and the ARL, in July '95 I accepted an extended contract with the club, taking me to the end of 1998. I made it very clear to the media early on what my position was about Super League when I told them: 'I thought about going to Super League for as long as it would take to think about jumping into a river full of crocodiles. There is no way I would ever have jumped in their direction; I considered what they had to offer then made up my mind very clearly what I wanted to do. I was also furious when the English Rugby League sold out a game which was established in 1895, to News Limited. The game didn't belong to them to sell.'

The extent of the Super League brainwashing, the propaganda at the height of the conflict, made life very difficult. It was hard to sort out the truth. Did Super League *really* have the 'vision' as they so stridently claimed via John Ribot, Maurice Lindsay and others? Were they really going to take over the rugby league world? I'm sure blokes like Robert Finch looked closely at the prospects presented and the money, and made the judgement that they had no choice but to go. We kept in touch for a time after Robert left the Knights in May '95, but things deteriorated between us. During the course of recruiting their team they did the

Knights a lot of damage. We were directly undermined and under seige from them all the time.

One evening, about three or four days after I had signed with the ARL, there was a knock on the door at home. It was Terry Lawler. Terry had obviously heard a whisper of the sort of money I was to receive through the deal. We sat and talked, it was quite friendly to start with, then it became less so. 'The fact that you have signed with the ARL may not be in the best interests of the club,' Lawler said to me. 'In fact we are disappointed that you have done it when the club has not yet decided the direction it is going to take.'

I answered him straight, 'Terry, I came out here to coach guys like Paul Harragon, the Johns brothers, Jamie Ainscough and the rest. The course I have taken is the only one I could have taken, considering the circumstances.'

Then he said something extraordinary, 'Well, you know all this money you are receiving, you know that you are going to have to share it with the other people in our organisation, don't you?'

'Well, I'm not so sure about that, Terry,' I told him.

It was effectively the end of our friendship, if not our formal association at club level.

Sometime after that the news came through that Michael Hagan was coming home to Newcastle, and could be a prospect for an administrative position with the club. I knew Michael's credentials, respected his football knowledge and regarded him as an awfully nice bloke. I thought he would be perfect for the football manager's job, Robert Finch having left by then. A week or so after he got back, Terry Lawler and I went to see him at the Apollo Hotel and offered him the job. He was obviously chuffed. 'I'm rapt – it couldn't have come at a better time for me,' he said. 'I'll just have to talk it over with Sue – then I'll come back to you first thing in the morning.'

The next day, when Michael hadn't rung by ten o'clock, I gave him a call. 'Listen, mate,' he said, 'I can't do it.' Michael told me he had had an offer from Super League and he believed the prospects were better with them. Some months later in conversation with Michael he told me of the firm view expressed by Terry Lawler that the club's long-term prospects weren't good and that he couldn't be guaranteed a job past the next 12 months. I was aghast.

Michael continued that first morning: 'So what I've done is taken what I think is a better opportunity – I've signed with Super League.'

The circumstances behind Michael Hagan's decision added to my belief that there had always been a hidden agenda. It seemed that Super League at that time were always one step ahead of what the Knights were doing. Unfortunately, confidential information and knowledge about player contracts and so on was used to the advantage of the Mariners as the new club struggled to plant some sort of footprint on the city of New-castle. David Morley, who eventually did become the Knights' football manager and a strong contributor to the Newcastle cause, told me some time later that he had been alerted to expect a phone call from the Super League administration – before Hagan was appointed. Before I had spoken to Michael, I had recommended to Terry Lawler that we should consider appointing Dave to do the job. News certainly travelled fast at that time!

Considering that Lawler was still chairman of the Knights at that time, it's no wonder that relations between him and me became strained to breaking point. Once it all blew up we didn't speak to each other for a long, long while; we just ignored each other. I am fairly sure he had made a decision quite early on that Super League was the direction to take. I have nothing personally against the members of the Knights' administra-tion who jumped the fence to Super League, and to the Mariners.

The city of Newcastle was an edgy and confused place in the white-heat months of the Super League wars. People took sides, with the overwhelming majority of them favouring the ARL's traditional right to run the game, and rejecting the News Ltd 'raiders'. Feelings ran deep and strong, and Super League-linked people had to be especially careful where they trod. Now and then it spilled over and there were some ugly incidents, like when rocks were rained on the Super League offices one night and considerable damage was done.

Not so remarkably, the players always got on very well – those who eventually went and those who stayed. The friendships built over the years of the shared experience of playing rugby league for Newcastle stood the test of even this. I certainly bore no grudge to the players who made their decision for Super League. Salt of the earth men like Robbie McCormack and Brad Godden – they were offered very little by the ARL. No one begrudged them anything. Or Paul Marquet ('Peppi'), a super fellow and a coach's dream . . . or Robbie Ross. No one wanted to see them go, but frankly our budgets were stretched tissue-paper thin and they had to go *somewhere*. The fact of another rugby league team in town offering huge wads of money was pretty unique. The other aspect of it was that I think all those players would have chosen to remain at the Knights had the offers and the money been comparable. Footballers' lives are short; players have to do the best they can in the time available. My feelings towards the players who left never changed. They did nothing wrong. They assessed the options available to them and made their decisions for their own reasons. Right down the line I tried to persuade players like Robbie Ross and Brad Godden not to leave but when they did, I never held it against them.

For all the obvious reasons – most to do with the fact that the game was literally tearing itself apart – my first two years back in Australian football, 1995 and '96, were difficult. Yet we managed to draw together tight as a football team in the face of 1995's challenges and constructed a season of some considerable achievement, although we were to fumble the ball in 1996. By then we had lost a dozen players to Super League, some good ones among them. Yes, when I look back on everything that happened in ''95 it is with some disbelief that I think about the sort of season we were able to construct out of all the wreckage strewn around us.

ELEVEN

Coach Down Under

The start of my coaching career in Australia with the Knights in 1995 was little short of a dream. Playing with increasing confidence, we won our first nine games straight despite all the administrative and legal battles raging around us in the game – it was a club record. Absolutely by choice, I eased myself gently into my new club. I think there is a tendency with some coaches and some executives – whether they be CEOs of sporting clubs or men in the corporate world – to come in and put a broom right through any new place they take over. Maybe the business gurus think this is the way to go, but to me this sort of management is way off the mark and I am not a believer in it. I think by taking that sort of approach you risk losing a lot of valuable allies. At Newcastle I settled in very slowly, letting a lot of people talk me through the way the club was functioning. Obviously it was already a club with a pretty solid structure; my task was to seek out all the positives and build on them.

I got on well with the general manager Brad Mellen, better than I did with his successor Ian Bonnette, but Mellen was gone soon enough, on his way to Super League with plenty of others. The fact was that the team I had taken over had been in fifth place only seven rounds out from the 1994 semis under the coaching of David Waite, only to lose their way badly and drop the last seven games. Much of the culling that took place was of the 'natural attrition' variety, although it was quite dramatic as the Super League war swept into town, cutting a swathe through both the community and the Knights.

My coaching career in Australia began the way I hoped it would. In a hard, physical game at Caltex Field we outlasted Cronulla 6–4 in the opening round of the 1995 premiership and I was out of the starting blocks as a coach Down Under. In the light of subsequent developments there were comments I made after that match that I regret a good deal. The Sharks teenage forward Adam Ritson took something of a battering in the game, and finished up the worse for wear. Two of our players – Marc Glanville and Adam Muir – were cited. There was an outcry from Cronulla, along the lines that they would seek protection for Adam, and that he was becoming a 'target' for high tackles. Asked the question, I made the technical point that I believed Adam's running style was the problem; that he was ducking at the point he hit the line and taking high shots that hadn't originally started out that way. I was as shocked and saddened as anyone at Adam Ritson's subsequent life-threatening illness, and my very best wishes are with him as he works his way back towards health and a normal lifestyle.

Rugby league is a hard game which extracts some sort of price from most people who play it over any length of time. It is always a tragedy on the rare occasions that that price is an extreme one; although in Adam's case, the medical judgement was that his league career had not been a factor in the problems that developed. Inevitably, the case of an old tour-mate of mine from 1970, Mick Shoebottom, comes to my mind. Mick was, and is, a great guy – a real livewire and the life of most parties on that tour. But the knock he took on the head in a match for Leeds against Salford many years ago changed his life for ever. For Mick it has been a long, hard road back. However, I saw him at Christmas 1997 and he's fine, he has improved a great deal and is enjoying life.

As we picked up momentum in that dream start to 1995, there were lots of tries and some big wins. People commented on the change in style, Newcastle's move to a more 'open' game. I am certainly a believer in letting footballers express themselves on the field, as long as it's in the best interests of the team. If a particular individual has special talent and it can be blended into the team pattern, it has to be beneficial all round. Sometimes, though, you can go overboard, and we did do that on occasions at the Knights. We tried to 'play football' to get out of trouble in matches. You don't do that; you go back to the fundamentals and start building again. You can't win games by just a big play. There must be a format; and then, when you've got the fundamentals right, you can play football. That pretty much sums up my philosophy about the game of rugby league in the 1990s.

The coach himself struggled physically for a time in '95. With both my knees giving me 'what for' I underwent surgery to have arthritic spurs, floating bone chips and loose cartilage removed. On crutches and then on a walking stick I managed to keep my coaching obligations rolling along.

The team was developing a seemingly unstoppable momentum against such strong odds. Always, the passion of our own supporters sustained us. It was a unique situation in a one-team city. There was always the chance that what was going on would tear the city apart. However, the great public support for the Knights and for the ARL's fight to save a game they believed they had the right to run provided strength for me and the team. It was all non-stop. People threw themselves behind us, with the very vocal 'Aussies for the ARL', headed by the feisty Barbara Davis, leaving *absolutely* no doubt where they stood as they gathered rank and file support for us – and for the fight being waged by Phillip Street.

I couldn't have been happier with the way the Newcastle players responded to what I was trying to build in 1995. It was a year in which we were right on the edge; I never thought we were any less than a genuine premiership threat. And when we came out of a late-season slump (six losses in our last seven games) to win successive semis, against Norths (20–10) and Cronulla (19–18), we were right in the thick of it. The Cronulla game was evidence of something that became a characteristic of the Knights over the next three seasons – the ability to fight back from seemingly impossible positions. The Sharks had us on the mat at 18–6, but we climbed back and Matthew Johns kicked a late field goal to steal the game for us. The media called the win 'Houdini-like'.

That was a really brave victory. We had a lot of 'wounded' players on the park against Cronulla, and the doctors had been busy with the needles. That sort of medical support – the use of painkillers – has never been a problem for me, as player or coach. I remember my limping exit from the 1973 grand final, and the urgent needling in the Manly dressing-room – three needles to try and get me through the game. Unfortunately that day the injury was incapacitating and even the needles couldn't nurse me through. My attitude is that I'll do anything to get a player on the park – and keep a player on the park. I think if the player represents the prospect of the team being more successful because he is out there, then you have to do it. But always the necessary checks and balances are provided by the specialist medical team. If a player risks doing more damage, then he won't be out there.

Inexperience probably beat us in the crunch game of the 1995 season, against Manly, the week following the win over Cronulla. There was a point midway through the second half when the score was close. With a little more experience we would have gone on with it, but it was Manly who steadied best under pressure, scored a try and then a couple of late ones to beat us 12–4 and end our season. It was disappointing, yet full of promise for the future.

When the disappointment of that day subsided I reflected with much satisfaction on what we had achieved in '95. I had arrived in Australia apprehensive about how the team would go, and what sort of reception I, as an 'outsider', would get, coming to a closely knit city like Newcastle. The difficulties caused by the battle taking place in the game's wider world hadn't helped the cause, but team performances on the park had been good, although I had identified that we were well below the strength levels of the Canberras and Brisbanes. That basically boiled down to the fact that the players hadn't been doing the specific training required. The Knights in fact were a few seasons behind some of the top Aussie clubs in physical preparation. Over the first three years I was there, we managed to peg teams back in that regard, leg strength increased and we became a bit more explosive, although not as explosive as I would have liked. Some of the guys dropped their body fat and were far more effective as a result of it.

The game has certainly come a long way since I was first running around with Castleford under the old-style coaching of George Clinton. The approach today is scientific and specific. When I looked at the Newcastle team of 1998, my last season before I came home to England, I could see players there who were still 20 per cent or so short of their potential. There were others who were running around performing week by week at 98 per cent of capacity, and a coach has got to be happy with that.

Two guys who can go all the way to the top in football if they maximise their potential are the Knights back-rowers Troy Fletcher and Peter Shiels. It's down to them. You can give footballers all the advice in the world, but they need the desire, the will to pursue the areas of improvement. Big Peter Shiels has everything it takes. He's six feet five inches tall and already weighs 107 kg. They call him 'Stretch'. His leg speed is pretty good, but his body fat is up around 17 or 18 per cent, and he has not yet seriously done leg strength work and upper body work. He can improve his physique, his physical strength and power by 20 per cent, and if he does that he could be anything. He's got great hands, great skills and he reads the game well. He needs a big off-season, and the same goes for Troy Fletcher, he needs to drop his body fat and put more muscle bulk on. Discussing such specifics of individual players' build-up was unheard of in the days when I was a player. It's a measure of just how much rugby league has changed and progressed in athletic terms.

Frankly we were still an inexperienced football team in 1995, despite the achievements, which were really remarkably good. The inexperience showed the next year, 1996, when we had one of those 'down' years sometimes suffered by good young teams on the way up. People have told me the story of the South Sydney team which built a great dynasty in the late 1960s, winning four premierships in five years and being runners-up the other time – and I can vouch for their abilities when I recall the momentous clashes that always ensued whenever my Manly team played Souths in the early '70s. Before all that started, Souths, as youngsters, had made the grand final of 1965 against the mighty St George side of that time – and had gone very close to bringing off an upset. Yet in '66, just when everyone was waiting for the team to ascend to the throne, they slumped. Thirty years on, we did exactly the same at Newcastle, letting our supporters down to an extent in a season of only moderate achievement which left us ninth on the ladder.

Mental toughness comes out of experiences. In '96 there was no questioning the physical toughness, the ruggedness of the side. I doubt that anyone enjoyed playing us. But one aspect of mental toughness is knowing precisely the job you have to do, then going out and doing it, under whatever adversity might present itself. In this regard, we lost our way. The consistency factor went missing in 1996. The key is being able to perform at a consistently high level, up around 90 per cent. If you do that you might not win *all* your games, but you're going to be mighty competitive. We were much closer to getting that right in my last year with the Knights, after the experiences of 1997. If we wanted to win a game badly enough, we could go up to 95, 98 per cent, and we'd play well enough to get away with it. The aim is never to fall below the 90 per cent level, and this comes only with team experience. However, in 1996 we just didn't aim up some weeks. I would estimate at times that we dropped as low as 65 per cent of potential in some of our performances. It was disappointing stuff, frustrating; and all I could console myself with was that I *knew* the team was capable of so much more, so much better.

It's a fact of football life that a team can go into a downward spiral very quickly. Suddenly confidence can dip and the spark can go out. Players who were previously buoyant can suddenly start doubting their ability to win. Even worse, they can go out with a real fear of losing. We went through that phase in 1996. I think every coach and every team has addressed it at some stage. The trick is how well, and how quickly, you can overcome it. It is a test of both the intelligence and toughness of players, of coach, of team and of club. The positive reality is that dreams are renewable. No matter what our age or condition there are still untapped possibilities within us.

Yes, '96 was a tough year with a tough ending. Money was especially tight and there had been a drain of players to Super League, plus the pending departure of three players to St George (Ainscough, Treacy and Andrew Tangata-Toa), of which I will tell you more. There was constant speculation about outside offers to the Johns brothers and Adam Muir, players who didn't come off contract until the end of 1997. The majority of our football staff took a pay cut, and reserve-grade coach Peter Sharp subsequently left for Parramatta.

The external distractions of 1996 didn't help, especially the formation of another team in the town (the Hunter Mariners), with our players having to contend with all the nuances that went with that – of seeing mates in the other camp, that sort of thing. That was difficult. In 1997, when the rival Super League competition finally got up and running, there was occasional talk of a home-town derby between the two Newcastle sides. I'm glad it never happened, although the crowd would have been enormous. I have no doubt it would have been a bloodbath – and not necessarily *on* the field. The fact was that the players got on well together. Off the paddock would have been the big worry, so deeply did the feelings run in the city. I believe such an event would have been extremely dangerous.

Yet for all the external dramas imposed on the club, the very worst blunder was of our *own* doing. In a tactical decision that was both short-sighted and disastrous in its timing, two of our good players – Jamie Ainscough (who established a club try-scoring record in 1995) and Darren Treacy – were told mid-season that they wouldn't be on board with the club the following year. Our CEO Ian Bonnette (of whom more later) was at the heart of this. It was a fact that Bonnette was dealing with financial reality – that the Knights couldn't keep Ainscough and Treacy on the sort of contracts they had at the club. Sure, Jamie had a problem or two, but he was an exciting player with bags of talent and, oh boy, it could have been handled better.

The news broke on a Friday before we were to play Canterbury in an important game. My memory is that Treacy and Ainscough learned the news for the first time when they read it in the papers! It was a delicate matter that called for discretion and sensitive handling. If the two players *did* have to go, for legitimate financial reasons, how much better it would have been if the club had handled it discreetly, perhaps testing the water quietly with other clubs. With intelligent handling it could have been a case of other clubs bidding for the pair. Instead, on the eve of a big game, they read in the press the news that they were no longer part of the equation at Newcastle, and that they were being offered around to other clubs (both went to St George eventually). This was slap bang in the middle of the season, and the two players were an integral part of our team and of what we were trying to achieve in difficult circumstances. It was blundering, heavy-handed administration – an important matter clumsily mishandled.

Accepting the reality of the financial situation, I still have no doubt the right way would have been to handle it in a manner that was not going to interfere with their performance on the park. The way it was done was a serious blow to the self-esteem and self-confidence of the players involved. I was never asked. No one ever came to me as coach of the side and posed the question: 'What do you reckon is the best way to handle this?' The chief executive, Ian Bonnette, and the chairman, Terry Lawler, just went ahead and did it their way, and it definitely caused us some trouble. The other players also weren't exactly enthusiastic about it either. 'I don't agree with letting them go,' fumed skipper Paul Harragon.

The episode was so demotivating. And surprise, surprise, Ainscough, one of our major strike weapons, went out and had a shocker against the Bulldogs, one of his worst games ever. Defensively appalling, he was responsible for two of the three tries Canterbury ran in during an overall team performance by us that was plain bloody awful. That day I did something I don't often do, and gave the team a tongue-lashing at half-time. I was frustrated and disappointed. 'There are individuals who aren't working hard enough on their goals,' I told the media later. We lost 24–14. The relationship between Bonnette and myself, already strained, certainly did not improve on the strength of that episode.

In that disappointing season of 1996, when we finished ninth with a 10–10 record, I felt that various people in the team were really struggling to mature as individuals, not just as footballers. We had young men there who had tasted some success the previous year, and now were trying to handle it, to search for their own identities. Those individual struggles didn't help the team very much, and I blame myself to a degree for not getting the blend better. There was one day when Andrew Johns turned up for a match against Manly with his hair dyed bright red. All he managed to do was put unnecessary attention and pressure on himself; he had a shocker.

There were some bad days, none worse than when unheralded Balmain knocked us over on our home ground at Marathon Stadium. That day the players suffered the painful experience of being jeered off their home turf, a new and jolting experience for all of them in this city where the Knights were such a focal point of the whole community in which the players lived. I remember that day vividly: the supporters booed, I was appalled, and the players seemed lost. As they slowly changed, a replay of the game featured on the dressing-room television, but the players turned away, they couldn't bear to watch. The season ended for us with another embarrassing day, a 22–0 last-round thrashing at the hands of Cronulla. At the end of it all we wore the unwelcome tag of 'underachievers of 1996'. As the coach that hurt – but we couldn't argue with it.

It was the year in which we lost our way, the season a major disappointment to a group such as Aussies for the ARL, which had backed us so resolutely. We didn't have a lot of luck on the paddock; but that's just football, never an excuse. Most of the problems were of our own making. For my own part I realised that there were things that needed tightening up. 'Sometimes understanding can be taken for softness,' I said in one press interview. 'We are just going to have to kick a few more backsides.'

When *Rugby League Week* looked at our 1997 prospects they concluded: 'Much would seem to ride on the ability of Newcastle players to put the past behind them and concentrate more on the football and less on their various pay cheques.' It was a reasonable call.

TWELVE

Knights to Remember

As has often been the way in rugby league, Jack Gibson has said it better than most: 'Winning starts on Monday, not ten minutes before the game. It's confidence all week long, and it's confidence for the month before that, and the year before that.' And, of course, that's the way it was for the Newcastle Knights of 1997 when we came steaming home to win a football premiership, putting a spring in the step of an entire city. And yet, for all the truth that lies in Jack's dissection of success, I have no doubt there was a single afternoon that provided the springboard for what we achieved in that unforgettable September.

It came on the day we played Balmain at home, just before the ARL finals began. The Tigers under coach Wayne Pearce had been on a real roll, just smashing everyone around. One of their forwards, Glen Morrison, had even gone public, suggesting that their forward pack was the toughest in the business. Stuff like that is always perfect motivational ammunition for a coach to use, and the quote did not go unnoticed among my blokes. The match was very special to us, and even more so for two of the forwards. For Adam Muir and Marc Glanville this was to be their last home-ground appearance in front of the Newcastle public in the red and blue of the Knights. Adam had signed a big contract with North Sydney and Marc, after 200 first-grade games and at the tail end of a fine career, was off to England to play with Leeds. Marc was a bit like the way I was back in '75 – running on knees that were better suited to the softer grounds of England rather than the hard 'on top' conditions in Australia. Adam Muir desperately wanted to stay a Knight, and we had spent numerous meetings trying to find ways of retaining him, trying to tie in an individual sponsor who might make the difference. But the fact was that Norths had made him a simply outstanding offer; from the point of view of his family and the future, he just couldn't knock it back.

All through the week I sensed that the players were going to make this a day to remember. All week I could feel the team gaining intensity and momentum; several times we sat through the video of Balmain dishing it out to Parramatta in the previous week's game. When the big day came, in a match played in a wonderful atmosphere before a big crowd, the team played superbly, steamrolling the Tigers in the forwards to set up a fabulous 34–10 win. If ever a match was won in the trenches, this was the one. The forwards to a man just lifted – and really 'gave it' to Balmain. Afterwards tears representing sadness and joy in equal quantities rolled down both Adam's and MG's cheeks.

It was a day of shared experience, with the crowd emotions lifting to new levels, aware of the fact that they were watching two of their favourite sons for the last time at home in Newcastle colours. I have no doubt that victory, and that whole day, was an important ingredient in what we went on to achieve over the next month. An intensified spirit of do-or-die was firmly planted in the team from that afternoon as we headed into the finals. From that day there was a quiet air of confidence that we were in with a big chance. I think it hit home with every single player that if we could play with that sort of passion on that day then nothing was impossible in the weeks ahead. I sensed just that – that with this team, anything was possible. The pending departures of Glanville and Muir had added an extra quality of personal emotion to the campaign. Very likely that was our 'X factor'.

This was the season in which Newcastle climbed back on to the rails after the disappointments of 1996. A combination of injury (Andrew Johns) and illness (Paul Harragon) threw the gauntlet down to the other players, gave them reasons for digging deep. Andrew missed a lot of football after suffering a badly injured ankle in a pre-season trial against Manly in Coff's Harbour, an event that gave one-time London player Leo Dynevor his chance at half-back, which he took extremely well.

Johns played only 11 games during the year, yet his contribution to what we subsequently achieved was immeasurable. And 'Chief' was struck down by severe migraines which caused him to miss six matches. The weather chipped in too, providing a series of grim, wet-ground home games at Marathon which cost the club two hundred thousand dollars or more in lost gate receipts. Unlike most English rugby league grounds, the Knights' home stadium has no cover apart from the main grandstand, so if it rains, the fans are going to get wet. Having said that, in all my long career in the game I've never experienced such an uplifting atmosphere as that provided at a packed Marathon Stadium on a crisp winter's afternoon in Newcastle. Against Souths, conditions were so bad the game was called off, and when we played Norths in mid-June, stinging rain pelted in horizontally from the south on the back of a chill wind. Out on the wing, Darren Albert got colder and colder, and ended up having to be treated for hypothermia. This wasn't quite Halifax, but it was a pretty tough day all the same — and, anyhow, everything's relevant, isn't it?

I remember that the only other time I saw someone come off with the sort of problem Darren had that day was the Aboriginal player Jamie Sandy, when I was coaching Castleford. We played York one day, and probably the only reason the game went ahead was because it was programmed for TV. If it hadn't been for that, there's no way we would have played. The frozen ground had thawed — to an extent — but only the top couple of inches. Under that the field was frozen solid and the melted ice lay as freezing water on the surface. Almost literally, young Jamie went blue after being out there for half a game or so. I can picture him coming to the sideline. 'Malcolm,' he said. 'I can't feel myself at all. I'm numb all over — you're going to have to get me off.' So we did, ushering him into a hot bath where he sat shivering for over an hour. Jamie Sandy pretty much won the Wembley final for us in '86, scoring a sensational try.

Whilst the momentum gathered all season with the Knights, it was also in 1997 that I got to coach the Rest of the World side against Australia. In that troubled, divided year with the establishment (ARL) and the new boys (Super League) wrestling for the hearts and minds of the public, the ARL programmed this match to give their season at least an element of international football. The match itself was no classic, but it was quite a fair struggle that hung in the balance for over an hour at Brisbane's Suncorp Stadium (better known to rugby league fans as Lang Park) before the Aussies slipped away to win 28–8. For me it was an intriguing challenge, trying to blend this mix of British, New Zealand, Papua New Guinean and Tongan players into an effective whole.

I chose to room a couple of the English lads together — Gary Connolly and Jason Robinson, both from Wigan — and that was a *big* mistake. Gary is something of a wild boy, who loves nothing better than a night out at a club and a late party. In contrast, the Jason Robinson of recent years is very much a committed Christian, quiet and careful in his ways. I think Jason's life was deeply influenced by Va'aiga Tuigamala, the ex-All Black who lives his life very much by the book, and is an inspiring sort of character. Jason had been something of a party animal himself in his younger days, but is now much changed. Not long after we had moved into our hotel there was a quiet tap on my door. It was Jason Robinson. 'Listen, Malcolm, I don't want to appear to be causing problems but would you mind finding another room for me,' he said. 'I don't mind a room by myself or I'll pop in with another player. You know, Gary and I just aren't on the same wavelength. I think you know that I'm a Christian . . . and Gary is just a larrikin.' So I put Jason in with the PNG player Marcus Bai (who's gone on to be a big success with the Melbourne Storm) and they trooped around together, very quiet, for the days leading up to the match.

A great distraction to the pursuits of the Knights as a single-minded football team in '97 came in the intense, continuing media speculation on the playing futures of Andrew and Matthew Johns. Would they stay together? Would they stay at Newcastle? Would they split up and take the money elsewhere? It was endless.

However, all this adversity did no harm whatsoever to a team of ambition. Very likely, in fact, it laid down a layer or two more of the qualities that eventually took us through to the premiership title. Belief and confidence grew in equal measure as we carved out a 14–1–7 record in the 22-game regular season, ending up equal second (with Parramatta) behind minor premiers Manly. And it was this confidence – in self and in the team – that enabled the side to do what they did over the four weekends of the finals. The play-offs make the month of September such a magical time in Australian rugby league – something I remembered so well from my time as a player with Manly – it's a time of intense, nerve-racking, sudden-death football, just like those Challenge Cup semi-finals I experienced in my days back home at Castleford.

The first semi for the Knights, against Parramatta, was the perfect example; at 18–0 they had us nailed to the floor. I'll admit I was pretty devastated early that day, yet never was there any thought that the game was 'gone'. Winger Adam MacDougall scored a double, then Adam Muir was over and it was 18–16 with half a match still to play. The rest of it was a gruelling knock-'em-down sort of affair in which injuries cut deeply into both sides. Our centre Matthew Gidley was carted off with a broken leg and full-back Robbie O'Davis was badly concussed. We all felt for Matthew that day – his dream of a grand final gone, for that year at least. Fifteen minutes into the second half, in scoring a brilliant solo try, Andrew Johns suffered a bad rib injury as Jason Smith drove into him on the ground over the line. Johns's ribs were to be the subject of many headlines in the days and weeks ahead. In the end we got home 28–20 against Parramatta, a truly epic victory in the circumstances of that afternoon. One paper called it our 'life after death' win.

Manly beat us 27–12 in the major qualifying final the following weekend, but this was a no-account game. Under the rather peculiar finals structure of 1997, the match meant nothing. Win or lose, both sides still had to get through another match to make it into the grand final. Winning would have been nice, certainly, and the game was played with fire and full intensity, but this day was more about crossing fingers and hoping to get through without further injuries. It was no psychological blow to us, I can

119

assure you of that. As soon as it ended we had drawn the line and were getting ready for the one we *had* to win, against Norths the following week. But that first Manly–Newcastle finals tussle whetted the fans' appetites for a possible rematch, two weeks down the track. There was much to talk about in the aftermath of the game, headed up by great controversy over a Nik Kosef 'torpedo' tackle on Matthew Johns after Johns had kicked the ball. It was a dangerous tackle, no doubt, and I was pretty amazed that Nik had done it. He and Matthew are really good mates, and have been for a long time. I can remember Matthew's own disbelief in the dressing-room afterwards, that Kosef would try to 'torpedo' him. You could draw no other conclusion than that Nik had set out with the intention of taking Matthew out of the game, launching himself at the legs when Johns couldn't have been more vulnerable. He went quite close to succeeding; Matthew suffered some medial ligament damage to one knee, but not enough to keep him out of the football that still lay ahead. After a great ruckus in the press, Kosef earned a week's suspension from the Judiciary.

John Hopoate was up to his tricks that day too, rubbing in the fact that Manly were on top. Honestly, I think Hopoate distracts himself with his behaviour, the sledging and the belittling of opponents. It's all so negative; he'd be far better off concerning himself with improving aspects of his own technical game. It's a joke the way he carried on in the years my Newcastle team competed against him, right up into our grand final meeting. And his presence certainly added an extra edge to games between the two clubs.

Even more edge came from the ever-present 'Clash of the Titans' – Paul Harragon versus Mark Carroll – but this was a much more positive prospect in any Manly–Newcastle game. They are two players who have never spared themselves, and the battles between them over the seasons have been positively gladiatorial, bringing out the best in both of them. I think the game needs action like that – it certainly had plenty back when I played for Manly and was a target for every Pommie-basher in the Sydney competition!

I have often thought the 'Chief' could have been kinder on himself, the way he played. But he was not a man for the easy option. I think the Carroll–Harragon clashes have been great for the game, just the sort of thing to set the turnstiles clicking. Yet for all the ferocity, there always existed between them a shared emotion: mutual respect.

We made the grand final of 1997 after a truly dramatic match against North Sydney. The drama came both on and off the field, with our share of it centred around the struggling Andrew Johns. Needled up to mask the pain of his damaged ribs, Andrew contributed a great deal for us in the first half, our two tries (scored by Robbie O'Davis and Billy Peden) resulting from kicks he put through. But close to half-time he was in real trouble after taking a heavy tackle. At half-time the doctor worked on him, but he was too injured to be sent straight back into the game, although I did get him back out there for a few minutes near the end.

I think with Andrew on for the full game we would have had a more decisive win than we did. He represented so much for the team – general kicking, goalkicking, field goalkicking, generalship, combination with brother Matthew. When he couldn't come out for that second half, it was a hurdle for us to jump, and I say this without any reflection on Leo Dynevor who took his place. A good attacking player with a high skill level, Leo did a darned good job for us in 1997.

Norths, so close in recent times to the 'big one' but never quite getting there, were desperate to beat us, and they came back at us strongly as the second half progressed. They scored two tries to level the scores at 12-all – and there were some desperation saves as we attempted to halt their momentum. Most memorable of all – and I'll *never* forget it – was Darren Albert's miraculous tackle on Norths' tearaway full-back Matt Seers. This was the moment that summed up the never-say-die, never-give-up spirit that lived in the hearts of the Knights.

First, Robbie O'Davis' despairing dive just clipped Seers's heels, checking him, costing him two or three metres. It was enough to give Darren Albert, flying from the opposite wing, the ghost of a chance. Yet right to the last second it seemed that Seers still must score as he sped down the eastern touch-line at the Sydney Football Stadium. Right on the cornerpost Albert nailed him with a mighty dive, spinning them both into touch. It was a fabulous moment, surely one of the great tackles of all time. Within days it was being compared to that in Australia, ranked alongside – or even above – the other most famous last-ditch saves remembered in the game's history.

I think after that tackle we were always going to win, despite the fact it was 12-all and that Norths had had the best of the second half. There were just two minutes left on the clock when Matthew Johns, on tired legs, lifted a 35-metre field goal between the posts at the southern end. The Bears gave one last gasp, trying a short chip over, but the 'Chief' regathered the ball and passed to Owen Craigie who was off and away for the try that wrapped up the match, 17–12. We were in the grand final. I'll admit that in the dressing-room the Newcastle coach shed a few tears, although discreetly. Then my son Glen came in and he was just as emotional as I was. I grabbed a mobile and rang my mum and dad in England to tell them the news.

We were now at the critical point; we had made the grand final. At that stage in years past there has been a temptation for many teams to let their shoulders drop a degree or two. As a coach I can understand why that could happen. Once you're there in the 'big one' a great deal of pressure is taken off straight away – that's certainly been the case in England when teams win through to Wembley and see their performances drop in the four or five league matches they have still to play before the cup final. The temptation is there, even subconsciously, to say: 'Well, at least we got there, plenty of others didn't.' With Newcastle in 1997, it was never that way. Personal and collective pride ran deep inside the Knights. Straight away after we beat Norths the emotion in the dressing-room was this: We have come this far. Now, after all the hard work we have done, there is no reason why we can't take the ultimate step. Inside our dressing-room that happy, emotional day there was only one question: What's the point of going this far – and not winning the damned thing?

The rest, as they say, is history.

THIRTEEN

Grand Final 1997

My wife Susan had been telling me all year we were going to win the Australian Rugby League premiership title in 1997. She knew, you see. Before a ball had been kicked in the season Susan had visited a spiritualist in Newcastle, who had conveyed the news with some sense of certainty. Kerry, wife of our English-import hooker Lee Jackson, had been given the same message. Susan had been so confident that she had tried to lay a bet, when the bookies had us listed at odds of 14/1 early in the season. But these were troubled times, featuring a game split like a watermelon into two camps and two competitions. Like many in and around rugby league, this one bookie at least was treading carefully. He wouldn't take the bet.

Unlike my wife, I had no prior knowledge from the 'other side', even if I was coach of this Newcastle team who were on their way to becoming premiers. But 30 years in the game at a high level gives you a certain sense of when things are smelling *right*.

So here it was, Saturday night, 20 September 1997, and we were in the Cricketers' Arms Hotel, Cook's Hill, Newcastle – my team and I – a wild mix of emotions. We were tired, elated, sore (the players, anyway), drained, overjoyed and buzzing with excitement and anticipation. Earlier that afternoon in a match of great tension and drama we had killed off yet another North Sydney dream, and won our way into the grand final. The next day Manly, coached by my one-time opponent, team-mate and good friend of quarter of a century Bob 'Bozo' Fulton, joined us in the grand final by beating Sydney City 17–16. 'Bozo' and his team stood as our last hurdle.

The gathering in the Cricketers' Arms represented the beginning of the last chapter in a book telling the tale of a very long journey. As I learned on my arrival in Newcastle late in 1994, the city had a rugby league tradition which stretched back into the mists of time. A Newcastle club was formed as soon as rugby league began in Australia, and teams from the club travelled to Sydney by slow train to play in the first two years of the competition, 1908–9. Born again in fresh, new garb in 1988, the Knights had been trying for the last decade to win the premiership. A city whose winter religion was rugby league willed them to do it. Now, with a football coach born 15,000 miles away – but in a coal mining community that was not so very different – they stood on the brink.

My preference as we began the final steps of the long march that last week before the grand final was to take the team away, to house them somewhere fresh, get them focused. However, we talked about it, and as always I listened closely to them, took on board their wishes. The players' clear preference was to stay 'in town', to share the moment with the people of their city and soak up the atmosphere. I had no problems with that. In hindsight, I have no doubt it was the right thing to do. The mantra for the team was something I had said in the dressing-room immediately after the Norths game: 'We have to get our feet firmly back on the ground. There's no point getting this far if we don't go all the way.'

I knew it would be a difficult, if exhilarating, week. I had been through it three times in England, with Castleford teams bound for Wembley. The atmosphere is frenzied, the demands on players and coach a hundred times above the usual level. The trick is to somehow find an island of calm in the middle of it all and keep taking care of business. So it was in Newcastle, September 1997. There was much to be done: media demands, marketing demands, and a trip to Sydney midweek for the obligatory grand-final breakfast. I suggested to the players that they cut themselves off from things said and written about the upcoming game. I couldn't stop them reading the papers, but I could at least suggest it. In our search for focus and clarity for what had to be done, I just didn't think that anything that was going to be printed in the final week would be of much positive help towards what we were trying to achieve. It is so easy to be distracted; one headline is all it takes.

We had an additional distraction in the huge media focus on our champion half-back Andrew Johns. His rib injury had been in the news for weeks, but there was greater interest now with the revelation that he had also suffered a punctured lung along with the rib damage. Will he play or won't he? asked the media. Should he or shouldn't he? The Manly and ARL doctor, Nathan Gibbs, stirred the controversy by claiming that Johns would be put at serious risk if he played, and to do so could be life-threatening. The *Daily Telegraph* latched on to it with a somewhat hysterical headline: HE COULD DIE! I believe that Gibbs's entry into the debate was ill-founded and unhelpful. He had no right to comment and I think what he did was more of a tactical ploy from the Manly camp than anything else. I was very upset about it. Nathan is a good doctor, I know that. But even if he had thought what he said in the press, he shouldn't have made it public. He had never examined Andrew and the fact was that Andrew was in the very *best* of medical hands and had been ever since he had first suffered the injury. Of course we wouldn't have played him if there had been any risk of serious repercussions. In fact a specialist monitored him all week – at training, before the game, and again at half-time.

Notwithstanding all the drama, the week was a good one – of solid focus, of finishing touches, of talking about what we had to do. We travelled down to Sydney on Saturday, the day before the game, and I'll never forget that. We were to meet at the ground, then travel down by coach. When I pulled up at Marathon Stadium my first reaction was: there must be a game on! The car park was jammed with people. In fact they were there to see us off, 10,000 or so of them! When we took off, a procession followed behind. Many of them joined us on the freeway, red and blue ribbons streaming in the breeze, and followed us all the way down to Wyong and beyond.

Along the way for the first 30 kilometres fans were lining the road and waving, saying their final 'good lucks'. On board the bus I'm sure there were more than a few tears. Things had never been too easy for Newcastle and we all knew what we were trying to do meant the world to a city which had known its share of adversity. The earthquake that in December 1989 had so shaken the soul of the community and taken lives was still sharply and permanently in the memories of local people. And, more recently, times had not been great; there was the depressed local economy, chronic unemployment and the BHP decision to close down the steelworks which had been so much a part of the city's lifeblood, a decision affecting some 2,000 jobs. I thought of how alike Newcastle was to some of the Yorkshire towns I knew, where the closing of mines and factories had snuffed out jobs and hope and changed these places for ever.

We stayed in Sydney at the Holiday Inn at Coogee, just across from the beach, easing in that late afternoon to the one 'official' function: our penultimate team meeting before the grand final. The meeting was strong and emotional and positive in content, and after it something extraordinary happened. The senior men – Chief (Paul Harragon), Butts (Tony Butterfield), MG (Marc Glanville) and a couple of the others – gathered the guys around them and held their own private players' meeting. It was something that I encouraged the players to do before a match, but this was something special. I left them to it; but I know it was an emotional occasion. There was focus on Glanville, a wonderful servant for the club who was off to finish his career with Leeds, and Adam Muir, who was leaving, reluctantly, but for good enough reasons considering the offer that North Sydney had put to him. The theme of that extracurricular meeting was: 'Why do you want to win this game?' – causing the players to investigate their own inner feelings and motives. There was a great deal of emotion and MG broke down, his show of feelings adding another layer of the intensity within this very determined football team. Paul Harragon talked later of the 'electric energy' generated within the team by the sight of Marc crying his eyes out.

In the material I prepared for the players for the grand final of '97 was an extraordinary document penned by a young Christian pastor in Zimbabwe, Brendan Manning, which was found in his office shortly after he was martyred for his faith in Jesus Christ. The passage was given to me by Jeff Poots, chaplain of the Knights for the first couple of years I was at the club, and a committed and loyal ally. I felt that whatever the religious beliefs of individual players, the essential message in what Brendan Manning had written could be useful. This is what he wrote:

> I'm a part of the fellowship of the unashamed. I have the Holy Spirit power. The die has been cast. I have stepped over the line. The decision has been made – I'm a disciple of His. I won't back down, let up, slow down, back away, or be still. My past is redeemed, my present makes sense, my future is secure. I'm finished with low living, sight walking, smooth knees, colourless dreams, tamed visions, worldly talking, cheap giving and dwarfed goals.
>
> I no longer need pre-eminence, prosperity, position, promotions, plaudits, or popularity. I don't have to be right, first, tops, recognised, praised, regarded or rewarded. I now live by faith, lean in His presence, walk by patience, am uplifted by prayer, and I labour with power.
>
> My face is set, my gait is fast, my goal is heaven, my road is narrow, my way rough, my companions are few, my guide reliable, my mission clear. I cannot be bought, compromised, detoured, lured away, turned back, deluded or delayed. I will not flinch in the face of sacrifice, hesitate in the presence of the enemy, pander at the pool of popularity, or meander in the maze of mediocrity.
>
> I won't give up, shut up, let up, until I have stayed up, stored up, prayed up, paid up, preached up for the cause of Christ. I am a disciple of Jesus. I must go till He comes, give till I drop, preach till all know and work till He stops me. And when He comes for His own, He will have no problem recognising me . . . my banner will be clear!

This passage I found very moving and very motivating, and it contained the sort of single-mindedness that we were going to need to beat Manly on that famous day in September 1997.

Grand final day dawned fine, the morning quiet at the Holiday Inn as players, and the rest of us, turned inwards to our thoughts about what lay ahead. Around midday we strolled as a group down to the beach and along the front, a couple of footballs passing from hand to hand all the while. This too was a time for quiet reflection and discussion; as always I found that the gentle activity of the walk was helping with the physical loosening up, and sharpening the mental focus. Then we went back to the last team meeting of that eventful year. A few words from the coach, saying what I wanted to say; then I left the players to it. I could do no more. The bus awaited us in the drive.

Dressing-rooms are strange places. We play a 'team' game but the preparation of the men who become the whole out on the paddock is idiosyncratic and individual. In our dressing-room on grand final day 1997, the song that had become something of an anthem for the day – 'Searching for the Holy Grail' – was pumping out. Steve Dunstan, the skills coach at the Knights, is quite a musical guy and he picked some powerful themes at times. Sometimes there is a preference for quiet. For a coach – and staff – at this late stage it's more or less just a matter of helping keep the players relaxed.

In the Sydney Football Stadium (SPS) dressing-room the strongest feeling in the air was determination. I kept myself slightly detached; watchful and, hopefully, mentally alert. There have been times when I've been involved with a team when I have found myself in exactly the same psychological frame of mind as the players, feeling as they are feeling, effectively getting ready to 'play'. That's a dangerous thing for a coach to do, although it does put you absolutely in tune with your players.

The room felt right this day. The vibes were good. Some days you walk in and sense that something is just a little off-centre. I'm sure that has happened to every coach. The music is too loud . . . or the room is *too* quiet . . . or the attitude is a bit light-hearted. It is part of the coach's' job to fine-tune the room if he can. There have been occasions when an experienced player such as Marc Glanville has alerted me: 'They're too quiet, Malcolm', and I have reacted in whichever way I felt appropriate. Getting the balance right is a delicate thing. It is no good being too far over the top, because in those situations you can give too much away by being reckless early in the match. You definitely need aggression, but controlled aggression. Attaining the ideal performance state (IPS) is crucial.

The preparation of a rugby league football team is vastly different to what it once was. We have all read stories of teams wrestling, slapping each other and headbutting lockers in the room, and of coaches roaring and screaming. I can remember an occasion in the '70s when Manly coach Ron Willey gave me whisky before a big game against Souths. Now, I'm a person who doesn't drink shorts; I have never drunk shorts in my life.

'Here, have a drop of this,' said Ron. I wasn't keen. 'It's OK,' said Ron. 'It's just a spirit . . . it'll relax you.' So I thought to myself, Well, if the coach thinks it will help me, I'll do it. So I drank it; I didn't like it at all. Ten minutes later Ron was around again: 'Here, have some more of this.' And he gave me another. When we got out on to the field my timing was so far out it was unreal. I was doing my best to make tackles, and I was way off line. I am aware of players in the old days who used to take a swig of sherry before a game or at half-time. As a matter of fact I had a couple of them in the side when I was coaching at Castleford and I used to pop a bottle of sherry in the bag before I went to the game.

Now that sort of behaviour has all gone. The challenge for coaches is to have the players revved up to a certain extent, but relaxed enough to do what they do best. On grand final day the mix seemed good. 'Chief' was serious, as always; Adam MacDougall was very different. He is a young bloke who is able to crack a smile as he takes the field, which he did on grand final day – a natural reaction to the anticipation of the pleasures ahead, of playing a game of rugby league. As the players headed down the long SFS tunnel and out into the sunlight, Marc Glanville crossed himself. It was his way. At the front of the western grandstand, in the Knights' area, I felt a chill go down my spine at the spectacle before me. My players were as one, interlocked in a line as the national anthem was played. It was a small but significant image, a spontaneous show of camaraderie which was not matched by our opponents.

As I took my seat, I knew we were ready for the game of our lives. But less than half an hour later, the first emotion of that grand final had really overtaken me – it was amazement. Amazement that we could be so fired up, so aggressive, so *ready*, yet be behind 10–0 on the scoreboard. And that's the way it was, far too early and far too easily, as Manly punched holes on the edge of the rucks. We seemed more intense, more fired up than they were; and there were a couple of reckless penalties, with 'Chief', looking very determined indeed, in the middle of it. Our defence was really solid and hard in the middle, but on the edges we were so soft. Manly handled superbly and John Hopoate was in after ten minutes, centre Craig Innes after 25 and the scoreboard blinked out 10–0. We hadn't beaten Manly in our last 11 meetings, and this wasn't looking great. But Andrew Johns got us on the board with a penalty at the half-hour mark, then Robbie O'Davis jinked in for a try six minutes out for 10–8. We should have had the momentum but Manly punished us again just before the break. 'Chief' turned the ball over and next thing old Cliffy Lyons – who played in the Leeds team I coached almost a decade before – had Shannon Nevin racing away for another try, and 16–8.

The half-time scoreline was exactly the same as it had been in the preliminary semi-final two weeks earlier, a match in which Manly went on to beat us 27–12. However, in the dressing-room at half-time there was no gloom, only that ever-present feeling of determination . . . that we hadn't come this far to run second.

Seventeen minutes after the break Andrew Johns kicked another penalty. 16–10. We were within reach. The match ebbed and flowed, heading end to end with thrilling attacks and always ferocious defence. There was talk later that we had set out to deliberately batter Manly captain Geoff Toovey out of the game. It's not true. All coaches and teams plan to send traffic at the smaller guys, but we knew too well of Geoff's courage, toughness and ability. He's a match-winner, as he has proved so many times in his long career with my old club. There was nothing intentional aimed at him on grand final day; although he did take some bad knocks, I like to think they were accidental.

There was a moment in the match when Andrew Johns was in trouble with his ribs, and was heading for the sideline. My direction to Mark Wright, my man on the headphones, was unequivocal: 'Get him back out there. Just tell him he's got to go back.' I think there are times in a football match, when pain and fatigue set in, that a player sometimes needs to be told, to be nudged to go that extra yard. Fatigue and injury make cowards of everybody, don't they? I'm not quite sure how far down the track Andrew was when this happened. I knew he wasn't well, but I also knew that his contribution to the team was so great, so important, that if we were to have any chance of winning he had to be there. So Mark intercepted him and said, 'Mate, Malcolm wants you back out there.' Andrew turned around and headed straight back into the fray.

With five minutes on the clock our full-back Robbie O danced and jinked and managed to plant the ball on the try-line, for 16–14. 'Chief' Harragon and Billy Peden were off the field at the time and on the video I've got at home you see 'Chief' give Billy, who is a shy sort of bloke, a massive shove and a hug. 'We're in this . . . we're still in this game!' said the Knights captain. Andrew Johns goaled and we were level at 16-all.

The crowd noise was unbelievable now, the red and blue army born again in the hope that we might yet do it. The momentum was with us, and three times we got set for field goals. I can still relive the slow torture of Matthew Johns's second shot. It was one of those times in life when everything seemed to slow down. The ball appeared to hang in the air for an eternity, spiralling towards the posts at the Randwick end of the stadium. When it hit the upright . . . and came back . . . I just thought: 'Oh, no . . . extra time for sure.' I reassured myself: We're finishing the stronger. We have every chance here if they give us another 20 minutes to win it.

There is still a sense of unreality about what happened in the final seconds of that game, no matter how many times I've watched the video of it – and they quickly became firmly installed in the legend and folklore of Australian rugby league. Andrew Johns darting out of dummy half on the short side . . . dummying . . . and giving the ball to Darren Albert.

Just seconds before, Andrew had gone for the drop goal and been charged down. This second chance that presented itself to him was a wonderful display of his awareness on the football field, his swift perception of the things happening around him. Darren Albert took Andrew's pass at pace and in a flash was over the line, dancing on those fast feet of his, and we had won the grand final. I'd like to say it was a move I had coached. It wasn't. This was just pure, instinctive, brilliant football – the sort of thing the game is really about. There were seven seconds left on the clock when Darren planted the ball behind the posts.

My emotion was more or less the same as it had been as we slid behind early in the match – amazement. Again I had the sense of things slowing down, of the last play happening in slow motion. My first thought was: What am I watching here? My second thought was that surely on such a day we must have had a little help from above.

In the wild excitement that followed full-time, I joined the players on the field. I was just so proud to be part of it. I joined them too for part of their lap of honour, but only halfway around. I declined the trophy. That belonged to the players; they had earned it and this was *their* moment of glory.

Out there on the paddock, 'Bozo' and I found each other, shook hands and embraced. It seemed we had been through so much together in different ways over the years. Words are never easy at those times. I'm honestly not sure what was said. I know I said that I felt for him, understood his disappointment; yet I could console myself with the thought that Bob had experienced the winner's feeling on many occasions before, he'd had his turn. It's one of the strange phenomena of sport – sometimes it's easier to be on the losing side.

Only later was I able to put the victory in the context of my whole career. From a coaching point of view it was right up at the top; I had never been associated with a team in which there was so much passion and emotion involved. Coaching and playing are so different. As a player things happen at a million miles an hour and you have less time to consider what you're doing, what you're achieving. Coaching is a more thoughtful, reflective sort of business. Probably of all the things I have achieved in my career, the most enjoyable still is winning at Wembley that first time, in 1969. To do it as a player is somehow more *personal*. Your own blood and sweat is involved. I have probably never again felt the way I did that day I walked out on to Wembley for the first time. To win grand finals with Manly – twice – at the Sydney Cricket Ground was also very special. Like Wembley, the SCG is such an historic place, with its own unique atmosphere. These are events I treasure in my life. And so it was on the late afternoon of 28 September 1997 at the Sydney Football Stadium.

I suppose 'pandemonium' is an accurate description of the way it was back in the dressing-room long after full-time when we finally arrived there. My wife and daughter, Susan and Lyndsey, were there at the ground and my son Glen, who joined me for a time in the dressing-room, was crying his eyes out. I called home to share the news.

Before we made the long, joyous trek back up the F3 there was a pit stop at a South Sydney pub, to round up some wine and beer. The drive home was amazing, punctuated by the blast of countless car horns as we made our way north. From ten kilometres out of Newcastle the road was lined with cars and people. A police escort picked us up around Wallsend and guided us in, through increasingly heavy traffic.

I remember at Wallsend, Andrew Johns came to the front of the bus. 'Can I get off for just a second?' he asked. I thought he must have spotted a pal in the crowd. So off he went, with brother Matthew right behind – and next thing they're up on top of a police car! 'For Christ's sake get 'em off . . . get 'em down,' I shouted. But no one worried. Like everyone else the policemen were celebrating what the team had achieved. If any damage was done to the car (and I can't imagine there *wasn't*) I'm sure that normal expenses covered it on such a day.

At the Workers' Club, when we finally made it, the scenes were just amazing – tens of thousands of people waiting in the streets for the team. One image sticks in my mind, of the team horse 'Rocky' trapped in the middle of the throng. I feared for what could happen if the horse got scared and turned or lashed out. However, Rocky never flinched, never moved, just stood there in this mass of red and blue colour and the seething crowd.

The party began. For some of the players it lasted for days. My own stay was not too long; a few beers and two or three hours, then I toddled off home, elated, my head still spinning with all that had gone on. When it comes to beer I'm a bit of a short-distance athlete. Generally it's three or four quick beers, then I'm on my way. I remember when I was at Castleford, John Joyner berating me. John would be just settling in and I'd be heading out the door. 'I'm not drinking with you any more,' he said one night. 'You're hardly here . . . then you're gone.'

Part of the reason for that behaviour is my belief that there must be some space between a coach and his team. In my view a coach should never fall into the trap of becoming one of the 'boys'. Share the celebrations, share the enjoyment certainly, but then take a step back and leave them to it. I'd like to think the players I've coached understand and appreciate that. The other thing is I don't like to get drunk. I think it's a stupid thing to do; and I don't like to see people drunk, because they're not in their right senses. I know when to draw the line and move on. But I do enjoy a drink and I greatly enjoy the players' company – and I certainly did on that special night in Newcastle.

Acclaim for the quality of the match, with its fairytale ending, was instant and universal. *A Rugby League Week* columnist summed it up, writing:

> For sheer drama and nerve-stretching tension I'll stick my neck out and say there has never been a greater grand final . . . this was high art on the sporting field – with the bonus of that breathtaking Agatha Christie twist at the end. Just when we thought it was all over, the winger did it!

The week that followed was a wonderfully happy one. I don't think I've ever before seen so many people so happy as the post-grand final days rolled by in Newcastle. My pride in what my team had achieved was immense. I read that I had become only the second 'import' ever to coach an Australian team to win the premiership – a New Zealander named Bill Kelly was the first, with Balmain way back in 1939.

Newcastle buzzed day and night with good feelings and the enjoyment of the moment. I had been to civic receptions before (in Castleford), but never to one with the numbers and emotion that Newcastle mustered to acclaim their team. The city was bound tight in one remarkable game of rugby league. The wonderful thing about the people of Newcastle is that you don't *have* to win for them. If you produce your best, give them a sense of pride in what you have contributed, then they'll give you everything in return . . . in support and loyalty. The book written about the foundation and early years of the Knights is titled *One Town, One Team*. And that's the way it was in the wake of the 1997 grand final – the town and its team . . . bound together as one.

FOURTEEN

Drug Wars

Early in June 1998, as we surged to the top of the competition, building resolutely on the Knights' achievement of the previous year, the club was rocked by a tremor as real in its own way as the one that had changed the city for ever in 1989. In a shock double whammy, two of our players, and then a third, were caught up in a drugs controversy that echoed through rugby league's world. First, our champion full-back Robbie O'Davis was reported to have returned 'abnormal' testosterone levels in a drug test, an indication of possible steroid use. Three days later the news hit the papers that back-rower Wayne Richards was to face the NRL's (National Rugby League's) Drugs Tribunal after also testing positive. And then Adam MacDougall.

The public naming of the players came via leaks from sources unknown. At the club we had been made aware of the problems that existed, but under the League's policy of confidentiality had kept the matters strictly in-house. Suddenly our players were headline news and the club's phones rang non-stop. For O'Davis, in the week of the third State of Origin match in which he had been picked on the wing for Queensland, it was a nightmare. And for the club, it was pretty much the same.

The drama escalated when the Drugs Tribunal decided it had no power to rule on the O'Davis case, accepting the defence put forward by the legal team and effectively finding that because O'Davis was registered with the ARL and not the newly formed NRL, the NRL therefore had no jurisdiction to rule on the case. It was a legal technicality, producing howls of protest from some quarters, but employed only after the most careful consideration by a club determined to be fully supportive of a player in whom there was unanimous belief.

It is not for me to comment on the technicalities of the case or the tactics, but I will just say this about Robbie O'Davis. He has been a model player in the modern game of rugby league – he works at it, I can tell you. Robbie is a compulsive trainer, a guy we sometimes had to tell to stop. His agility is excellent, his skills superb. He is meticulous about diet and only an occasional drinker. I have described him as a 'class act', and that is exactly what he is in terms of ability, commitment, preparation, demeanour, sense of fair play and concern for the game he plays.

His 'crime' in this case was that he took a substance (Andtrib-400) which was unquestionably legal when he first acquired it, in November 1997. Unbeknown to Robbie O'Davis, androstendedione, which is contained in the formulas, was placed on the NRL's banned list in January 1998, in line with a change in International Olympic Committee (IOC) policy. Effectively he took something in absolute good faith (and I would suggest that just about every player in the Australian game is 'on' a supplement of some kind), and then the goalposts were shifted without him realising it. Robbie O'Davis was never a drugs cheat. What he did was take a legal product, without realising that it had suddenly changed to being an *illegal* product.

The cases of Robbie O'Davis and Wayne Richards – the pair of them representing a very different set of circumstances – sent the storm clouds gusting over the city of Newcastle. Everything had been going so well; now we were a club under siege in our home city. For me there were mixed emotions: support for a player I believed in (O'Davis) mixed equally with embarrassment. People talked of our grand final win over Manly being 'tainted' and there were dark rumours of a 'drug culture' at Newcastle. It was shattering stuff, some of the barbs inevitably reaching me, as coach. This cut deeply. Yes, as both player and coach I have been a man who loves to win, someone who prepares thoroughly, trying to dot all the i's and cross all the t's in seeking the edge in getting ready for the weekly contest. But I abhor the use of illegal drugs in sport, while accepting absolutely that footballers (and all sports people) are fully entitled, if they so choose, to use one or other of the many *legal* substances available in their search for professionalism and maximum achievement.

I accept fully that rugby league *has* had its share of problems with drugs, and particularly steroids. I also believe that this was more the case over ten years ago than it is now. We have all seen them. Players who end one season looking more or less the same as they had looked over the years, then suddenly starting the next season looking so different; much, much bigger and much more powerful. I recall a well-known Australian player who came over to England ten years or so ago. I won't name him, suffice to say I used to train with him and he was a well-built lad, 94 or 95 kg. When he came back to the UK again a few years later he was *huge*, bulked up to about 108 kg and immensely powerful. He had taken a giant leap.

The question is: can players possibly build up to that extent without using illegal substances, that is, steroids? The story that these men always gave would be that they were hitting the gym hard (which no doubt they were) and were on a new diet based on a vast intake of bananas and so on. I'm afraid it was only half the story. I don't think there's too much doubt that some players have reached for chemical assistance at times in the game – and certainly so in Australia before the NSWRL brought in its drug-testing programme some seasons ago. The player I mention above, but cannot name, made his giant step at a time pre-testing, when rumours of steroid-taking in the game were rife. I was made very aware after I went back to Australia in 1995 of at least one grand final out there about which the rumours still persist. These rumours suggest that some players in the winning side had been on a steroids programme, adding substantial strength and bulk and an unfair edge. Members of the beaten team claim to this day that they were beaten by drug cheats.

It was in that sort of climate that Maurice Lindsay, then boss of the English Rugby League, sent a letter to his Australian counterpart, Ken Arthurson, expressing concern that some players in Australia were talking performance-enhancing drugs and asking for assurances from Australia that the problems of drugs in the game were being pursued as professionally and enthusiastically as they were in the UK. I don't believe there could ever be the slightest doubt about the determination of men such as Ken and John Quayle to rid the game of drugs. The question was pretty much the international one being faced by many sports: whether off-season steroids programmes undertaken by individuals had slipped through the testing net. Maurice's letter contained quite a lot of psychology as he looked for ways of unnerving the Aussies – but it was a reasonable point to make.

As I have mentioned more than once in these pages, the problem we (Great Britain) faced in our battles with Australia in the period around the late 1980s was in trying to compete *physically*. In the various tests we had done, we were always 10 to 15 per cent down in the physical areas of the game. Much of that had to do with the vastly superior and more sophisticated training programmes that Australian clubs had undertaken. I accept that totally. Yet in some individual cases – via players who may have taken the next step either by themselves or with the covert blessing of their clubs – there was always the thought too that there was more to it.

When I first joined Newcastle in 1995, I sensed there might have been some drugs in and around the club. Without any announcement, I organised an in-house test – none of the players had a clue it was coming. We tested everybody one Monday. The results came back on the Wednesday: three positives for social drugs. Only four people knew of the outcome: the club CEO, football manager Robert Finch, the drug-testing people and myself. On the Thursday, the result was in the papers. I never had any idea where the leak came from.

In my fourth and final year at Newcastle (1998) we once again had an in-house drugs programme in place. It was to do with both an awareness of a wider problem that now exists in society – not just in football clubs – and also with the Knights' image as the then champion club of the league, and role models to many young people. I simply approached the players at the start of the year and said, 'Right, we're going to do this for the good of the club.' It's a system that covers the two grades, based on random numbers pulled out of the hat.

I am aware there were some mutterings about the strength and 'build-up' of some of the Newcastle players in 1998, and it is a fact that some of them had bulked up considerably over the off-season. One example was the promising young centre Matthew Gidley, who played at around 87 kg the previous year and came back for the new season at 94 kg. But I knew for a fact he hadn't taken drugs; our testing programme confirmed that. Matthew's growth was partly natural – he's a young man and still growing – and partly due to an extremely good weights programme and the supplement of some (legal) powders. It is possible to put on that much weight without the use of steroids. And when you're used to being around gymnasiums – which I am – you can tell. Rugby league players like Matthew just don't have the *definition* of some of the huge guys – obvious steroid-takers – around gyms.

The first time my Newcastle team played Canberra in 1995, it was so obvious how much more explosive they were than us (and, it should be remembered, Canberra were the 1994 premiership winners.) Their leg strength was 30 per cent or more up on our guys. And this is certainly the sort of thing you can build with the right programme, the type of heavy-leg programme that the Knights' players began to undertake during my time there. The reality is that you can't get pure speed without strength. First of all you develop the strength; then you turn that strength into explosive power. We had a very good guy at Newcastle, Bruce Gulliver, who is also a sprinter, who devised some outstanding programmes. Some of the players now leg-press enormous weights. The problem in-season is to find the window of opportunity to do it. A real good blow-out with a specific leg session knocks a player about afterwards, and he will need about five days to recover before a game.

I suppose footballers have been taking 'foreign' substances ever since the first rugby league (Northern Union) ball was kicked back in 1895. I have talked elsewhere of Ron Willey giving me a glass of whisky before a game at Manly, and of the players at Castleford years ago who would swig sherry before a match.

I can reveal now that years ago at Castleford – and I'm going way back

– we took a substance that I can only presume would be on the banned list these days. There was no drug-testing then, of course, and a doctor used to bring it to us – it was a red syrup that we'd take in Lucozade in the dressing-room before the game. We would take a tablespoon each. Now, I don't know exactly what it was, but it certainly made a difference. I can only presume it was some kind of amphetamine because I know that I would have a hell of a job trying to get to sleep after a match. My mind would be racing. It was obviously some sort of 'speed'.

The red syrup only appeared for one season. Next year when I enquired about it, the doctor said, 'I'm sorry, I can't get it any more on prescription.' Obviously there had been pressure at some level and the stuff had been withdrawn.

My view of 'performance-enhancing' substances is that as long as they are strictly legal under the rules of the sport being played, there's nothing wrong with them. I've taken them myself. It's a fine line. There are a lot of useful legal substances you can get today without going over the edge into the banned steroids and so on, although the ground is constantly shifting, sometimes dangerously so, as Robbie O'Davis discovered. The compound that a player is taking now might be perfectly legal; then in two weeks' time a memorandum arrives through the post bearing the news that it has suddenly been deemed an illegal substance. I think any player today who takes something without first getting a clearance from his club doctor is a fool.

Yet all players take *something*, as they seek the 'edge'; just as I did in the past, most dedicated athletes these days take three or four different vitamins and powders and things like that. It is part of the daily routine, and in many cases probably of not too much use at all if the diet is a good and balanced one. For players it is no more than an insurance policy, just to make sure they're not deficient in vitamin C or B or whatever. There's also a bit of a psychological kick – knowing for sure that you've got the right balance in your body before you go out to play.

Players are a lot more responsible now about what they do to themselves away from football, although the game has still got a few of the old-timers who will knock themselves around on alcohol. For rugby league players, there is not too much wrong with alcohol – but moderation is the key. If they are going to drink to the point where it affects their performance or their behaviour, then not only are they doing themselves harm, they're doing it to the team, the club, the city or town and the game. It was also established quite a while ago that alcohol and injury-recovery do not go together.

I can reveal that, yes, there is still beer in the vicinity of my team's dressing-room after a game. But it is not on display the way it used to be in the changing-rooms when I was a player. These days you're much more likely to see the players sipping on a nutrient drink after a game, a cocktail of bulking agents, carbohydrates, protein and bananas. It's a meal in itself, although we always feed the players – in more traditional fashion – after a game as well.

I think more than ever in its history that the rugby league governing bodies and the clubs, in both Australia and England, need to be constantly vigilant in dealing with the players, who are the game's lifeblood. The dual effect of the ridiculously high salary packages brought on by the Super League split and the move to full-time professionalism at most clubs has created a new breed of wealthy young men, with time on their hands. This can be a dangerous mix and the predators – drugs, alcohol, gambling – await some of them. There is an obligation for clubs to provide firm and positive guidance and education. They also need to provide a climate that leads to the maximising of their opportunities in playing days, plus the chance for the creation of a worthwhile future when football is finished for them.

FIFTEEN

The Front Office

I agree in the main with the contention that the success of any football club at a high level depends on the efficiency of the 'front office' – the administration. I think it was Jack Gibson who first made the claim in rugby league. However, in my view Newcastle swam firmly against the tide during my four years there. We managed to gain success despite serious disruption in our administrative team in 1995, and some significant vagaries in its operations in the ensuing seasons. In '95, of course, we were often in disarray, and no blame could be afforded. The Super League raids on players and officials as the battle for Newcastle unfolded left us flying by the seat of our pants for much of that year. The success we gained was much against the odds.

It was in 1996 that Ian Bonnette came to the club as chief executive, an appointment largely pushed by Terry Lawler who was still then at the helm as chairman and who, no doubt, saw Bonnette's financial expertise as being what the club needed. Whether there was any other motivation in Terry's obvious preference for Ian ahead of any more sports-experienced candidates who may have come from a wider advertising of the job, I have no idea. I understand that Bonnette had an accountancy background tied in to his corporate career in engineering and the financial struggle, to stay afloat, was certainly very much a key issue at Newcastle then.

It's fair to say that Ian Bonnette and I never hit it off. I think the guy's all right, but we just didn't see eye to eye on many issues. From the beginning I found it difficult to work with him; he would scrutinise, make difficult every single thing I tried to do in relation to the purchase and development of players. Instead of asking my advice on football issues, he would go elsewhere. In trying to do my own job professionally and with an expertise backed by many years in the game, everything became a struggle. We were continually at loggerheads.

Towards the end of Lawler's reign, when Bonnette had been at the club only two or three months, I went to a board meeting and told the directors I could no longer work with him, because he just didn't know enough about the game. This was about the time that his protracted handling of negotiations to re-sign one of our talented backs, Brett Grogan, cost the club in the vicinity of one hundred and eighty thousand dollars. The negotiations had gone very smoothly in the early stages, and Brett, represented by Sam Ayoub – one of the best-known player agents/managers in Australian league – was ready to sign for a figure that both sides saw as fair. Brett was on a contract under which he was certainly being paid less than his talent deserved, peanuts in fact. This can happen when a player suddenly blossoms in talent and confidence. My view has always been that clubs should pay players what they're worth. If you cheat on a player, if you have a player on your books who is genuinely under-paid, then you're going to have an unhappy and probably underperform-ing player. It's got to be a win-win situation. Beginning the negotiations, I believe I offered Brett a deal which was absolutely fair, considering the market place. I believe that Brett and Sam Ayoub thought it was fair, too. But it got off the rails and some of the club's ensuing offers to Brett were ridiculously low. Negotiations that should have been locked up quickly and amicably dragged on and on. When it was finally settled, the cost to the club was vastly more than it should have been. Brett Grogan got a *great* deal.

I make the point about the problems I had with Ian Bonnette at Newcastle to illustrate just how important the link between coach and chief executive – or the person who's effectively running a club – is in a highly professional sport like rugby league has now become. Whilst administrators need to have the necessary administrative knowledge and skills, people who have no practical knowledge of the game should not be overriding those who do by making important decisions concerning players and their preparation for the game. We have to remember that rugby league is a sport, and one based on great passions and emotions, involving both the players and the supporters from the communities they represent. Big business may have been the root cause behind the Super League war that changed the game so dramatically, but it can't be allowed to take away that basic enthusiasm and passion for the game that makes players want to play and supporters want to support – and, I might add, coaches want to coach.

In my earlier days as a player I saw how that passion was just as evident in the leading administrators of the clubs I was involved with – Ken Arthurson at Manly, a football man through and through who had played for and coached at the club; Phil Brunt at Castleford, a hard-headed businessman who wanted to balance the books just as much as any modern-day chief executive or accountant, but who was a lifelong dedica-ted supporter of his local rugby league club and the game as a whole. In the British game we've often had situations where the club chairman, or directors, would care so passionately for their team that they'd put in sizeable amounts of their own money to purchase and pay players. I saw that kind of backing with Tony Gartland at Halifax, and since my return to England I've seen it with Ken Davy, the Huddersfield chairman. When men like these are prepared to invest so much, the very least they deserve is to be given good advice on players and the game from people with genuine knowledge gained from experience. And, likewise, a coach needs to know that the problems and challenges he faces in creating a successful team are being understood and supported, not undermined, by those in the 'front office'.

In my time as Great Britain coach I also had an excellent working relationship with Maurice Lindsay whilst he was the international team manager. I know some people have expressed surprise at this, suggesting Maurice and I were like 'chalk and cheese', but we honestly got on fine. Maurice was a very astute judge of footballers, although he wasn't a former player or coach himself, and he had his own opinions on the game, which I respected and was always prepared to listen to. Certainly whilst Maurice was the Great Britain manager we had no problems getting anything we needed for the team and its preparation from the RFL board – nothing was too much trouble. It was interesting to note that after he had given up the manager's role when he became chief executive of the League, things became much more difficult for his successor as team manager and myself to get what we felt was best for the team.

At Newcastle Ian Bonnette and I eventually fell out – big time. I don't feel I ever had his support for some of the things I wanted to do for the betterment of the club and its players. It just seemed that everything constructive I proposed was blocked. Our confrontations were on a weekly basis. My fight for an improved training ground for the team was a case in point. Bonnette gave me the impression that he thought it was just another issue somewhere down the priority list that honestly didn't warrant anything much in the way of urgent attention. The only time I ever seemed to get any action with him was when I really bashed it – when I went in and beat a really big drum.

On three separate occasions I felt so let down by the absence of support from my CEO that I felt obliged to take the problem to the Knights' chairman, Michael Hill. Only after the third time did things really improve, to the point that in 1998 Bonnette seemed inclined to just let things go through when it came to my wishes. I suppose that must have been the direction given to him by Michael Hill, who is a genuine football man, whose support and friendship I valued at the club. If he hadn't been around I would have been absolutely lost. Into season 1998 things eased a bit between Bonnette and me; the fact was that we didn't talk much at all. But until that slight thaw in the temperature in my final year with the Knights, I effectively didn't have a working relationship with him at all.

There are impressions I have about the man that have stuck with me long since I left Newcastle to fly home to England. I doubt I'll ever forget his manner after the round 19 game in 1996, a high-voltage Monday night scrap with Parramatta which we just *had* to win if we were going to make the semi-finals. We lost 18–16, on a late and controversial penalty. I was distraught, really upset. We had played poor football; some of the guys had gone out and just done their own thing. There had been bad mistakes and poor judgement. I can still picture 'Chief' Harragon, absolutely inconsolable, sitting with his head in his hands. I was annoyed with myself, the team, the loss, the repercussions – and the players felt exactly the same way. Then in walked Ian Bonnette, laughing his head off. I can see him now, as bright as a button in that sad, sombre room. I had felt all along with him it was a case of 'them' (the players) and 'us' (the administrators). From that day I decided that that was the way it would be with me too – in reverse.

I have another small recollection of how Ian Bonnette illustrated my point about the gap that can exist between a corporate figure and a rugby league club CEO. In 1997 Vince Karalius, one of the greatest of England's post-war forwards and a man who is a living legend in Australia, came to Sydney for a few days with his wife. At the Sydney Football Stadium after our sensational preliminary final win over Norths, I bumped into Vince in the upstairs bar. 'Hello, Vince, it's nice to see you,' I said, and we stood and chatted amicably for a time. A mate of mine, Jock Graham, was nearby, and I introduced him to Vince. Jock, a good rugby league man, couldn't believe who he was meeting. He eventually rejoined the group he had been with.

'Guess who I've just met!' he beamed excitedly. 'Vince Karalius!'

Ian Bonnette's response was at least honest. 'Who's Vince Karalius?'

'Well,' said Jock, 'have you any idea who Sir Donald Bradman is?' It's just a story, not a criticism.

The Knights, with Bonnette as CEO, had to take a lot of flak for the fumbled handling of the Robbie O'Davis affair in 1998. I'm sure Bonnette didn't want it to work out the way it did – which was pretty bloody bad. For me as a coach, things were too often more difficult than they should have been. Before the '98 season I had to go over Bonnette's head (to Michael Hill) to secure Neil Pincinelli and Peter Shiels, two players I was very keen to have on board, and who subsequently proved invaluable contributors to the cause. Bonnette didn't want them – told me early on: we've no money for them.

Once again, in trying to do something I knew would benefit the club, it was a battle.

I can't say that things turned out very well between Peter Sharp and myself, either, although they started out all right. Sharp was my reserve-grade coach in 1996, and he certainly had my full support when he came to the club. We got along all right – although I had the impression that Peter was mainly for Peter – and I actually pushed hard to get him a full-time job at the club. Super League had offered him some terms and I was keen to keep Peter because of his knowledge of football and footballers. I made that very clear to Bonnette. Peter had been an electrician, but we got him a nice full-time job at the club, with a car, handling development work as well as coaching the reserves.

Some time after the 1996 season I took a couple of weeks off and headed away to the house of some friends, at Airlie Beach, before flying home to England for the holiday I had planned with the family at Christmas time. In total I was to be away five weeks, albeit a crucial time in the business of recruiting players. Money was very tight – I think we only had about two hundred and fifty thousand dollars to spend on players – and I was comfortable that Peter Sharp was there in a specific role to look after what had to be done, once our plans were in place.

This was after we had lost a dozen players to Super League, and Treacy, Ainscough and Andrew Tangata-Toa to St George. 'Just have a good look into the guys you believe can do a job for us,' I said to Peter. 'The guys that you think can come through.' I left him to it, and in the fortnight I was at Airlie Beach I was in constant touch with Peter and Dave Morley, our football manager. Peter was the one with the specific knowledge of the players though, and the ball was in his court. The messages I was getting back were a little vague. We finished up signing guys like Evan Cochrane and Mick Jenkins who were on our list, but nothing much seemed to be happening at that time. 'Look, we are trying out best,' Peter said to me one night. Later we picked up some excellent buys such as Leo Dynevor, Adam MacDougall and Wayne Richards.

On the day before I flew to England, I spoke to Peter three times. On one of those occasions he said to me, 'Look, I can't talk just now – I'm in a meeting.' I headed off in the expectation that in the three weeks I was away, he would be stitching up the deals, signing some players who would be handy to us, notwithstanding the tight budget.

When I arrived at Heathrow I hadn't even picked up my luggage when I took a call from Australia: 'Can you come back? Sharpey has resigned and gone to Parramatta!' Things like that just don't happen in 24 hours, although Sharp was to tell me later: 'The notice was that short; they gave me just twenty-four hours to make up my mind – and I couldn't contact you.' The excuses were lame and in the end I just put the phone down on him. I was bitterly disappointed; I felt badly let down. His handling of that was the reason I could not recommend him for the job at Newcastle when I had made my decision to step down at the end of 1998. I felt very bitter about the way Sharp left the club. He certainly did not have my support when his name was put up as a possible replacement coach at Newcastle on my departure. I reminded people that he had 'jumped ship' at the club and told the *Newcastle Herald*: 'He turned his back on this club at a very inappropriate time with only one thought in mind, to feather his own nest. He didn't have the decency to tell me he was interested in the Parramatta [reserve grade] job, let alone going there.' Ironically, a year later in 1999, Peter Sharp took over as first-grade coach at my old club Manly, when my long-time friend Bob Fulton decided to relinquish the post for his own personal reasons.

No, I'm not sure the 'front office' at Newcastle was anywhere near as consistently good as it could have been during the first three years of my stay. But I drew close to the team, did my best to insulate them from frustrations that were making things more difficult for me than they needed to be – and we won a premiership.

SIXTEEN

Press-ganged

I have had my ups and downs with the media over the years, the Australian media in particular. I know journalists have to make a living, but in my view some people abuse the positions they hold, pushing things way too far. Gossip becomes fact and the feelings of the subject are ignored. I consider myself to be a touchy person, fairly private in my life, and I have had some angry and uncomfortable days through unfair things written about me in the newspapers now and then over the years. There have, of course, also been many positive and good things, and I am appreciative of those.

Probably my worst experience was during my time as a player in Australia back in the early '70s, and involved a paper that no longer exists, the old Sydney *Daily Mirror*. The *Mirror* and the Sydney *Sun* were tabloid afternoon papers – fierce rivals, and relentless chasers of stories, especially about rugby league which, as the major winter sport in the city, was always the number one topic of conversation. Bill Mordey, headed for later fame, and possibly fortune, in the boxing world, was the chief rugby league writer for the *Mirror*. E.E. 'Ernie' Christensen, a man with whom I always got on well and respected, was his opposite number and keen rival on the *Sun*. Hard-nosed journalists, Bill and Ernie played a cut-throat game, but managed to be good pals too.

In 1972 Bill Mordey pursued me to put my name to a series of articles to appear in the *Mirror*. The stories were to run over three days, and I was to be paid a fee which was negotiated to the mutual satisfaction of myself and the paper. We talked at considerable length on a couple of occasions and covered a great deal of detail about football, my career and so on. But when the stories were published it seemed to me that the paper had a preconceived idea of what it wanted. Only about 25 per cent of the material I had discussed with Mordey was used and, in effect, the series depicted me as some sort of animal on the football field. I recall one of the words used was 'monster'. I don't know whose doing it was; Mordey may well have been acting under direction from above to shape the stories a certain way. However, in my view it was pretty nasty stuff and it certainly didn't sit well with me.

So I put my own ban on the *Mirror*. I refused to talk to journalists from the paper and when there were photographers around – in dressing-rooms and so on – I always checked which paper they represented. If it was the *Mirror*, it was no go. This lasted for about two years. Then, on the joyous occasion of Glen's birth in January 1974, there were a number of requests from newspapers seeking to photograph the new member of the Reilly clan. One of them was from the *Mirror*. The thing had dragged on long enough by then and I was overjoyed about the arrival of a healthy son. I thought to myself, well, they can't do anything wrong with this – a picture of a newborn baby and happy father – and so I said OK. When the story appeared the headline was: *Son Born to the Monster*.

Bill Mordey and I have never made much ground on patching things up since then, even over a quarter of a century later. I'm sure he's a genuine guy and has many friends, but he is certainly no friend of mine.

I also took a strong stance against another *Mirror* journalist in Australia, Peter Frilingos, several years later in 1988 whilst I was coach of the Great Britain team. Frilingos had given us a big serve after the second Test of that tour, singling out Andy Gregory for special treatment. Andy had been in hot water in our undisciplined and disappointing performance in Brisbane, earning time in the sin bin for a head-high tackle he aimed at Andrew Ettingshausen. I was close to my team, who were doing their best under serious difficulties, and I took the criticism very personally, leading to the dressing-room confrontation with Frilingos after we had won that momentous victory in the third Test in Sydney. When Frilingos came in and offered me his hand with the words, 'Congratulations, Malcolm,' after that game, I just saw red. 'You've got two choices,' I said to him. 'You can either walk out of here now, or . . . ' Frilingos left without much hesitation.

Strangely enough, I think all the negative publicity we got after the Brisbane Test on that tour helped us considerably as we prepared for the third. In the face of all that flak there was something of a siege mentality that grew within the team – healthily so – and qualities of pride and determination re-emerged on the way to that morale-boosting victory.

I probably found the going a lot tougher as a coach than I had as a player in my dealings with the media. Thankfully, I've got better at it as time has gone by – well, I think so. However, back then I used to take things very personally, it was just my nature. As a player I was able to take on board negative things that happened and turn them into positives. It's harder as a coach; you don't have that physical release out on the paddock and the emotion tends to stay bottled up.

I'm pleased to say that time did its job and patched up the serious rift that developed between Frilingos and myself back in 1988. Peter is chief rugby league writer with the Sydney *Daily Telegraph* these days, and during my time with the Newcastle Knights he and I had a courteous and entirely workable arrangement, coach to journalist. There were no problems. My philosophy in dealing with the media has not really changed over the years. I just look for fairness and honest reporting, of me and my teams. If criticism is warranted – and given – I can live with it. I just expect fairness; if people are fair with me, I'll be fair with them. However, the fire is still in me, and if there is dishonest or unfair treatment, I'll definitely take offence. And I don't forget very easily.

One of the realities of a coach–journalist relationship is that very often the journalist sees the coach only at times of considerable stress and tension, most obviously after football matches in which there will very likely have been drama, controversy, pain and aggravation. In Australia, during my most successful season with the Knights in 1997, one writer, Paul Crawley of the Sydney *Sun-Herald*, offered a profile of me which sort of summed up the way perceptions can be. He wrote:

> Tough town, tough man. Malcolm Reilly can make Mike Tyson look like one of the good guys. After games you see him. Mad as hell, his face on fire and twisted with emotion. Answering questions like a drill sergeant. Rapid fire – rat-a-tat. Next question please. 'Sometimes, you guys [the media] see me when I am in an emotional state,' explains Reilly. 'People might look at me and think: "What a miserable bastard this guy is. What turns him on?" Well, I don't believe you have to be smiling to be having a good time. The thing about my coaching is that I am an emotional person – I find it hard to contain my emotions.'

My occasional problems with things said or written have not been confined to the Australian media. In 1992 I gathered the travelling British media corps around me in the dressing-room after a game on tour – and just gave it to them. At that time I felt that some of our (British) press were naïve in comparison with the Australian journalists when it came to writing about the game. At a press conference I had said that I thought we had played dumb football. The message that went back across the wires to England was that the coach thought his *players* were dumb. There's quite a difference. So after the next game I called the media blokes in: 'Excuse me, can you come in here?' – and told them exactly what I thought.

Considering all the years I've been in the game I guess things haven't been too bad. There are media people in both hemispheres who I count among my friends, and a few I would much rather not invite home to dinner. I have never asked too much of the media, really, no more than just to be reported straight and fairly. Press people who have treated me that way have been treated respectfully and fairly in return. I see the press gang as another part of rugby league's family; they have their job to do, and I have mine.

SEVENTEEN

Ellery and Me

Ellery Hanley was a truly remarkable footballer, and a rather solitary character, very much his own man. For much of the time we were together – me as Great Britain coach, Ellery as my captain – we had a good working relationship and a relatively successful partnership. However, in the end the respect ran out. Ellery and I have no contact now, and I have no special plans to change that.

The relationship between Ellery and myself went into decline in the early '90s on a trip to Perpignan in France where we were to play a Test against the French. It was a part of France I know quite well, through rugby league and occasional holidays there. Close to both the Spanish border and the Mediterranean coast, it is a fine part of the world.

Arriving in the afternoon two days before the match, I decided it would be best from the team's point of view if I kept them 'occupied' that night. The alternative was to let the players run their own race, which for sure would have meant them strolling into downtown Perpignan, which is quite a lively place with more than enough diversions for a football team on tour. I chose instead to organise the team bus to take the whole squad for a trip to Saint Cyprien, a quiet sort of holiday resort on the coast which was pretty dead at that time of year in the middle of winter.

I have no doubts that Ellery, the captain, would have much preferred a stroll into Perpignan. Ellery was a player who prepared himself superbly for football, a non-drinker who paid close attention to his diet. His interests away from the football field included an active social life. There would have been no great problem from the point of view of that weekend's Test match in him wandering into town; it was one or two of the others I was more worried about. It was quite clear that Ellery's preference was to stay in Perpignan that night, but I had to make a decision which I believed was in the interests of the team as a whole. So I took them to Saint Cyprien.

It was fairly quiet there, as I knew it would be. We parked the bus and agreed to meet back there in an hour or so. Most of the team headed off for a coffee or a mineral water; I went to a bar with the medical staff and the physio and had a couple of quiet beers. Ellery didn't even get off the bus; I'm sure he realised exactly what was going on and he just sat there and played some music.

Just before we set off for the trip back, I heard someone say, 'Who's running this mini-tour anyway?'

The atmosphere was a little edgy, as it can be just prior to a Test, and I took offence. What I had heard just wound me up. I thought I knew who had made the remark and charged up the aisle. 'Did you say that, Ellery?' I asked. I was really fired up; I was going to crack him.

'No, no . . . not me,' he said.

I stared at him, then left it and went back to my seat, fuming. That was really the beginning of the deterioration of our relationship. I felt that in his attitude to what I had organised for the team that night, Ellery, as captain, had not provided me with the necessary support. The link between a captain and his coach is an important one. But there was now a gap between us and things were never quite the same after that night.

There was also another occasion. We were staying at the Post House Hotel just outside Leeds before a Test against France at Headingley. There was an eleven o'clock curfew on the team. Some of the guys went bowling, and others went to a cinema near the hotel. I was there when they wandered back in at the appointed hour. Ellery was the only one not among them. He was rooming with Phil Clarke – and he didn't get back to the hotel at all that night. Now, Ellery lived just ten minutes down the road, and I knew that. The point was that if he'd come to me quietly and said, 'Listen, Malcolm, I want to go and sleep at home – I'm more comfortable doing that,' there wouldn't have been a problem. My answer would have been: 'That's fine – just make sure you're here for breakfast.'

But Ellery made matters worse by trying to deceive me. The next morning he told me outright lies; that he had in fact slept in the hotel, in another room. 'Which room?' I asked him. 'If you can tell me which room and verify it with the hotel people, no problem.' He couldn't. Once again on that occasion he was my captain. I expected more.

Things didn't get any better. I had occasion to take Ellery and a couple of other players to task after another match, and I didn't hold back. Afterwards Ellery and I had a one-to-one outside the dressing-room. He was saying that I operated by intimidating people but I didn't worry him, things of that nature. We had words, and basically that was that.

Having told of the decline and fall of dealings between me and Ellery Hanley, I will now say this: that while I may not agree with aspects of the way he has conducted his life, I don't think I've come across a finer player or athlete or anyone who contributed more to an international side. He was simply outstanding. At times I have seen him do things on the football field that were absolutely freakish. A true athlete: I have no doubt that if he had taken up any track or field sport, he would have succeeded.

He seemed to have great stores of natural power. Ellery never did a lot of weights; he was just physically very strong. His preparation for matches was impeccable and he was very mentally tough. I am aware of many occasions on which he played with injuries; before he won man of the match against the Australians in that great victory at Wembley in 1990 he had injections for a painful groin injury. He was a player who could be carrying quite serious injury, yet still go out and do the business on the football field. For most of our time together he never let me down as Great Britain captain. I had a lot of confidence in him, and he was an inspiration in the dressing-room and an example on the field.

Ellery was also one of those rare players who can help 'make' coaches. With the utmost respect to what they achieved, I doubt that either Graham Lowe or John Monie would have had quite the success that they did with Wigan if they hadn't had Hanley in the ranks, although Lowe and Hanley had their difficulties at the club.

The strange thing about Ellery was that he wasn't particularly skilled as a player. Genetically the game will eventually produce someone like him but with, for example, Andrew Johns's skills. You know, someone at 98 kg who can pass both ways and who has it all – strength, power, speed, skill, vision – you name it.

Ellery's great strength was just that, strength, and especially leg strength. I have seen him run sideways faster than most people can run forward. He would almost always run left to right, using a powerful fend to keep defenders at bay as he crabbed across the field. He was great in both England and Australia – a special player, Ellery Hanley.

EIGHTEEN

Bozo and Me

The story of Bob Fulton criss-crosses the pages of this book as it does almost my whole life in rugby league. Team-mate at Manly, much admired opponent and close friend, the man they call 'Bozo' has been very much a part of my own journey through football. I hold him in the highest regard, as the ultimate professional and as a loyal friend. In an article that appeared in the *Sydney Morning Herald* in 1995, Peter 'Zorba' Peters, ex-league journalist and a team-mate of us both with Manly in the wild grand final of 1973, revealed a story that shows how close Bob and I are as mates, even when head-to-head in a battle for the Ashes. Peter wrote:

> Bob and I drove up to a little country pub and met Phil Lowe and Malcolm. The media didn't know about it and even though the [1990] Test series was one-all, not once during the night was the third and deciding Test match spoken about. It didn't need to be. They've got a great deal of respect for each other. Both are keen students of the game who relentlessly pore over video footage to try and prepare the perfect game plan. Not much goes by in the game without the two of them knowing it. They are two highly influential, powerful people who have made a great fist of what they are doing.

For Bob and I, there was never even a thought that there was anything wrong with getting together in the week before a Test whilst he was Australia's coach and I was Great Britain's. Friendship goes a lot deeper than that. And I have been proud to call 'Bozo' a friend over the years, much admiring what he has made of his life in football. I recall being asked to pen some thoughts on him for one of the Test match pro-grammes in 1990, and was able to state that during my time at Manly I came to regard Bobby Fulton as the epitome of the professional rugby league footballer. Whilst the Australian game in the modern era has been full of such focused and dedicated characters, Fulton was years ahead of his time – the trailblazer. His preparation for matches, the way he thought about the game and the opposition, and his supreme physical fitness made him a role model for the countless players who followed him into the green and gold jersey. He was wonderfully skilful too.

Australia's dominance during the '80s owed much, I believe, to the fact that the 1978 Kangaroo touring party was skippered by Fulton. His influence must have been considerable on guys like Boyd, Price, Rogers, Reddy, Young, Boustead and Krilich, who all returned with the 1982 'Invincibles' squad. Bob was a player who would never jeopardise his chances of playing in the forthcoming week's match. If he had a slight knock he'd get the ice pack on it immediately. And he would abstain from drinking alcohol if it meant being ready for the next game. Having said that, he was a good team man and a good socialiser when the occasion was right. We enjoyed some wonderful times together.

Of all the games we played together for Manly, I'd have to choose the 1973 grand final defeat of Cronulla as the one in which Bobby Fulton made the most indelible impression on my mind. As has been mentioned elsewhere in this book, it was a tough, rugged contest, probably the most brutal in grand final history. It wasn't a game which left me with pleasant memories because I was forced to come off injured early on. But Fulton reigned supreme that day, scoring both Manly tries from nothing and sealing a 10–7 victory. He was world class that afternoon; his contribution was immeasurable.

The amazing thing about Bob was that he was so physically fit and had this amazing strength. He could hold off the biggest forwards and get to the line. He just had so much energy on the field. It was always apparent that he would become a great coach because he was a very deep thinker on the game and had proved to be an outstanding captain of both Manly and Australia. Even back then as a player, he would dissect the opposition prior to a game until he knew every player's strengths and weaknesses. Bob did a fine job as coach of the Australian team, always making them thoroughly well prepared for anything they had to face.

It's fascinating, sometimes, to think about how Bob Fulton's life has run parallel with my own in so many ways. A lot of British fans probably don't realise this, but we were both born in the north of England during the extremely harsh winter of 1947–48. Bob was born in Warrington, on 1 December 1947 – making him just 49 days older than me. The Fulton family emigrated to the New South Wales south coast in Australia when young Bob was just a nipper. Although he came back to England to play as a guest for the town of his birth in the 1969–70 season, we never got to play against each other that year because Warrington and Castleford did not meet in the league fixtures. But we did meet as international players in 1970 on three occasions – in the third Test of our memorable Ashes-winning series, and then twice in the World Cup campaign in England later that year. After that controversial World Cup final, which the Aussies won, Bob and I never played against each other again. We did, of course, lock horns again — metaphorically speaking — as coaches of our respective countries. I took over as Great Britain coach in 1987, and Bob as Australia's coach in 1989. He had the better of it as a coach, winning the Ashes series in 1990 and '92, as well as the World Cup final in '92. By 1995, with the outbreak of the Super League wars, we were back on the same side, battling to help the ARL keep control of the game. And it may have seemed like fate that we should eventually come together again as rival coaches for that famous grand final in 1997, me with Newcastle and Bob with Manly.

Late on that emotional afternoon, in the midst of the pandemonium that reigned out on the Sydney Football Stadium, Bob Fulton and I shared a handshake and amidst the emotion struggled out our words of consolation/congratulations. The friendship of a life in football continued — as it always will.

NINETEEN

Into a New Millennium:
The Player of the Future

The perfect rugby league player of the future will stand about six feet one inch tall and weigh in at around 98 kg. It is very probable that he is already out there somewhere, learning his football. He will have tremendous skills, and great vision and awareness of the game around him. It is my view that almost certainly as the game changes we are moving towards a more 'standardised' prototype of the ideal rugby league player. He might be a half-back (sort of a taller version of Andrew Johns) or he might be a front-rower – with more agility, cardiovascular endurance, more speed and more power than today's crop.

I think the way the game is going is that the smaller players (and I remember playing alongside such 'little maestros' as Alan Hardisty and Roger Millward) will inevitably find it harder and harder to compete at the top levels because of the defensive requirements under the ten-metres rule. Those players not blessed with great physical strength or size are going to have to develop something really extraordinary about their games to survive, such as freakish speed off the mark.

My views on modern rugby league are that we are, generally, on the right track. I think it is a better game now than it was when I played. The ten-metres rule gives teams the chance to introduce more attacking flair, and I firmly believe the game will continue to develop offensively. I have no doubt there is room for improvement in the offensive side of the game. In some ways (certainly more so in Australia) it has tended to become too structured, too close to the American football style. The room for change and improvement lies in relation to the skills area, in such things as passing and the possibilities that can exist in attacking situations.

I am concerned to an extent that we are breeding a new race of kamikaze forwards; players short on skill, high on courage, who are trotted out as cannon fodder by some coaches week after week. The bravery of these men is never in question. Again and again they charge into the 'valley of death', headlong into the packs of hefty defenders waiting to punish them. They do not step or swerve or run 'angles'. Rarely do they pass the ball. In some ways they seem very removed from what rugby league was (and I believe is) meant to be – a skilful game of running and passing in which mental and physical skills are of equal value, and one in which the broadsword has always been a comfortable associate of the rapier.

I worry about young players like Cronulla's Martin Lang or Bradford's Stuart Fielden. They're like bulls at a gate, and if they don't introduce some subtlety into the way they play, their careers could be short-lived. They perhaps don't realise the damage they could be doing by the punishment they guarantee themselves via the way they play. Even those sort of players, the 'hit-up' men so necessary to get the yards in the modern game, need to use some variety in what they do. I have talked to Paul Harragon a lot about that, about how with the introduction of variety to what they do these sort of players don't have to take vast amounts of punishment week in and week out. 'The Chief' was not the sort of guy who would ever spare himself, and was almost always the target because he was the player who gave our team the lead. However, he managed to add extras to his game: the ability to bounce back off tackles and slip the ball to support. A brave, proud and ambitious player, Harragon will be remembered as one of the greats of the modern game.

I'd keep the scrum in rugby league's future, even though it is no more than a pale shadow of what it was intended to be. The beauty of scrums – in whatever form – is that they do provide open-field situations and opportunities for the backs. If we went to a 'turnover' instead of the scrum, that lack of clutter, with the forwards locked away, however briefly, would just no longer exist. The scrum today is a formality. The challenge is that we don't make a complete joke of it and embarrass ourselves and the game in the process. Perhaps the ideal for the scrum lies a little closer to the rugby union model, in a clean-looking formation in which there is *just* the chance that a team with some skill, a big push or maybe just a touch of luck, can win one against the 'feed'. I can't ever see scrums going back to what they were, to the situation where every scrum was a battle. For all the fury of the contest, they were extremely messy things. Fifty per cent of the time the ball wouldn't go in on the first attempt, or the second . . . or maybe the third. Everyone would be striking and struggling and scrabbling for the ball. It wasn't a great spectacle.

To be up front in the old-time scrums was no place for the faint-hearted. I have played in matches in which the Great Britain trio of Hartley–Fisher–Watson have simply demoralised the opposition . . . frightened the living daylights out of them by virtually smashing them physically. All three today wear the marks of their profession. Tony's ears and Dennis's ears . . . well, they're not much like ears really and I'd rather not talk about them. And Cliffy. Well, I'll just say that Cliff is not the *bonniest* fellow you'd ever meet. I'll put it as gently as I can and say that he has the appearance of a man who has packed into some scrums!

I know a lot of old-time rugby league men – in both England and Australia – will, at the very mention of that fearsome Great Britain front row, get nostalgic for the game in its old unlimited tackles format. Certainly in my early days as a player the game could be pretty wild compared to the modern game, and I had my share of battles up front. But it should be remembered that I played my entire professional career under the limited tackles rule – and that never-to-be-forgotten Ashes win in 1970 was the *only* series ever to be played under the four-tackles rule.

Back in the early '70s, when I was playing for Manly, rugby league in Sydney was very tough and sometimes brutal. Probably the reputation I got during that 1970 Lions tour had a lot to do with it, but I seemed to find myself right in the middle of things on a regular basis. Season 1974 was a particularly troubled one for me. I earned a couple of weeks' suspension on a headbutting charge and in the first game back, against Western Suburbs at Lidcombe, I was marched again – by Australia's answer to 'Sergeant Major' Eric Clay, the very stern Laurie Bruyeres. This time I was suspended for a month on a late head-high tackle charge, which I thought was a bad call. In my view the tackle was a legitimate shoulder charge, but I was left to rue a month on the sidelines, and the loss of around twelve hundred dollars in playing wages.

In those days Manly versus Souths was pretty much state of the art when it came to both football and the rough stuff. The anticipation was this: you knew full well you were going to get hurt, and you knew there was every likelihood of you hurting someone else. Both psychologically and physically you had to be very well prepared. I know the sort of focus I had to have in those days has helped me as a coach when it has come to getting my team focused. Although in the modern game players are focusing on very *different* aspects to the things that were concerning us then.

There was one infamous afternoon which is still talked about in Australia over 25 years down the track – the day that South Sydney's hooker George Piggins and I fought like a couple of Kilkenny cats in the centre of one of the world's most famous arenas – the Sydney Cricket Ground. I still get asked about it after all this time, and now I'm prepared to admit it – it was my fault. The one-on-one battles that was rated one of the fiercest ever seen on the hallowed turf of the SCG was my doing. I provided the intimidation and the provocation – and that's about as much detail as I'll give. But Piggins wasn't the sort of man to back down in any challenge. He took on board what I had to offer that day then came right back at me, giving me just as good as I gave him.

George and I fought our own personal, nothing-barred battle on a patch of ground on the Ladies' Stand side of the SCG, ignoring the brief warning given to us by referee Laurie Bruyeres as he passed us, and trailed the play. I can only hope the ladies weren't watching!

When referee Bruyeres finally won the day – as referees invariably do – and sent us from the field, we were both a fair bit worse for wear. The newspaper photographs of the incident and its aftermath left no doubt about that. They showed me with an eye that was closing fast and both of us looking wild, ragged and torn. It had been quite a fight, and we got three weeks apiece for our troubles. Perhaps the intense media coverage of the game in Sydney played a part in it, although I'm not apportioning blame after all these years. But the truth of it was that in the build-up to that Souths–Manly match, which were always very special occasions anyway in those years, much media attention was paid to Piggins and Reilly, with predictions that there would be certain fireworks. Really it was just a matter of who was going to instigate, George or myself. In the climate of the match the confrontation was automatic; there were no maybes, it was just a matter of when. The repercussions continued well after George and I had been dispatched for early showers, with some angry exchanges between the two rival club secretaries, Charlie Gibson (Souths) and Ken Arthurson (Manly) over whose fault it had been.

I copped plenty of criticism. In an open letter published in a newspaper after the brawl with Piggins, the former Australian full-back Les Johns offered me some advice:

> Your action on the field on Saturday left me somewhat sick. What in the dickens are you trying to prove? We all know how tough you are so what about settling down and playing football? You are a sucker for the slightest provocation. You have to learn to turn a blind eye to the stirrers. The best way you can show them who is boss is by your skill – on the score of skill and class you have no rival.

George and I can laugh about it now – and we have done. Very likely we would agree that it was an honourable draw; well, maybe not so honourable. There were no hard feelings about it then, when we met on the Monday night at the Judiciary, or, certainly, now. In fact the event probably cemented a friendship between George and me that exists firmly today. I know there is mutual respect. We may have been partners in infamy that day and earned ourselves a niche in the folklore of Sydney rugby league, but while it's not forgotten, we have both moved on a long way down the track. In fact, I am a big admirer of George Piggins. I believe his resolve and his strength through the Super League wars were nothing short of admirable. George was of the view that a vast injustice was being done to the game by a corporate invader, and he said exactly what he thought. I found myself on much the same wavelength. A hard man, George Piggins, but a very straight one. Rugby league could do with more of his kind.

I recall another interesting afternoon during my time as a player in Australia involving myself and another English back-row forward, Bill Ashurst. Bill was a talented player – very talented – with an extremely good kicking game. He came to Australia around the same time as Mick Stephenson and Phil Lowe, and joined 'Stevo' at the Penrith Panthers, giving a struggling side quite a boost. Bill got plenty of good press and he really could play and mix it up – the tough stuff, clever stuff with the hands, a smart kicking game. There was a particular match at Brookvale which the media had really built up as a battle between 'the two best second-rowers in the world' (Ashurst and Lowe).

Before the game Bill was really talking it up, the message essentially being how good he was. Big Phil didn't react at all; he wasn't that sort of person. He was just a fast, big-framed kid who loved to run the ball. During the week as the talk flowed, mainly from Bill, I arrived at a point where I thought: I'm sick of this. Without anyone realising, I got myself really wound up. When it came to the game, we had a real good set-to, or several actually. Bill was down for the count a couple of times and then sparked an incident when he tried to headbutt me, right in front of the referee. I just held him at arm's length, and the referee, Don MacDonald, immediately sent him off. However, the next thing that happened was a touch-judge charged on to the field, flag upraised. He had seen a slightly earlier incident. The ref listened to his story, then sent me off too. I have seen Bill in recent years and he is a very changed person; he became a born-again Christian.

One man who was very taken with that battle between two Poms, was the then *Rugby League Week* editor, Geoff Prenter. He wrote:

> It was the most explosive 20 minutes of football I've seen for four years. It was the type of clash that rugby league fans have been starved of. The Mal Reilly–Bill Ashurst battle at Brookvale was dynamic box-office stuff . . . which had the crowd screaming for more. Despite the feud, both continued to play brilliantly.

Prenter suggested that the game 'lost its appeal' when referee MacDonald sent us both off. In the same magazine, in a light-hearted column, they added me to a list of 'Top Ten Enforcers' after the set-to with Ashurst. I'm not sure how I felt about that! But, for the record, the list was: Vince Karalius, Rocky Turner, myself, the old French prop Louis Mazon, Bumper Farrell, Peter Dimond, Kevin Ryan, John Sattler, Noel Kelly and George Piggins. I was certainly in lively company!

In those days, it was a case of survival of the toughest – or maybe the luckiest, if it happened you could manage to dodge the referee's wrath. In any game there would be a testing time right from the start, the traditional 'softening-up' period. I learned a lot in Sydney, probably every week. Early on I was easily distracted by things that happened on the field, by any 'baiting' from the opposition. However, increasingly I was able to drag positive motivation from aspects of the game, whether it was a hard tackle that had been made on me, a bad refereeing decision or whatever. These triggers, and the way players respond to them, are a vital part of the game. The more mental triggers you have to lift your effort, your determination or your skill, the better.

Back then there was no shortage of them for me. Increasingly people saw me as a target, and it had to be up to me how I was going to react. In the case of the George Piggins battle I admit I was the instigator, mainly for the reason that I knew it was inevitably going to happen and thought we might as well get it over with.

Sometimes if a referee was giving me or the team a hard time I just took matters into my own hands. There was a game I played against Canterbury at Belmore one day when the Bulldogs had the talented trio of the Hughes brothers – Graeme, Mark and Garry – in their side. The ref had given us – especially me – a really rough deal. I had been penalised a couple of times for illegal play and near the end when I took the ball up, the Canterbury blokes really gave it to me. The ref took no action. My next tackle was on one of the Hughes brothers – I can't remember which one – and it was just an ordinary tackle, quite friendly in fact. The referee sent me off! I was so frustrated at the ref's inconsistency that I diverted course and kicked the second-rower Graeme Hughes right up the arse, just to make a point! The formula that day – frustration multiplied with bad discipline – cost me another three weeks on the sidelines.

I doubt you're ever going to see that sort of thing repeated these days. As we head towards the next millennium the game is just as physical as it was 25 years ago, but it is a cleaner game. There is far less chance of a player getting his jaw broken, or a depressed cheek fracture, or getting king hit (or even getting kicked up the backside!). These things were almost everyday occurrences back then. However, today's game is tough and uncompromising, and the collision factor is severe. We're talking about bigger, faster guys with more muscle bulk and less fat. Today's players are more explosive and are stronger than we were.

The very positive difference is that players in the modern game are more free to concentrate on skill and technique without having to look over their shoulders all the time. These days the second man in the tackle goes in to lock the ball up. Once, the second man went in to knock your head off, to do as much damage as possible. The players are protected a lot more than they were by the rules of the game, and by the referees. And I think that's great. I would have loved to have played in the changed circumstances of today's game – and I can just imagine how my little mate Roger Millward would have starred in the modern game when you consider all the broken jaws and head injuries he copped back in the old days. I don't think some teams make the most of it. There is a tendency to play very conservatively, despite the reality that the men who are capable of being playmakers can ply their art without being illegally bashed out of games by their opponents.

Having said that, I must say I have some sympathy for the (many) first-grade players who these days get only 30 or 40 minutes a match. It's just the way the game has evolved. However, I can tell you that in my career I would have hated to have been brought off the field. I believe quite strongly that the interchange rule has changed fundamental things about rugby league, and that the changes are not for the good of the game. The way the game is now – with players on and off the field – detracts from the elements of toughness and endurance that have been the backbone of the game throughout its history. Once rugby league was a personal test, one man against another. No longer. The essential quality of determination is not as much of an issue as it once was. These days, just when a player has reached the point where he has to dig deep into the areas of courage and determination, the coach will intervene: 'Wait on. This guy is down a bit; get him off, he's vulnerable.' And off he goes.

It was once a tactic of the game that you targeted players of ability, trying to wear them down and bring them back to the field. It's much harder now, with coaches watching every move and swapping players quickly if they see a problem. You can still catch a player who is fatigued because it's difficult for coaches to time substitutions *exactly* right, but it's a lot less frequent these days. Because of the way the game has been shaped there is a lessening, I believe, in the character of the players. No longer are many of them required to express the 'second effort' qualities of toughness and endurance. The great strength of a player like Wayne Pearce was exactly that: his ability to push on and on in a match, and be going stronger than anyone else in the last 20 minutes. It was the same with Bob Fulton. 'Bozo' had the ability to run just as fast at the end of a game as he had done in the first five minutes. That was a tribute to what he was and what he did – the sophisticated additional training that put him ahead of the field. To quite an extent these sort of players are penalised by unlimited interchange. The skills they had, the inner qualities, the 'edge' brought about by the extra price they had paid in training is negated by the fact of coaches being able to continually wheel players on and off the field.

These days the unfolding of a match, with players recycled on and off the paddock, is a bit like a relay race. And to be honest, these days there are players around who simply couldn't do the 80 minutes, or who are not up to the expectation that coaches would have of them, anyway, due to the increased demands and intensity of today's game.

Some doctors have come out strongly in favour of the unlimited interchange they have in Australia, emphasising the 'safety' factor. The game, though, is no harder today than it was, although it moves at an overall quicker pace, and especially so under the ten-metres rule. I doubt that players are at any more risk now than they were before unlimited interchange. The rule has been mainly coach-driven. It makes life more certain for coaches – being able to replace again and again – but there is a great deal of opposition to the rule in Australia, and I understand that. At Newcastle our system was that the half-backs and the three-quarters generally didn't get a rest in the match unless there was something wrong with them. The half-backs (and at Newcastle we had the outstanding Matthew and Andrew Johns) are such an integral part, the building blocks of the team over the 80-minute journey of any match. But we had nine forwards which we rotated in every game, the hooker included.

I'm not sure how much I would enjoy that aspect of being a forward playing the game today, being on and off the park. Regularly replaced players have said to me how difficult it is to play 'stop-start' and to get their second breath once they're thrown back into the fray. I just tell them: 'Look – it's what you get paid for. Just go out there and do it. You're an impact player; you must make an impact. The first three or four times you touch the ball I really want you to take advantage – run at some of the weaker guys, the blokes who are more fatigued. Just get out there and bust your arse and settle into the game.' The timing of that is not easy. Some players go out there and try too hard and finish up in an exhausted state after six or seven minutes.

It isn't always easy for a player to accept that the coach wants to pull him on and off the field, I know I wouldn't have liked it. And that certainly appeared to be the case with one of Newcastle's best-known players, Mark Sargent, although it wasn't until a long time later that it was driven home to me how deeply Mark had been cut by the way I chose to use him in the

Knights' team of 1995. When that hidden anger did finally surface a couple of years later, Mark and I were suddenly at each other's throats in an incident that could easily have got way out of hand.

In 1995 when I arrived, Sarge was Newcastle captain, a foundation player at the club, their first ever Australian international, immensely popular and well respected. He was also moving into the latter stages of an excellent career as a front-row forward. I used him accordingly, alternating him with 'the Chief' and Tony Butterfield. With the ten-metres rule in play in 1995, it was very difficult to have Sarge and Chief on the park at the same time, because their east-west defence, lateral defence, was a bit limited. One on the field was fine; to have them both there at the same time was a bit of a problem.

The other thing about Mark Sargent was that he was a very good impact player. When he came on fresh against a tiring defence, he was terribly difficult to stop; he just ploughed into them. Mark was obviously a very proud individual, and he had a career he was entitled to be proud of. The way I used him, off the bench when he was captain, definitely rankled a lot more than I realised at the time. He had obviously been deeply offended. However, there was never any great drama on the surface, until a night in September 1997. Up to that time, we seemed to be OK even after he went to Super League and the great chasm had opened up between the two sides. We'd pass in the gymnasium and say hello. Mark had told the media in February 1996 after making the switch to Super League: 'As far as my relationships with the Newcastle players are concerned there have been no problems. I guess the only problem was the working relationship with Mal Reilly became a little bit tense after I made my decision.' There was no evidence of any *great* problem. But after the game in which we beat North Sydney to reach the grand final in September '97, I bumped into Mark in the Cricketers' Hotel, where we had stopped for a celebratory drink.

'Hello, Sarge,' I said, and offered him my hand. He refused to shake it. So I just told him to piss off, and that I'd be about any time he cared to make an issue of it. I was fuming; it had been a wonderfully successful day and I didn't need this. My blood was boiling. And, as you may have gathered, there is an element of latent aggression in me that can boil to the surface at times like this. I stood there eyeballing him from across the room; then Sarge headed towards the men's room and beckoned me to follow. I didn't need asking twice; I just threw my coat off and followed him in. Some of the players had seen what was going on and followed me in. Eventually, apart from some angry words, nothing came of it – and I'm glad it didn't. It wouldn't have helped anything, but it would have been interesting.

It's obvious that the situation of 1995 had been eating away at Sarge all that time. Maybe it was my fault; maybe I didn't explain things as clearly to him as he required. I honestly thought I did; we certainly had plenty of talks about it. I definitely didn't want to humiliate the man. I respected him; he was captain of the Knights whether he was on the field or not. But I think there comes a time in every player's career when they have to assess themselves and say, 'Maybe this is the role I should be playing now.' And accept it. I know I had to do that when my bad knee first told me I couldn't play on the hard Aussie surfaces any more and I should head home for Castleford, and eventually that I couldn't be a hard-running loose-forward any more but had to move up to the front row and take on more of a ball-distribution role. On that night in 1997 it became quite apparent that Mark Sargent had never really accepted the way things were for him back in 1995.

TWENTY

Coming Home

I had made up my mind even before a ball was kicked in the 1998 season that, despite all the great promise for my Newcastle Knights in the euphoria of winning that dramatic grand final the year before, my time in Australia was drawing to a close. Soon I would be back home in Yorkshire where I was born, picking up the threads of that other half of my life. I knew that when the last ball was played for Newcastle in '98 it would be the end of the road for me in Australia – well, as far as rugby league goes, anyway.

Throughout my stay with the Knights I had lived with the fear that grips all sons and daughters of ageing parents when they are far from home. My mum Annie and my dad Robert had battled indifferent health in recent years, making my decision to leave England, as I did in late 1994, a difficult one. Dad had had a chest problem, and what seemed to be angina. To be honest, I was even more worried about my mum. She also has angina, and tends to get very het up and worried about things. She is no longer strong. It was a dread that was ever-present in me, that something would happen to one or the other of them while I was far away in Australia. I made a point of going home every Christmas, but when you're 15,000 miles away and heavily involved in your work it's difficult to do much more than that.

A couple of years ago Dad had a nasty turn one afternoon after doing some work in the garden of my home at Ledsham. He just collapsed and fell off a kitchen stool, unconscious. That time he spent a couple of days in hospital. He then seemed to recover quite well, although he progressively lost weight. He still kept himself active, by gardening and walking the dog.

One night in March 1998 Mum rang me. 'Dad's in hospital,' she said. 'He's had a bit of angina again.' It was more than that, as we learned from a friend who works at the heart unit at Seacroft Hospital, on the outskirts of Leeds – Julie Varley, the wife of the well-known rugby league photographer Andrew Varley. Julie and Susan were in constant touch by e-mail, and she told us the news that it wasn't angina, but a lot more – a quite serious heart attack. I was greatly worried, of course, and kept in constant touch. I remembered how he had been the previous Christmas. He had seemed worried, and a little frightened. The message from home, however, was always reassuring: 'He's all right – don't worry. He's coming home next weekend.'

Dad wasn't all right, of course. In the early hours of Thursday morning, 19 March, I got the phone call at home in Newcastle. My father had passed away. He was 73. For me, so far away, it was a nightmare come true. I have never felt so helpless.

Long before that, I had already made up my mind that I would be going home at the end of 1998, at the completion of my contract with the Knights. I just wanted to spend a few years making sure my parents were OK in the latter years of their lives. After all, they had put much of their lives into my sister Jennifer and me. Now Dad is gone, and it hurts me a great deal that I missed such a lot of those last few years of his life. Back home I would see my parents two or three times a week; we were a close family and there were regular visits. So, for those reasons, we headed back home to Ledsham. I can only hope that Mum has some good years ahead, some years as enjoyable and healthy as they can be for her.

And me? I flew out of Australia with some deep-down regrets, just as I did 23 years before. I knew I was leaving behind in Newcastle a football side of wonderful ability and potential. I left with an aching heart because I feel at one with Australia and the lifestyle there, and had come to love Newcastle. To me it is one of the country's better kept secrets, with its fine beaches, proximity to the beautiful Hunter Valley and its salt-of-the-earth people, so warm and friendly and loyal. The supporters of the Newcastle Knights were nothing short of magnificent in my time in the city. I will never forget them. When the time came for us to finally say goodbye, there were so many farewell receptions – from the mayor, the city, the club, supporters, sponsors and individual friends – Susan and I were overwhelmed. It was very emotional for all the Reilly family, I can tell you. I would love to have been able to stay and coach the Knights for another three years. But it was not to be. I did what I had to do. I have had to live with the feeling that I neglected my duty at home, and it was time for me to go back.

I still have a house in Newcastle, currently occupied by my successor as coach of the Knights, Warren Ryan, which gives an indication of how amicable the parting of the ways was. It has been a wonderfully fortunate outcome of my life that I have been able to share my career between two countries I love with comparable – if different – passions. My love of the countryside has been part of my enjoyment in both my 'homes', England and Australia. Two places so different, and yet both so beautiful in their own ways. I grew up within easy reach of the rolling hills and dales of Yorkshire's open country, not far from the moors which can be so desperately bleak and dangerous, yet which have never for a moment lost their appeal for me, even during all my years far away in Australia.

Yes, I love the countryside, love nature, love animals, which may surprise those people who can still picture me at the heart of so many violent rugby league battles of yesteryear. The village I'm lucky enough to call home in England, Ledsham, is a truly beautiful place. It's one of those little hamlets from which you can head out on a nice day, and just keep going across the open fields, and on and on through the countryside. To do that, whatever the season, is one of the pleasures of my life. Foxes and pheasants pass through our garden. In England I like the contrast between seasons, something that doesn't really happen in the parts of Australia in which I've lived. Even winter in England – the first snow – I think everyone finds very special. The problem is that winter just runs on a bit long; about three or four days would be nice! Autumn, when the leaves are tumbling, is terrific and so is spring, when the weather is softening and the countryside coming to life. And summer with its long days and long twilights . . . I really do take pleasure from all of them. I think the ideal situation would be to live in Australia for six months of the year and in England for the other six.

Ledsham is only half a mile away from the busy A1, yet in many ways it's 'old England', a privately owned estate in the southern part of North Yorkshire. There's a gamekeeper, a shooting lodge, a church, some old alms houses, a village pub, three or four farms, about 40 houses, and about 120 people in all. I know virtually everyone who lives in the village. It truly is home for me, we've lived here since I first came back to play for Castleford from Manly in the mid '70s, and since we returned from Newcastle at the end of 1998 we've been building an extension on to the house. The Yorkshire roots are very strong, although we do have a wonderful picture of the coastline of Newcastle hanging in the lounge which I only have to look at to evoke some of those great memories of my days with the Knights.

Apart from family, it's football that dominates my life, as I'm sure it does anyone professionally involved in the game these days. To switch off is not easy; as well as everything I do around the 'team', I also try to keep up to date by reading of developments in other sports. I guess every single football coach in the world is looking for that extra bit of information that might just give him the 'edge'.

Away from rugby league I do admit to a secret passion – cooking. It's always been an ambition that one day I might own a restaurant. Now and then on a Saturday I plan the evening meal, and I can tell you I take it very seriously. I browse through cookbooks and finally land on something, then I head out to round up the ingredients. Considering the cost of the things I buy, I am sure that it often works out that it would be far cheaper to eat at a restaurant. But that's not the point! Seafood has been my favourite ever since I first discovered it back in Australia during the 1970 tour, and seafood chowder is my speciality. I made up a recipe for the *Newcastle Herald* one day — a chowder — and I just put everything in it, scallops, prawns, leeks and potatoes and plenty more. Living in Newcastle for four years meant we were on the fringe of the beautiful Hunter Valley, where some of Australia's best wines are made. Susan loves the Australian wine and has become quite a connoisseur, but I have always remained more of a beer man myself.

However, despite the quiet pleasures of these other things, the reality of my life is rugby league; it has been — and is — and hopefully will be for me for a few more years yet. It was always my plan to stay involved in the game on my return to England. I said before I left Newcastle that the next challenge in football would probably be my last, that I didn't intend to stay around too long. And as a coach, if I ever for a moment thought I was dragging behind with techniques, or getting behind the pace of the game's developments, I would call it a day pretty quickly.

Having made the decision to come home for my own personal and family reasons as I have explained, I quickly had a couple of tentative enquiries from English clubs when my intentions to come back became public. A couple of clubs called me, asking if I would like to coach them. One was Huddersfield, the other option would have meant not being in the Yorkshire area, which really defeated the object of me coming home to be close to my mum. So, Huddersfield it was, and I joined the Giants towards the end of 1998.

TWENTY ONE

Extra Time

In the seasons since I left home – again – to go to Australia in 1995, rugby league has undergone profound change in England, with the move to summer football. I still have mixed feelings on the change, as I look on with sadness at the decimation of the great traditions of international football now there are no Kangaroo tours, no Lions tours, and no battles for the Ashes. But, obviously, from a coach's point of view, the intro-duction of full-time professionalism and the opportunity to train your team in good weather, in the daylight, is a big attraction.

My view is that the 'close down' period, caused by the worst winter weather that has been a fact of most years that rugby league has been played in England, certainly hasn't helped when it comes to matching the physical excellence of the Australians. In any given season there would come a time when proper training would be near impossible to stage – plus some games would be postponed for reasons of frost, snow or fog. Teams, and individuals, would lose physical and mental momentum.

I remember watching a second-team game at Thrum Hall one night when the fog came seeping in. We (Halifax) scored three tries – and I didn't see a single one of them. Then we 'lost' a player; he was injured down near the corner post, and no one could see him. You could see about halfway across the field; for the rest of it players just disappeared like ghosts. If we hadn't spotted a particular player for a while we'd send someone out to see if he was OK. Certainly it is much more conducive to the physical preparation of footballers and it must be much more pleasant to play in dry, firm conditions – something I always preferred myself as a player – but will the switch to summer work for the game as a whole? Time will tell.

Obviously I realised that I was taking on a very difficult job at Hudders-field, but it was put to me as a three-year project with the prospect of buying in some new players, with my challenge to be able to elevate the overall position and footballing operations of the club. The bottom line has always been that I enjoy what I do – the day-to-day involvement with a team, working with the players – if I didn't enjoy it I wouldn't do it. But it has been a bigger struggle in my first season with Huddersfield than I could ever have imagined, and the situation when we conceded 86 points against Leeds at Headingley, then followed up with several more thrashings, was something that I've never encountered before in my career. I'm used to being involved with highly competitive teams, Newcastle Knights being the ultimate, and even when I was at Castleford we may not have been in the top two or three teams but we were always very competitive. Sundays were certainly a lot more enjoyable than many of them have been for me in 1999!

The season started off pretty optimistically. Huddersfield had finished bottom of the Super League table the previous year by a clear margin of seven points, with only two wins from 23 games, so to start my first season with the Giants being very competitive, and getting a few wins quickly on the board, was a big improvement for them. In the first half of the season we lost several games by very marginal scorelines, and we certainly weren't copping any floggings. Even when we came up against some of the top teams like Bradford, Wigan or St Helens, I went into the game confident of the outcome. I still firmly believe that sport is one area of life where you can make the impossible happen – it is not always the strongest or the quickest who wins. There are other elements which can play a key role, like determination and persistence.

Maybe I was naïve when I took the job because I didn't fully realise just how lacking in the fundamentals some of the players were. I had grown accustomed to Australian club standards where it was so refreshing from a coaching point of view to work with players of such high skill levels and positive mental attitudes. But I realistically thought that, at Huddersfield, if I had a bunch of committed and enthusiastic guys, I was confident in my own ability to smarten them up – get them a bit fitter and improve their skill level – enough to win plenty of games that would mean mid-table was a reasonable target.

What quickly became obvious to me was that Huddersfield weren't on a level playing field compared to the other teams in the Super League. The club had been outside the élite of the game for so many years, it had a massive gulf to make up. The other clubs had had the last three or four years in Super League to build up their organisations, both on and off the field. Everybody knows there was a 'war' in rugby league started in 1995, and there were some enormous amounts of money flying around, with many players being given the kind of contracts that the game just cannot realistically afford. The ambitious clubs – like Bradford, Leeds, Wigan, St Helens – already had their professional administrations in place, both in the recruitment and development of players and their marketing set-ups. They capitalised on the opportunities offered by the changes in the game and built on what they already were doing, with the result that they have accelerated even further ahead of the others. Things may have improved from the days when Wigan totally dominated the British game, but in 1999 we now have a situation where the top four or five clubs in the Super League are operating on a higher level to the rest and creeping further away from the other clubs.

I knew it would take a minimum of three years to get Huddersfield up to the level of the top clubs, but it is so much harder to attract new players to a club that hasn't got a successful reputation. I've always found that if you're talking to a quality player who has offers from two clubs, both on the same financial terms, the player with ambition will invariably choose to sign for the club that already has a track record of success. Players want to win – and nothing is better in rugby league than the feel-good factor and confidence that being part of a winning team transmits. Huddersfield could have turned that around, but it can't happen overnight. To start the long haul back they need to get together a nucleus of good players who are proud to go out and play for Huddersfield, who can convince the supporters that they are going to give total 100 per cent commitment in every match.

I think that some of the players came to the club for the wrong reasons, and that is what contributed largely to the bad results they suffered. I believe that money has been the prime motivation for these players to join Huddersfield and they're really not too bothered about whether they win or they lose. When the going got tough they weren't prepared to dig deep. They've got no passion for the club and they did not sign for Huddersfield because they were looking to achieve any kind of success in the game – it has been purely and simply because it met their financial requirements. It has also been a matter of convenience for them because, in several cases, the Super League clubs they were previously with realised they didn't want them any more. At Huddersfield I inherited a number of former St Helens players – quite obviously they had been allowed to leave Knowsley Road because the Saints coach at the time, Shaun McRae, knew they weren't up to the required standards for Super League any more. Some of the players appear to have very limited ambitions in the game, and certainly striving for international recognition is not high on their list of priorities. It would appear that the Huddersfield chairman Ken Davy was not getting very good advice when it came to signing players, and I'm sure that with hindsight he would have done things a lot differently, and not agreed to some of the deals that were done. Somebody should be held accountable for the kind of team-building and recruitment that went on, because it's quite obvious to me that the club's resources were not being spent wisely. It's an ulcer in the club that they've got to cut out and start afresh – now in the new joint venture with Sheffield.

Some people secured contracts with Huddersfield that offered them far more money than other, better-established Super League clubs were prepared to pay them. I know one player – Ian Pickavance – did say that he came to the club because the Huddersfield offer was twice as much as he could earn with St Helens. And these are the sort of people you don't want at a club if you're genuinely striving to build a successful future, because all they're coming for is their own financial gain. Everyone needs rewards out of football – there's got to be an incentive somewhere – but I believe the prime motivation has still got to be your own personal pride, your desire for success and to be a part of a successful team. The game has passed players like that by – they are dinosaurs of the game. Rugby league has accelerated significantly over the last few years and it is leaving those sort of people behind. Full-time professionalism must demand people with the right attitudes of self-motivation and pride in performance.

In contrast to the example quoted above, I approached one Australian player during 1999 with a view to bringing him over to Huddersfield. I won't mention any names, but he's a very experienced player with probably another couple of good seasons in him. We discussed terms, and made him a pretty reasonable offer. But he told me, 'I'll have to think about it – my first thoughts are that the way I want to commit myself I don't think I can justify that contract.' It was the kind of honesty a coach wants to hear from his players. People know what their own commitment to a particular cause is going to be, so they know what they're worth. In rugby league you've got to get people like that who understand and accept that they've got to pay a price, so they will push themselves to achieve the level of performance required.

That night Leeds put 86 points past us was probably the lowest point of my whole career in rugby league; as both player and coach I'd never experienced anything like that before. I could never have imagined that a team I was involved with could lose like that. It was a night when all our problems of having such a weak squad came to a head. We had nearly all of our most experienced players out that night – men like Danny Russell, Craig Weston, Jim Lenhigan, Andrew Tangata-Toa – so our problems were compounded because we had to bring kids into the first-grade team that really weren't ready for that level of football. We caught Leeds on a red-hot night – and the rest is history as the scoreboard went into overdrive.

I was shellshocked; I still get very emotional about the game. Normally, if we have had a loss on the weekend and the team hasn't played particularly well, it might take me until Tuesday to start feeling relatively positive again. By then I can start transmitting positive energy to the players, and get them into a positive mode. It's never been a problem for me. But after that flogging at Headingley, the feeling of deep disappointment and embarrassment – a kind of numbness – still hadn't gone away by late the following week. In some ways I don't think it ever will, it's like a recurring nightmare for me. And what has really got to me is that some of the players just don't care – they don't hurt after games when they've copped floggings and played so poorly. For me it has been a terrible experience; I have been ashamed and felt humiliated at times. Going back to my own time as a player, sometimes at Manly it wasn't just winning that interested me, it was playing well. There were times when Manly may have lost but I would have been very happy with my own performance if I'd achieved what I believed to be a good contribution to that particular game. Likewise, there were occasions when the team won, but if I felt I'd fallen below the level of commitment or performance that I set myself I wouldn't be satisfied. And that's the criteria I'm looking for in players now: you've got to be able to assemble a team of people with that level of personal pride in their own performance. Once you've done that, success as a team will follow.

People have asked me: 'Where can Huddersfield find the type of players to bring them up the level of the top clubs?' My answer to that is that they'll find them in the same places as Leeds and Bradford find them – and they'll discover some prospects and bring them through by educating them in the ways of professional football. When I arrived at Huddersfield I found a lot of guys at the club were mystified by some of the techniques required to play the modern game at this level. In the past, they just haven't prepared themselves for this level of competition.

The biggest difference – and it remains an enormous difference – between rugby league in England compared to Australia is the strength of the junior game. To be honest, I doubt we'll ever be able to match the Aussies in the production of top-class players because they have such a vast network of junior areas. I know the situation is different because rugby league maintains its position as the number one sport in New South Wales and Queensland, whereas in England we always have such overwhelming competition from soccer, but the bottom line remains that we need to get far more kids playing the game in this country and ensure they get good quality coaching and football education.

In the four years I was away at Newcastle I was led to believe that the British game was making a lot of progress. I was both shocked and disappointed to find that little had changed when I came back at the end of 1998 – this despite the influx of all those millions of pounds from Rupert Murdoch's backing of Super League. And the alarming statistic that around 40 per cent of players in the Super League are overseas imports – that's a damning indictment on those responsible for fostering and developing the game over here. There have been plenty of jobs allocated, and there's been a lot of talking about it, but they were talking about it years ago when I was the Great Britain coach. Then we always had the problem of two rival governing bodies, the RFL and BARLA. But now, rather than unification, I've arrived back in England to find the game split yet another way with Super League (Europe), as well as the RFL and BARLA. Until we get unified and everybody in the game knows we're all going in the same direction, it's going to be awfully difficult to compete with what the Australians are doing over there.

Not that Great Britain can't compete again at Test level, or that we don't have individuals on a par with the Aussies – we do. As I have often said, a lot of it comes down to actually believing that we can beat them. We managed to conquer that hurdle of self-belief pretty well in 1990 and '92, but I sense that maybe it's gone adrift again with our British players in recent years. Certainly the Super League 'world club challenge' games in 1997 did nothing to boost self-confidence. But if you look around at the game over here, we've still got some dynamic players; guys like Iestyn Harris and Adrian Morley from Leeds would do well at any level in Australia. It's the same on the coaching front. Very few Super League clubs have English coaches, it seems to be a question of self-confidence again. I don't think there's a great deal of difference between English and Australian coaches. When I first went there to coach (at Newcastle) I was pretty apprehensive; I knew I was on a learning curve. But I was accepted very quickly, and I found it wasn't all that tough.

The big difference, just as it was during my time as the international team coach, is that we could probably put together a squad of 17 or 18 Test-class players – and after that the quality would start to deteriorate rapidly. In Australia they could pick at least 60 or 65 players of top quality; that strength in depth, and the intense competition for first-grade places in all the clubs, is a product of their network of junior systems. You can appreciate that strength in depth when the Aussies can send over a team of players like Gateshead. They are all players who weren't really wanted by Australian clubs, yet they were in the running for a top-five place over here at the very first attempt – and Gateshead will only get stronger as time goes by. None of them are 'flash' players, but they all do the fundamentals very well.

Physical preparation is an aspect of the game I have constantly referred to throughout this telling of my own story in rugby league, and undoubtedly the British game has made some big strides forward in that department. When I first started pre-season training in the gym with the

Huddersfield guys, I found that the Giants forwards were stronger in the upper body than several of their counterparts at the Newcastle Knights. But it's not just upper-body strength that counts – it's the explosive power, the technique, and the different fundamentals of the game that are needed. Especially in the defensive side of the game. In Australia you find that defensive awareness and techniques have been orientated into players throughout their time as juniors, sometimes from 11 years old upwards. Their work ethic is stronger, they are prepared to work harder, and their game awareness is greater. I just feel that at the moment we in England don't possess an abundance of players who have those qualities, and they are the qualities needed to play rugby league at the highest level.

Leg strength remains so important in such an explosive impact sport, and this was where the Australians were way ahead of us. To be fair, we have caught up a lot in this department, but not enough to the point where we have fierce competition for international places. The Aussies still have four or five guys of the same high standard for each position. And they also have a clear edge in the psychological aspect of the game – players believing in what they can do and really stretching themselves to the limit. Too many of our players aren't tough enough mentally; if things don't go well their heads start to drop. Maybe I'm judging them by different standards, because in my own days as a player, mental toughness had to be proved every time you went out on the field. It was a bit of a war game in those days, every opposition team had one or two guys who were aiming to take your head off, and you knew you had a battle to fight before you could play your football. Things went on then that you just couldn't get away with in the modern game.

But, having said that, rugby league remains basically the same game; the motives are the same now as they were 30 years ago. It's about personal pride in performance, going out and challenging yourself, followed by the satisfied feeling afterwards of having achieved something. That's what the game is all about, and having some fun while you're doing it, because if you're not having fun, naturally, you won't perform very well.

Clubs in England, like Huddersfield, who want to improve their status so they can challenge the big guns, really have to try and defend their own areas these days, because there are some very big contracts being offered to juniors by the handful of wealthy clubs. Even before I went back to Australia in '95 the big clubs were signing them well under age, and clubs have to be quick-footed if they are to secure their 'own'. Just before I left Halifax in the 1994-95 season, we picked up a very promising young junior, Andy Hobson, who was six feet one inch, 14 and a half stone, and was still at school. There were all kinds of ways you could do it without being seen to break the Rugby League's rules on signing juniors – such as giving the player a loan and then writing it off when they turned 17, or making a payment to the parents.

In my view the key to success, when it comes to producing and developing players, one thing all clubs need is for players to have pride in the club – and to have a real sense of identification with the jersey they are wearing and the community they are representing. Newcastle was a perfect example of that; nearly all the Knights players were locals who had come through the juniors. It was the same when I was at Manly, and it's always been the same with clubs like South Sydney or Balmain. That pride helps you go that little bit further when the going gets tough because you know you're not just playing for yourself, you're playing for the community in which you live. And that's the way it used to be in England, certainly for towns like Castleford and Featherstone. It's something that worries me about the game at home now, apart from recession times and the general industrial decline in the north of England, television coverage of sport – not just rugby league – has also hit the smaller clubs. When I was growing up, kids would support their home-town team with some certainty. Certainly in Kippax, 95 per cent of people would be staunch Castleford supporters, but now I see hordes of new Leeds Rhinos fans there. It seems people are very fickle in the modern age; they follow the glamour of whoever happens to be a winning team – there are no firm roots there. Now, because of television, you see hordes of Manchester United fans travelling out of Castleford every week. This increasing failure to capture that local element of support can only be damaging to the long-term future of the small-town rugby league team. In Australia the situation was, and is, so different. If you're a Souths fan, or a Balmain fan, or a Manly fan, you never lose that allegiance – even if your team is running bottom of the competition.

It's that strength of loyalty, and sense of tradition, that makes the subject of mergers such a difficult one. But the fact is that things have changed dramatically in rugby league, and society, in England. Sad as it may seem, it would appear that a club like Featherstone Rovers now have no chance of getting back to former glories among the élite of the game – there's no chance that Featherstone will win the cup at Wembley again. The little clubs have been left behind by the changes in the game since the Super League war.

Of course, that doesn't mean people have to stop trying, and Huddersfield had a great opportunity to try and rebuild a tradition for rugby league, every bit as strong as the ones I've experienced at Newcastle or Manly. As the town that is the birthplace of the game, Huddersfield has so much potential for emotion to take over, once the right nucleus is in place and starts bringing more people through. Huddersfield is big enough to build a major force in the game; just like Bradford and Leeds have cashed in on being big-city teams, Huddersfield has a big catchment area and the right stadium for a Super League club. But until the team starts achieving success on the field it can't start realising any of the huge marketing and commercial potential that Huddersfield offers. Whether it can build the momentum to the tidal-wave proportions that I experienced at Newcastle, time will tell. But the significant point to keep emphasising is that the Knights' strength came from its vast infrastructure of juniors in the area. That bred so much local pride among the players, and everyone connected with the club. Maybe that was intensified because we were perceived as the 'country boys', from outside the city of Sydney. But I know from just listening to the players talk how very emotional and motivating it was to be associated with a group of guys so passionate for the area they came from.

That strength of local pride was a great motivational factor. There was an enormous amount of peer pressure on the players and they took that responsibility on board and got the job done. If one individual player was letting the team down in one particular area, the peer pressure alone would ensure he knew about it and had to shape up. I, as coach, didn't have to say a great deal, the players would do it themselves. I'd liken it to being in a relay race in which one man wasn't running his leg up to the standard of the others. He's got to apply himself harder – and that's what happens in rugby league in Australia. There was far more one-on-one involvement with the coaches for the players, and that better grasp of the fundamentals of the game I mentioned before was also inherent in people off the field, as well as the players. At Newcastle all the support staff I had were first class; the conditioners had great knowledge of the defensive requirements of the game – defensive patterns and techniques – and they provided a lot of information that helped me as head coach. At the same time the players were much more aware than the ones I'd encountered before in England; they thought a lot deeper about the game and their individual role in the team performance.

When I first joined Newcastle in '95 and became involved in the Optus Cup, as it was known then, I was struck by the gap that existed between the individual club player in Australia and in England. I would estimate that as a general rule the Australian players were on average 30 or 40 per cent more skilful than their English counterparts. I remember my office at the Knights overlooked the pitch at Marathon Stadium, and regularly after training was officially over and the players weren't required to be there, I'd look out of the window and see the Johns brothers out there practising their passing and kicking skills, doing various drills, for hours at a time. Nobody asked them to do it, they just wanted to get better.

And that's the kind of enthusiasm, call it innocent enthusiasm if you like, for this game of rugby league that every player starts out with as a youngster. Even after over 30 years in the professional game it still gladdens me to see it, and it fires my own enthusiasm for the game that has been my life. Happily, even in the dismal performances endured at Huddersfield in 1999, there were rays of optimism in the performances of teenagers like Martin Gleeson and Jimmy Carlton. Both are at a great age where they want to learn – they haven't come just for the money like some other players, they genuinely want to test themselves and achieve something as footballers. With a good off-season behind them they will start maturing into real first-team prospects. Unfortunately, because of injuries and lack of competition from more experienced players, we've had to throw them in at the deep end in their first year.

Certainly my first season back in the English game was bitterly disappointing, to say the least. I feel especially disappointed for the Huddersfield chairman, Ken Davy; despite the lousy results, he remains positive, he is still flying the flag for the club and optimistic about the future. Both Ken and his wife Jennifer have been tremendous supporters and the Huddersfield club owes them an awful lot.

One of the most frustrating things about the whole situation, before events unfolded that saw Huddersfield announce their merger with Sheffield, was the fact that we had so many big things planned for next year. Whether they get the chance to put those plans and player recruitments into practice still in Super League remains to be seen. For Ken Davy's sake I hope so, but I still believe that if a team finishes bottom then it deserves to be relegated. Obviously, the matter of promoting a team now needs to take into account their ability to compete as a full-time professional club, and their potential for growing into a successful operation if we genuinely want to have the right criteria for making the Super League an élite, high-profile competition. You need a sound administration, you need a decent stadium, and most of all, you need a decent team. Most evidence suggests, and a glance at results in the Challenge Cup in 1999 will confirm this, that the gap between even the lower half of the Super League and the teams in the Premiership is getting wider year by year.

Trawling through the memories of my career for this book isn't something that has come naturally to me, because I'm not really the kind of person who likes to look back. In rugby league I've always thought that if you look back too much it can stop you going forward. And the game must go forward – the damage and fall-out from the 'war' of 1995 and onwards is still being felt by the changes brought on the game in both hemispheres. I look on with sadness at the prospect of famous old clubs like Balmain and Souths being forced into mergers or extinction in Australia. Make no mistake, whilst we (the ARL) may have won the initial battle, it was Super League (News Limited) who won the war, and they are controlling the purse strings and, effectively, the future of the game in Australia – and thereby the rest of the world I guess. My personal loyalty to Ken Arthurson did a lot to shape my views on that, because nobody had more influence on my life in rugby league, and my whole destiny, than Ken.

When the plane took off from Mascot in October 1998 and climbed above that marvellous Sydney coastline, there was a lump in my throat as big as a football. I had to accept that I wasn't going to be back in Australia, not in the name of rugby league, anyway. It was the start of a climb back to reality for me, back home to Yorkshire, to where it had all started for me, and to where this grand game that has been my life was also born.

Sure, I've got those great memories of famous Wembley finals, Test matches and grand finals, and when I came home and joined Huddersfield I was still hoping there would be another magic moment in rugby league for me, another achievement, somewhere down the track. But, with the bitter disillusionment that grew with every crushing disappointment in the 1999 season, for the first time in over 30 years I started to question whether I wanted to carry on in the game. Even several weeks before the end of Huddersfield's '99 season, when there was still a possibility the club could avoid bottom place and thereby hang on to Super League status, I wanted to go on record how I was feeling at this time, that even if the club managed to avoid relegation I wasn't sure that I would want to carry on. The recent humiliations have left a scar on me, and it's something I've never had to experience before at any time in my career. At some stage of your football career I guess the time comes when you question your own motivations, whether the quest for sporting success is still your prime concern, or whether rugby league is no longer the be all and end all of everything. It's a time to ask myself: Do I need this responsibility (being coach of a football club) when I have my own responsibilities to my wife and family, who so often over the past 30 years have made sacrifices to help me in my rugby league career? As I wrote this in August 1999, I was agonising over what the future might hold. It was a time of torment because I had players who I knew wanted to come to Huddersfield – good players – with whom I have had an association in previous years. They had agreed to come largely because of that personal association, but I didn't want to lure them under what might seem like false pretences if I decided that I wasn't going to carry on. But, by the time this book appears, everybody will know that events have overtaken my thoughts at that time. A decision has been made that Huddersfield are to merge with Sheffield and that I won't be taking the coaching job with the new club. I want to wish my old Castleford colleague John Kear the best of luck in his new role.

However, it is hard to imagine a life without rugby league. I've enjoyed everything in my career except the experiences of the second half of the 1999 season at Huddersfield. I caught the bug a long time ago, back when the world was a different place and league a very different game (albeit with the same basic aims, challenges and passions). Over many years it has afforded me much pleasure and enjoyment. And some pain. It has also given me a chance in life that I doubt could have been there through any other avenue; and a chance to share my life in two different countries I have come to love with equal passions.

At least, I suppose, I'll always have 'the knee' to remind me of so many great people and wonderful times.

TWENTY-TWO

Mind Games:
And Help from Some Friends

Throughout my coaching career I have always been a believer in employing the wisdom of others in the weekly search for excellence in my football teams. On a certain day in a football season a quotation from some source – even if penned hundreds of years ago – can strike just the right chord with the team and its men. For years I have been a collector of messages and inspiration, and I never hesitate to use them if I think they might help the team on a certain day. Sometimes the source will be unexpected – an anonymous letter or a poem from a supporter, digging deeply into the feeling a community may have for its football team.

In my time at the Newcastle Knights I got lots of letters from fans. There were inspirational and spiritual messages from the chaplain Jeff Poots, and there were poems, drawings, complaints and suggestions from members of the public, all of them written because people care about the club. Some of the poems became very special to me and I still keep them today. Soon after I joined the Newcastle club, the 'Merlin' letters began to arrive – they were anonymous, on decorative paper, unsigned, but each bearing the name 'MERLIN – Supporting Newcastle Knights'. I don't know who wrote them, but I had my suspicions. They were positive, helpful, sometimes hard-hitting and welcome. I enjoyed receiving them, and even though I am now back in England I still receive the occasional letter from 'Merlin', and I still write back to him (or her). I have no name, or address, just a PO Box number.

Before I sum up my views on league's final frontier – the game in the mind – I'd like to share some of the quotations I have gathered over the years. They are a legitimate part of a coach's armament, now and then helping to add an extra dimension that we all seek in the quest to create a winning feeling in our teams. The quotes that follow are very diverse and come from many different places – and I am very appreciative to all the authors for putting into words such essential messages about success and the human condition.

Be more concerned with your character than your reputation, because your character is what you really are, while your reputation is merely what others think you are.
John Wooden, college basketball coach

I care not what others think of what I do, but I care very much about what I think I do. That is character.
Theodore Roosevelt, twenty-sixth US President

Truth has no special time of its own. Its hour is now always.
Albert Schweitzer, French clergyman and physician

Loyalty, up and down the line. That's one quality an organisation must have to be successful.
Woodrow Wilson, twenty-eighth US President

No building is better than its structural foundation, and no man is better than his mental foundation. When I prepared my original Success Pyramid years ago, I put industriousness and enthusiasm as the two cornerstones with loyalty right in the middle of the pyramid – loyalty to yourself and to all those who depend on you.
John Wooden, college basketball coach

One thing I learned from football is that you must have respect. It is not so important that people like you, but it is an absolute must that you have their respect.
Jim Brown, NFL full-back and actor

I believe it is very important to show respect towards individuals who live up to their obligations and responsibilities, whether or not you like the individual concerned. Respect is a virtue that goes far beyond the emotion of liking.
Reggie Jackson, Major League baseball player and sports broadcaster

You cannot do a kindness too soon because you never know how soon it will be too late.
Ralph Waldo Emerson, American writer and poet

How desperately difficult it is to be honest with oneself. It is much easier to be honest with other people.
Edward F. Benson, English author

It's the old story. You might be able to fool your coaches, or your team-mates, or your opposition. But, you can never fool yourself in anything. I believe that the more critical you are of your own performance – the higher standards you have – the better you become at what you do.
Don Maynard, NFL wide-receiver

The people I feel closest to are people who don't compromise their basic nature and the way they feel.
Dustin Hoffman, American actor

You have to develop a style that suits you and pursue it, not just develop a bag of tricks. Always be yourself.
James Stewart, American actor

I was involved in some pretty bad things, the kind of things you do to impress other guys. It was a way of being accepted. I had to learn to be somebody strong. You have to be an individual and let people accept you for what you are.
Art Still, NFL defensive end

Class is striving hard to be the best at what you do while taking the needs of others into consideration.
Roger Staubech, NFL quarterback and broadcaster

Class is an intangible thing. Different people show it in different ways, but it does not take long to surface and it is easily recognisable.
John Wooden, college basketball coach

Never tell a young person that something cannot be done. God may have been waiting for centuries for somebody ignorant enough of the impossible to do that thing.
Arthur J. Rooney, NFL team owner

Show me a satisfied man and I will show you a failure.
Thomas Edison, American inventor

The resources of the human body and soul, physical, mental and spiritual, are enormous and beyond our present knowledge and expectations. We go part of the way to consciously tapping these resources by having goals that we want desperately – it is the only

way we currently know how to use these hidden resources. Wanting desperately to achieve taps that hidden resource that every one of us has.
Herb Elliott, Olympic gold medallist

I've always believed that desire must come from within, not as a result of being driven by coaches or parents.
Dawn Fraser, three-times Olympic gold medallist

The long span of the bridge in your life is supported by countless cables called habits, attitudes and desires. What you do in life depends on what you are and what you want. What you get from life depends on how much you want it – how much you are willing to work and plan and co-operate and use your resources. The long span of the bridge of your life is supported by countless cables that you are spinning now, and that is why today is such an important day. Make the cables strong!
L.G. Elliott, American author

I've always believed that everybody with a little ability, a little guts and the desire to apply himself can make it. He can make anything he wants to make of himself.
Willie Shoemaker, professional jockey

Even when I went to the playground, I never picked the best players. I picked the guys with less talent, but who were willing to work hard, who had the desire to be great.
Earvin 'Magic' Johnson, professional basketball player

To succeed in life one must have determination and must be prepared to suffer during the process. If one isn't prepared to suffer adversities, I don't really see how he can be successful.
Gary Player, golfer

Football is a professional game, you play it to win at all levels. There is no room for sentimentality. Either you play or you don't play. I was determined to play. I knew all along deep down inside that I could do it, that I was good even though nobody else seemed to agree with me. My determination more than ever made up for a lack of speed, height, weight, or whatever else I wasn't supposed to have.
Jack Lambert, NFL linebacker

You set a goal to be the best then you work hard every hour of every day, striving to reach that goal. If you allow yourself to settle for anything less than number one, you are cheating yourself.
Don Shula, NFL coach

The only thing that counts is your dedication to the game. You run on your own fuel: it comes from within you.
Paul Brown, NFL coach, general manager and team owner

The most important thing is to love your sport. Never do it to please anyone else – it has to be yours. That is all that will justify the hard work needed to achieve success. Compete against yourself not others, for that is who is truly your best competition.
Peggy Fleming, Olympic gold medallist

I am a firm believer in the theory that people do their best at things they truly enjoy. It is difficult to excel at something you don't enjoy.
Jack Nicklaus, golfer

The most important thing that a young athlete must do is pick the right sport. Not one that they like just a little bit but one that they love. Because if they don't really love their sport, they won't work as hard as they should.
Babe Ruth, Major League baseball player

I love to work. You've got to love what you do. It takes time, patience, long hours of work trying to improve yourself each day.
Jack Dempsey, professional boxer

Success is a peace of mind which is a direct result of self-satisfaction in knowing that you did your best to become the best you are capable of becoming.
John Wooden, college basketball coach

The one strongest, most important idea in my game of golf, my cornerstone – is that I want to be the best, I wouldn't accept anything less than that. My ability to concentrate and work towards that goal has been my greatest asset.
Jack Nicklaus, golfer

I learned to fight. I worked and studied it. If I got beat up or got sloppy in the gym, I'd go home and work on it till I got it right.

Man, it was hard work but I didn't want to be just good. I wanted to be the best.
Thomas Hearns, professional boxer

My ambition is not to be just a good fighter. I want to be great, something special.
Sugar Ray Leonard, professional boxer

Actually, all I ever genuinely wanted was to be the best in my field.
Lou Holtz, college football coach

There is no doubt that a man is a competitive animal and there is no place where this fact is more obvious than in the ring. There is no second place. Either you win or you lose. When they call you a champion it is because you didn't lose. To win takes a complete commitment of mind and body. When you can't make that commitment, they don't call you a champion any more.
Rocky Marciano, professional boxer

I know I'm nowhere near my potential. I'm looking forward to breaking the world record. All I care about is finding out what I can do, how fast I can go. Honestly, it is almost like the faster I go the easier it becomes.
Mary Decker, distance runner

I refuse to accept less than what I'm capable of achieving at any time. My goal every year is to play better than the year before.
Hale Irwin, golfer

True success is one of our greatest needs.
Reggie Jackson, Major League baseball player

Every guy who lives on God's green earth who may be doing good is stupid if he thinks he can't do better. I want to be the best ever.
Earl Campbell, NFL full-back

Being courageous requires no exceptional qualifications, no magic formula, no special combination of time, place and circumstance. It is an opportunity that sooner or later is presented to us all.
John F. Kennedy, thirty-fifth US President

To dream anything you want to dream. That is the beauty of the human mind. To do anything that you want to do. That is the strength of the human will. To trust yourself to test your limits. That is the courage to succeed.
Bernard Edmonds, American writer

The most sublime courage I have ever witnessed has been among the class too poor to know they possessed it, and too humble for the world to discover it.
George Bernard Shaw, Irish dramatist

Courage is the first of the human qualities because it is the quality which guarantees all the others.
John L. Lewis, United Mineworkers Union President

The stories of the past courage can define that ingredient. They can teach, they can offer hope, they can provide inspiration. But they cannot supply courage itself. For this each man must look into his soul.
John F. Kennedy, thirty-fifth US President

Nothing good comes in life for athletes unless a lot of hard work has preceded the effort. Only temporary success is achieved by taking short cuts. Set a goal and go after that goal with integrity, self-confidence and a lot of hard work.
Roger Staubach, NFL quarterback and broadcaster

I am wondering what could have happened to me if some fluent talker had converted me to the theory of the eight-hour day and convinced me that it was not fair to my fellow workers to put forth my best efforts in my work. I am glad that the eight-hour day had not been invented when I was a young man. If my life had been made up of eight-hour days, I don't believe I could have accomplished a great deal. This country would not amount to as much as it does if the young men of fifty years ago had been afraid that they might earn more than they were paid for.
Thomas Edison, American inventor

I believe there is a price tag on everything worth while, but it is seldom a monetary one. The price is more often one of dedication, deprivation, extra effort, loneliness. Each person decides whether

he or she wants to pay the price. If you do, you achieve beyond other people.
Jim McKay, broadcaster

The dictionary is the only place success comes before work. Hard work is the price we must all pay for success. I think we can accomplish almost anything if we are willing to pay the price. The price of success is hard work, dedication to the job at hand and the determination that whether we win or lose, we have applied the best of ourselves to the task at hand.
Vince Lombardi, NFL coach

In order to succeed greatly, you have to sacrifice greatly. Nobody ever said it would be easy.
Mike Pruitt, NFL full-back

Before I get into the ring, I'd have already won or lost it out on the road. The real part is won or lost somewhere far away from witnesses – behind the lines, in the gym and out there on the long road before I dance under those lights.
Muhammad Ali, professional boxer

I learned that the only way you are going to get anywhere in life is to work hard at it. Whether you're a musician, a writer, an athlete or a businessman, there is no getting around it. If you do, you'll win – if you don't, you won't.
Bruce Jenner, Olympic gold medallist

If I work on a certain move constantly, then, finally, it doesn't seem so risky to me. The idea is that the move stays dangerous and it looks dangerous to my foes, but it is not to me. Hard work has made it easy. That is my secret. That is why I win.
Nadia Comaneci, five-times Olympic gold medallist

Repeated actions are stored habits. If the repeated actions aren't fundamentally sound, then what comes out in the game can't be sound. What comes out will be bad habits.
Chuck Knox, NFL coach

I work from dawn to exhaustion. If there's not a crisis I'll create one.
Lou Holtz, college football coach

Discipline is the whole key to being successful. We all get 24 hours a day. It's the only fair thing; it's the only thing that's equal. It's up to us as to what we do with those 24 hours.
Sam Huff, NFL linebacker

You can't get much done in life if you only work on the days when you feel good.
Jerry West, professional basketball player, coach and general manager

Always have a plan and believe in it. I tell my coaches not to compromise. Nothing good happens by accident – it happens because of good organisation. There must be a plan for everything and the plan will prevent you from overlooking little things. By having that plan, you'll be secure and self-doubts will never become a factor.
Chuck Knox, NFL coach

You cannot run away from weakness, you must sometimes fight it out or perish: and if that be so, why not now, and where you stand?
Robert Louis Stevenson, Scottish novelist and poet

Winning is the science of preparation and preparation can be defined in three small words. 'Leaving nothing undone.' No detail too small. No task too large. Most of the time the difference between winning and losing, success or failure, can be the smallest detail or as they say in baseball, just a matter of inches.
Reggie Jackson, Major League baseball player and broadcaster

Being ignorant is not so much a shame as being unwilling to learn to do things the right way.
Benjamin Franklin, American diplomat and inventor

Don't mistake activity for achievement – practise it the right way.
John Wooden, college basketball coach

I only play well when I'm prepared. If I don't practise the way I should, I won't play the way that I know I can.
Ivan Lendl, tennis player

Our theme has been that hard work equals success. We haven't done it with magic or with better plays or anything like that.
Don Shula, NFL coach

If I see something that can be successful and even if it's not my style, I'll investigate it a little further. If it looks worth while, I might incorporate it. I'm not so hard-headed as to ignore something just because it might be a little different than what I'm doing.
Don Shula, NFL coach

Practice does not make the athlete. It is the quality and intensity of practice that makes the athlete, not just the repeated practising.
Ray Meyer, college basketball coach

The challenge for rugby league's players of today is to be the best they can be – the eternal challenge of top-level sport. I think the best way someone can succeed is to accept that, *every* time, the person you are competing against is yourself. If you can accept that, and keep working on all the facets of what you do and listen to the right guidance from people who know, then you're in with a chance. Modern rugby league is about so many things: it's nutrition, it's peaking at the right times, it's rest and recuperation, it's getting the right advice in relation to strength, speed, power, technique; it's about continuing re-evaluation of self. It's doing it.

The territory of the mind is the last frontier for the footballer. At Newcastle we linked up with an excellent sports psychologist from the Australian Institute of Sport, Geoff Bond, who worked with the club regularly on scientific monitoring programmes of individual players. OK, it may sound a long way from those days at Castleford 30 years ago when 'Rocky' Turner was giving us his pre-match talk, but the principle remains the same – the fact of life in rugby league is that psychological readiness to perform is what makes the difference between a player's potential and his performance. The quality of clarity in a player's mind on what has to be done is so important in the preparation. I recall one (of many) of Muhammad Ali's sayings: 'I won the fight well away from the boxing ring; I won the fight a long time before I ever got into the ring. It was in the slog of the hard road runs, in all the sparring sessions, the mental hype.'

The film of Ali's battle with George Foreman, *When We Were Kings*, is a wonderful inspiration to anyone involved in sport. The psychological approach he adopted for that fight stands as a beacon for anyone in sport. No one gave him a chance, yet single-handed he turned it all around. His trainers, who had been 'down', were converted. They became buoyant, feeding off his energy and confidence and he in turn fed off their confidence. Ali incited the crowd with his chant (a word meaning 'Ali, kill him'), and he then fed off the crowd's chanted response. The whole exercise was a brilliant display of mental toughness. Footballers can do that too – feed off the emotions of a home crowd in a close game.

Successful rugby league teams – and at times my Newcastle team did this during the 1998 season – sometimes display a little bit of arrogance, a *certainty* in some games in which they trailed that they would get out of trouble. That's not such a bad thing, as long as it doesn't go too far. The mark of a top side, the indicator of the necessary mental toughness, is the ability of a team to prepare adequately for *any* match, whether against the top team or the bottom one. That's a very personal thing; it's about the individual player and what he will accept on any given day. Some players accept far less than they should. Sometimes it is apparent there is an attitude against a lower side; a player thinking it's enough just to 'turn up' and go through the motions, knowing that one or other of the stars will manufacture the expected win. But if there are four or five, or half a dozen, players who have that attitude, then the team is in trouble. Mental toughness is a week-by-week thing, a player getting himself to the ideal performance state where he is going to be at his top or close to it, then aiming even higher the following week.

Happily, British rugby league players have taken a lot of these lessons on board, and they've come a long way since the Lions tour of 20 years ago, in 1979, proved to be such a turning point (downwards) in our history. It was the year after Bob Fulton had led the Kangaroos to the Ashes in England, and the tour that proved to be the moment when Australia really 'jumped' British rugby league and stole a huge march. It was the forerunner of the unprecedented Test hammerings at the hands of the 1982 'Invincibles', and a decade of trying to play catch-up to the Aussies. The critics labelled it the 'Dad's Army Tour'; my reasons for missing it were absolutely legitimate, but as it turned out it was a very good tour to miss.

Over the years I spoke to a number of the players who went on that tour – guys who were genuinely concerned about success – who told me that without doubt there were some who had just gone to enjoy themselves. The training sessions were apparently very ordinary and it showed in the results. The blame for that state of affairs that befell British rugby league at that time rested equally with the players, with those who selected the party and with the coaching staff. I was told of one occasion in New Zealand when the manager allegedly stuck his head out of the bus en route to training, realised it was raining and issued the instruction, 'We'll give this a miss,' ordering the driver to turn around and take the team straight back to the hotel. It was that kind of attitude that sowed the seeds of the vast gap that opened up between rugby league's two oldest rivals.

In total contrast came Great Britain's win over Australia at Wembley in 1990, or Newcastle's grand final triumph in 1997. Those victories were the rewards for positive thinking, mental clarity of preparation, and determination of unrivalled intensity. Sport doesn't get much better or more dramatic than the rugby league that fans saw on those two occasions. The quality of such contests is what Vince Lombardi was talking about when he produced a quote which has always been among my favourites:

> All of the rings, all of the colour, all of the display, linger only in the memory. The spirit, the will to win, those are the things that endure and those are the qualities that are so much more important than any of the events that occasioned them.

That just about says it all.